CONTENTS

SCHOLASTIC YEARBOOK

Illustrations

CHARBAK DIPTA AND PRIYA KURIYAN

SCHOLASTIC
New York Toronto London Auckland
Sydney New Delhi Hong Kong

Editors: Prerna Mathur and Ashley Kumar

While the Editorial research team has made every attempt to authenticate the news and information that has been included in the *Yearbook*, we regret any unintentional errors or omissions. Events in this edition span from August 2024 to July 2025.

Published by Scholastic India Pvt. Ltd.
A subsidiary of Scholastic Inc., New York, 10012 (USA).
Publishers since 1920, with international operations in Canada,
Australia, New Zealand, the United Kingdom, India, and Hong Kong.

For information regarding permission, write to:
Scholastic India Pvt. Ltd.
A-27, Ground Floor, Sigma Centre
Infocity-1, Sector 34, Gurgaon 122001 (India)

First edition: October 2025

ISBN: 978-93-5954-092-4

Printed in India at : Shiv Shakti Printing & Trading Co., Haryana

EVENTS
All Major Events

AUGUST 2024

Bangladesh Prime Minister Sheikh Hasina (76) resigned on 5 August and fled the country after more than a month of violent demonstrations. The protests started against 30 per cent government job quotas for kin of 1971 Bangladesh liberation war veterans. Hasina was the country's PM from 1996-2001 and was in power since 2009 till her ouster.

Wrestler Vinesh Phogat (29) got disqualified from the Olympics final in the 50 kg freestyle category in Paris for being overweight by just 100 gm. She took significant nightlong efforts to bring down her weight—from abstaining from food and water to sauna, but to no avail. A day earlier, she had become the first Indian woman wrestler to reach the final of an Olympics.

A second-year PG trainee doctor was raped and murdered at RG Kar Medical College and Hospital in Kolkata on 9 August, triggering nationwide protests over the next few weeks.

The Justice Hema Committee report, formed to study workplace conditions of women in the Malayalam film industry, was made public on 19 August, despite its submission to the government back in 2019. The 235-page report, based on depositions and statements from multiple witnesses, made shocking observations on widespread exploitation of women.

Afghanistan's Taliban rulers banned women's voices and bare faces in public under their new laws, approved by supreme leader Hibatullah Akhundzada.

Indian cricketer Shikhar Dhawan announced his retirement.

Pavel Durov (39), the founder and chief executive officer of social messaging app Telegram, was arrested after he arrived at Le Bourget airport outside Paris on a private jet. He was arrested in connection with an investigation into crimes like child pornography, drug trafficking and fraudulent transactions on the social media platform.

Aiming to boost manufacturing within the country, the Indian government decided to build 12 new industrial cities across 10 states, with an investment of over ₹28,500 crore. The cities, including Agra and Prayagraj in Uttar Pradesh, Gaya (Bihar), and Jodhpur (Rajasthan) among others, will have such places where businesses can be easily set up and operated ('plug-n-play'), creating over 10 lakh direct jobs and over 20 lakh indirect jobs by 2027.

Canadian company Lucara Diamond Corporation said they unearthed a 2,492-carat diamond—the second-largest in the world—at Karowe mine in Botswana using X-ray technology.

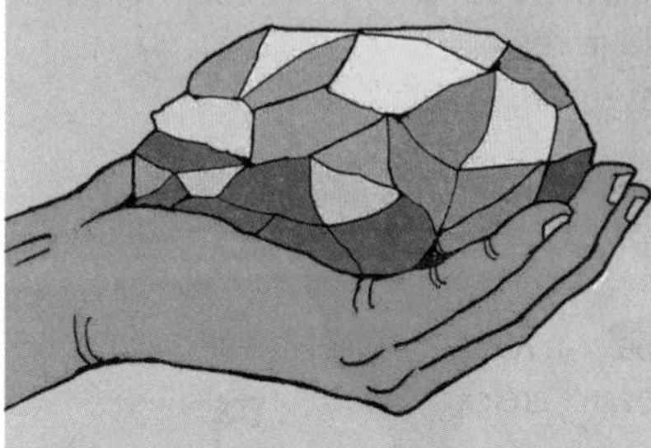

PEOPLE METER

Defending Olympics champion in javelin Neeraj Chopra won India's lone silver medal at the 2024 Paris Olympics with a throw of 89.45 metres on 8 August. Chopra is the only Indian to win Olympics medals in athletics.

Swapnil Kusale (28) won India's first Olympic medal in men's 50-metre rifle three positions on 1 August.

Twenty-two-year-old Avani Lekhara on 30 August became the first Indian woman to secure two Paralympic gold medals by winning the women's 10-metre air rifle event. Lekhara surpassed her own record of 249.6 set in the 2020 Tokyo Paralympics (held a year later due to the prevailing pandemic).

India's Jay Shah was elected unopposed as the chairperson of International Cricket Council (ICC) on 27 August. Shah, aged 36, became the youngest to officially take over the role on 1 December 2024.

Gautam Adani (62), with a wealth of ₹11.6 lakh crore, overtook Mukesh Ambani as the richest Indian in 2024 Hurun India Rich List on 29 August. India now has 334 billionaires, a 29 per cent rise in the number from last year. Mukesh Ambani secured the second position with ₹10.14 lakh crore.

Apple, in August, named Indian-origin Kevan Parekh, then vice-president (financial planning and analysis) as its chief financial officer.

DEATHS

Padma Vibhushan Bharatnatyam dancer Yamini Krishnamurthy died on 3 August at the age of 84 after suffering from age-related issues. Krishnamurthy, also a distinguished Kuchipudi and Odissi dancer, was awarded the Padma Vibhushan, India's second-highest civilian award, in 2016, after being honoured with Padma Shri in 1968 and Padma Bhushan in 2001.

Former England batsman Graham Thorpe passed away at the age of 55 on 5 August. Thorpe, who played 100 Tests between 1993 and 2005, scored 6,744 runs, including 16 centuries.

Former West Bengal chief minister Buddhadeb Bhattacharya died on 8 August at the age of 80 at his Kolkata flat following a cardiac arrest. He held the office for eleven years from 2000 to 2011.

French actor Alain Delon died on 18 August, aged 88. He had suffered a stroke in 2019, after which he had been in poor health, mostly keeping himself confined to his estate at Douchy in France's Val de Loire region.

Noted lawyer and author Abdul Ghafoor Noorani passed away on 29 August at the age of 93. He was confined to bed for over a year after a fall, in which he suffered a shoulder injury.

SEPTEMBER 2024

At least 50 people were killed and 271 wounded after Russia hit a military institute in Ukraine's Poltava with two ballistic missiles.

Olympian wrestler Vinesh Phogat joined the Congress following which she was nominated from the Julana Assembly constituency in Jind district for the Haryana Assembly elections.

The Union Cabinet on 11 September cleared health insurance cover of ₹5 lakh for people aged 70 and above as the Centre expanded Ayushman Bharat Pradhan Mantri Jan Arogya Yojana (AB PM-JAY). As many as six crore people will benefit from this expansion, as per the government.

The Supreme Court granted bail to Delhi Chief Minister Arvind Kejriwal on 13 September in the excise policy case. Kejriwal was arrested by the ED on 21 March and the CBI on 26 June. Kejriwal resigned on 17 September and handed the reins of chief ministership to AAP leader Atishi.

For the first time, a Houthi missile landed in central Israel on 15 September.

As many as 274 people were killed in Israel's strike on Lebanon on 23 September in one of the deadliest strikes in the country in decades.

India defended its Asian Champions Trophy hockey title, defeating hosts China 1-0.

In a historic triumph, two Indian chess teams won gold medals in the 45th Chess Olympiad. The Indian teams grabbed gold in Open and Women's categories in Budapest, Hungary.

Former US president Donald Trump survived an assassination bid on 15 September after the FBI foiled the attempts, while Trump was golfing in Florida.

The Union Cabinet on 17 September approved the recommendations of a high-level committee headed by former president Ram Nath Kovind to hold elections simultaneously in the country. The panel, in its report, said Lok Sabha and Assembly elections can be held together and should be followed by local body polls within 100 days.

Calling it 'unconstitutional', the Bombay High Court struck down the central government's amended IT rules that gave the Centre powers to identify 'fake news' on social media platforms through its Fact Check Unit.

India and the US have signed agreements to set up a semiconductor fabrication plant to make chips for use in 'national security, next generation telecommunications, and green energy applications'.

PEOPLE METER

Para-shuttler Nitesh Kumar made history at the 2024 Paris Paralympics by winning the gold medal in the Men's Singles SL3 category. The 29-year-old became the third Indian to achieve this feat.

Aryna Sabalenka defeated Jessica Pegula to claim the US Open women's title.

Randhir Singh (77), a five-time Olympian, became the first Indian to be appointed as the president of Olympic Council of Asia.

Jannik Sinner won his second Grand Slam after outplaying Taylor Fritz in the men's US Open final. Sinner became the first Italian man to win the US Open.

Javelin icon Neeraj Chopra on 14 September fell short by just one centimetre to claim his second Diamond League title. With a best throw of 87.86 metres in the final, Chopra lost to Grenada's Anderson Peters (87.87 metres).

Air Chief Marshal A P Singh took charge as the Indian Air Force chief. He succeeded Air Chief Marshal V R Chaudhari, who retired after a tenure of three years as the head of the air force.

DEATHS

Aruna Vasudev—regarded as the 'mother of Asian cinema'—died aged 88 due to age-related health complications.

Alberto Fujimori, former president of Peru, died on 11 September at the age of 86. He was the country's first president of Japanese descent.

Former Italian striker Salvatore Schillaci died aged 59. Schillaci was the top scorer in the 1990 World Cup and was named as the winner of the Golden Ball and Golden Boot in the tournament.

Veteran CPI(M) leader M M Lawrence died aged 95 on 21 September. He was among the group of leaders that attacked a police station in Kochi during the communist uprising in Kerala in 1950.

Hanif Kureshi, who popularized Indian street art, passed away after suffering from cancer. He was 41.

Keki Daruwalla, a renowned English-language Indian poet, died on 26 September. He was 87 and a recipient of Sahitya Akademi Award and the Padma Shri.

Renowned actor Maggie Smith passed away aged 89. Smith was known for her works in the *Harry Potter* series and British period drama *Downtown Abbey* among others.

OCTOBER 2024

Actor Govinda accidentally fired at himself, injuring his left leg. Police said the actor was hospitalized and out of danger.

AIX Connect formally merged into Air India Express on 1 October. With the merger, AIX Connect, which was formerly known as Air Asia, along with Air India Express, has become part of the Tata Group.

In one of the largest such operations in Chhattisgarh, at least 28 Maoists were killed by security personnel in an encounter in Dantewada district.

In the Assembly elections results announced on 8 October, the NC-Congress alliance secured victory in Jammu and Kashmir (J&K), while the BJP won in Haryana. Omar Abdullah was sworn in as first chief minister of the Union Territory of Jammu and Kashmir. Nayab Singh Saini took oath as the chief minister of Haryana.

At least 20 miners were killed when terrorists attacked a private coal mine with rocket launchers and automatic weapons in Pakistan's Balochistan.

Nationalist Congress Party (NCP) leader and MLA Baba Siddiqui was shot dead in Mumbai. Siddiqui was a three-time MLA and leader of Ajit Pawar faction of the NCP.

In a 4-1 verdict, the Supreme Court upheld the constitutional validity of Section 6A of the Citizenship Act 1955. The Act sets 24 March 1971 as the cut-off date for entry into Assam in a bid to get Indian citizenship.

After spending more than 18 months in jail, AAP leader and former health minister Satyendar Jain walked out of Tihar jail on bail. He was arrested in a money laundering case.

In a mission to examine whether Jupiter's moon Europa can sustain life, US space agency NASA launched a spacecraft from Florida. The probe is scheduled to enter orbit around Jupiter in 2030 after travelling about 2.9 billion kilometres.

PEOPLE METER

Justice Sanjiv Khanna took oath as the 51st Chief Justice of India. President Droupadi Murmu administered the oath. Justice Khanna succeeded D Y Chandrachud as the Chief Justice of India.

Claudia Sheinbaum, 62, took oath as the first woman president of Mexico.

Star gymnast Dipa Karmakar, an Olympian and Commonwealth Games bronze medalist, announced her retirement from the sport.

As part of the National Awards, President Droupadi Murmu presented Dadasaheb Phalke Lifetime Achievement Award to actor Mithun Chakraborty. Rishab Shetty won the Best Actor Award, and Nithya Menen bagged the Best Actress Award.

Basketball legend LeBron James and his son Bronny became the first father-son teammates to play an NBA match. The match saw LeBron's Los Angeles Lakers defeat Minnesota Timberwolves.

DEATHS

Christopher Charles Benninger, prominent architect and urban planner, died on 2 October. He was 81.

Ratan Naval Tata, chairman emeritus of Tata Group, passed away. He was 86. Tata took over as chairman of Tata Sons from his uncle J R D Tata. He was at the helm of various group companies, including Tata Steel, Tata Motors, TCS, and Tata Powers. Noel Tata, half-brother of Ratan N Tata, was appointed as chairman of Tata Trusts.

Greek composer Mimis Plessas died aged 99 just a week before his 100th birthday. His composition 'O Dromos' remains one of the highest selling albums in the history of his country.

The Netherlands football legend Johan Neeskens died aged 73. Neeskens was part of the Netherlands team that reached two successive World Cup finals in 1974 and 1978.

Former AIIMS director P Venugopal passed away at 82. He conducted India's first heart transplant, and, in a career spanning four decades, performed more than 50,000 surgeries.

Acclaimed Singer Liam Payne (31)—former member of band One Direction—died after falling from a hotel balcony in Buenos Aires, Argentina.

T P Gopalan Nambiar, founder of BPL group, died at his residence in Bengaluru. He was 94.

NOVEMBER 2024

Usman Lashkari, a Lashkar-e-Taiba commander, was gunned down in an encounter in Srinagar's Khanyar. In another encounter, two more terrorists were killed in Jammu and Kashmir's Anantnag district.

The Indian team lost all three Test matches of a series at home as New Zealand clean swept to a 3-0 series win.

In a 4-3 ruling, the Supreme Court overruled its 1967 verdict, which had deemed Aligarh Muslim University (AMU) as not a minority institution.

The Canadian government ended a fast-track student visa for 14 countries, including India. The programme, Student Direct Stream (SDS), was launched in 2018 to enable faster visa processing for students who have completed their secondary education from these 14 countries.

In its biggest such attack in Moscow since the start of the war, Ukraine attacked Russia's capital with at least 34 drones. On 17 November, in a major drone and missile strike, Russia targeted energy infrastructure in Ukraine.

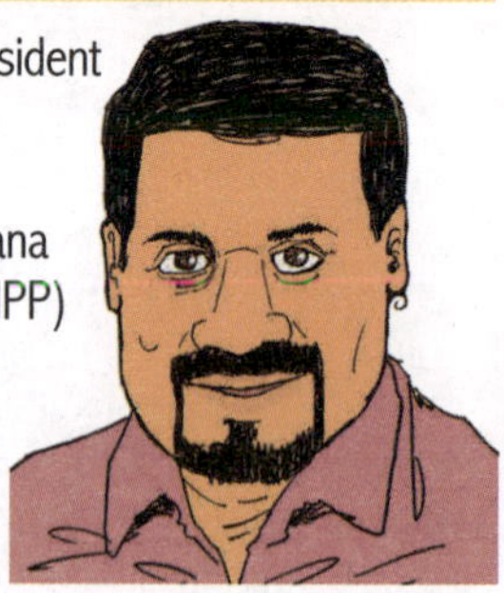

Sri Lankan President Anura Kumara Dissanayake's party Jathika Jana Balawegaya (NPP) won two-thirds majority in the country's Parliament elections. The NPP, which is a coalition of more than 20 parties, secured 159 of the 225 seats in Parliament.

The central government has reimposed the Disturbed Areas status under the Armed Forces (Special Powers) Act (AFSPA) in six police stations in Manipur.

Maoist leader Vikram Gowda was killed in an encounter in Udupi district, Karnataka. Gowda, 44, was wanted for more than 20 years.

Narendra Modi became the first Indian Prime Minister to visit Guyana in 56 years. He met Guyanese President Mohamed Irfaan Ali. India and Guyana signed 10 agreements to enhance cooperation in hydrocarbons, digital payment systems, pharmaceuticals, and defence.

Prosecutors in the US indicted Adani Group Chairman Gautam Adani, his nephew Sagar Adani, and six others for allegedly offering ₹2,029 crore as bribes to officials of the Indian government in a bid to secure solar energy contracts with state electricity distribution companies.

The BJP-led Mahayuti alliance won the election of the Maharashtra Assembly. The alliance of BJP, Nationalist Congress Party, and Shiv Sena defeated its rival group mainly of the Congress, NCP (Sharadchandra Pawar) and Shiv Sena (Uddhav Balasaheb Thackeray).

In Jharkhand, the Jharkhand Mukti Morcha (JMM)-led alliance won the Assembly elections. The alliance consisting mainly of the JMM, Congress, RJD defeated the BJP-led NDA.

PEOPLE METER

Krisha Verma won the gold medal in the 75-kg boxing category in the inaugural U-19 World Championships in the US.

Donald Trump was elected the president of the United States. Trump, 78, defeated Vice President Kamala Harris, to win his second presidential term. Trump won 312 electoral college votes, while Harris secured 226.

Opposition leader Navin Ramgoolam was appointed as prime minister of Malaysia after his Alliance du Changement (ADC) coalition won 60 of the 62 national assembly seats.

British writer Samantha Harvey won the leading literary award, Booker Award, for *Orbital*. The winner gets £50,000 while each of the six shortlisted authors get a sum of £2,500.

Sri Lanka's President Anura Kumara Dissanayake has reappointed educationist Harini Amarasuriya as the island country's prime minister after claiming a massive victory in the snap parliamentary elections.

Vaibhav Suryavanshi, 13, became the youngest player to be signed for the Indian Premier League (IPL). Suryavanshi from Bihar has been picked by Rajasthan Royals for a price of ₹1.1 crore.

Jharkhand Mukti Morcha (JMM) leader Hemant Soren was sworn in as the 14th chief minister of Jharkhand.

DEATHS

Bibek Debroy, economist and chairman of the Prime Minister's Economic Advisory Council, died aged 69. Debroy's death was caused by acute intestinal obstruction.

Prominent fashion designer Rohit Bal died of cardiac arrest aged 63.

Colm McLoughlin, an Irishman who helped lead Dubai Duty Free into becoming an airport retail giant generating billions of dollars, passed away. He was 81.

Quincey Jones, a giant in American pop music, died aged 91. Jones began his career as a jazz trumpeter and rose to a lyricist, composer and record producer.

Sharda Sinha, popularly known as Bihar Kokila, for her classical and folk songs passed away at 72. She was suffering from multiple myeloma. Sinha was known for her songs in Maithili, Bhojpuri, Magahi, Sanskrit, and Hindi.

Dinanath Batra, educationist and first principal of RSS-run Vidya Bharati school, passed away. He was 94.

Pandit Ramnarayan, who popularised the musical instrument Sarangi, died aged 96.

Justice Kuldip Singh, former judge of the Supreme Court, died following a brief illness. He was 92. Known as the 'Green Judge', Justice Singh presided over the Bench that heard the M.C. Mehta V. Kamal Nath, which was used as a benchmark for cases related to the environment.

DECEMBER 2024

'Brain rot' has been declared as Oxford's Word of The Year. Oxford University Press said that the word's frequency increased 230 per cent from the year before.

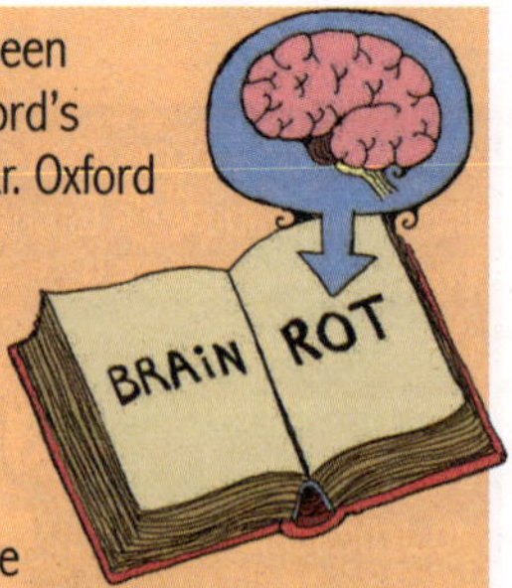

A controversial decision by a referee at a football match triggered violence that killed 56 people in Nzerekore, Guinea.

The Indian Space Research Organisation (ISRO)'s PSLV successfully placed into orbit two satellites of the European Space Agency as part of Proba 3 mission.

Over 100 Palestinians were killed as Israel kept pounding in the Gaza Strip through the month.

Rebel fighters took control of Syrian capital Damascus to end the regime of president Bashar al-Assad. The latest development put an end to the five-decade rule of Assad's family.

Taliban Refugee Minister Khalil Haqqani was killed in a suicide bombing in Afghan capital Kabul. He is the uncle of Sirajuddin Haqqani, the acting interior minister of Afghanistan.

At least 13 people died after a Navy super boat crashed into a private ferry heading to Elephanta Island off the Mumbai coast.

Abdul Rahman Makki, brother-in-law of the 2008 Mumbai attacks mastermind Hafiz Saeed, died of heart attack in Lahore. Makki was also one of the plotters of the Mumbai attacks.

India and Kuwait elevated their bilateral relationship to a 'strategic partnership' during Prime Minister Narendra Modi's two-day visit to the country. Modi's visit was the first by an Indian prime minister in 43 years. Amir of Kuwait Sheikh Meshal Al-Ahmad Al-Jaber Al-Sabah conferred upon Modi The Order of Mubarak Al-Kabeer, the highest national award of Kuwait.

At least 179 people were killed after a plane crashed while landing in Muan in South Korea. Video footage showed the Boeing 737-800 aircraft operated by Jeju Air coming off the runway before hitting a barrier and bursting into flames at Muan International Airport. Of the 181 people in the flight only two members of the flight crew—a man and a woman—survived the crash.

Mentioning the need to protect the country from 'North Korean communist forces' and 'anti-state forces', South Korean President Yoon Suk Yeol declared imposition of emergency martial law across his country on 3 December. Hours later, the decision was overturned by South Korea's Parliament following a vote. Yoon Suk Yeol was subsequently impeached for the move.

PEOPLE METER

Gukesh D, aged 18, became the youngest world chess champion after defeating China's Ding Liren. Earlier, Russia's Garry Kasparov was the youngest-ever world champion at 22 years of age.

Star off-spinner R Ashwin announced his retirement from international cricket on 18 November. In his Test career of 106 matches, Ashwin took 537 wickets at an average of 24, and scored 3,503 runs that included six centuries.

Devendra Fadnavis took oath as the 21st chief minister of Maharashtra. This was his third term as the CM of the state. Former Chief Minister Eknath Shinde from Shiv Sena and Nationalist Congress Party's Ajit Pawar were sworn in as deputy chief ministers.

Red Bull's Max Verstappen won the Qatar Grand Prix. It was Verstappen's second consecutive win in Qatar and ninth of the season.

Scottish artist Jasleen Kaur, who has an Indian origin, has won the prestigious Turner Prize 2024 for her exhibition 'Alter Altar'. The award is named after radical painter J M W Turner.

DEATHS

Urban planner Shirish Patel, who designed the first-ever flyover of India at Kemp's Corner in Mumbai, lost his battle to cancer. He was 92.

Architect Ranjit Sabikhi, who pioneered urban design in India, passed away at 89.

Former prime minister of India Manmohan Singh died at the age of 92 after a 'sudden loss of consciousness'. Singh was the prime minister from 2004 to 2014. He played a key role in 1991 as finance minister when India carried out major economic reforms.

Zakir Hussain, regarded as the greatest tabla player, passed away. He was 73.

Shyam Benegal, widely regarded as the pioneer of parallel cinema in India, passed away. He was 90. Benegal, a recipient of Padma Bhushan award, is known for movies like *Nishant*, *Manthan*, and *Zubeidaa*.

Om Prakash Chautala, supremo of Indian National Lok Dal (INLD) and five-time chief minister of Haryana, passed away on 20 December. The 89-year-old was the son of former deputy prime minister and Haryana chief minister Devi Lal.

Tulsi Gowda, an environmentalist, who was regarded as 'Tree Goddess', passed away. The Padma Shri recipient was 86.

Eminent Malyalam writer, author, and screenplay writer M T Vasudevan Nair died at the age of 91.

Acclaimed novelist Bapsi Sidhwa, one of earliest English-language writers from Pakistan, passed away at the age of 86. Her novel, 'Cracking India', became the basis of Deepa Mehta's film 'Earth' starring Aamir Khan in 1998.

The draft rules for the Digital Personal Data Protection (DPDP) Act, released by the Ministry of Electronics and Information Technology, made 'verifiable consent' of parents must for children to join social media platforms in India.

Justin Trudeau announced he will step down as the Canadian prime minister, ending his nine-year regime, under growing pressure from his own party.

The 18th Pravasi Bharatiya Divas convention was held in Bhubaneswar from 8-10 January on the theme, 'Diaspora's Contribution to a Viksit Bharat'. Pravasi Bharatiya Divas is celebrated once in every two years for the engagement of the overseas Indian community with the country and reconnecting them with their cultural roots.

On 15 January, the India Meteorological Department (IMD) marked the completion of 150 years of its establishment.

Actor Saif Ali Khan was stabbed multiple times at his Mumbai penthouse during a robbery bid by an illegal immigrant from Bangladesh, Shariful Islam Shehzad.

President Droupadi Murmu gave away the National Sports Awards 2024 to 47 sportspersons, including Major Dhyan Chand Khel Ratna Award, to four people—Gukesh D (chess), Harmanpreet Singh (hockey), Praveen Kumar (para-athletics), and Manu Bhaker (shooting)—at a function in Rashtrapati Bhavan.

Uttarakhand implemented Uniform Civil Code (UCC) from 27 January, bringing significant changes in marriage registration, inheritance rights and divorce laws. It became the first state in the country to do so.

A series of ferocious wildfires that erupted on 7 January, roared across Los Angeles in the US throughout the week, killing at least 29 people. A new wildfire was again reported on 22 January, covering 10,425 acres. However, it was contained in a day.

Centre announced the formation of the Eighth Pay Commission for salary revisions of approximately 49 lakh employees and 65 lakh pensioners, effective from 1 January 2026.

India won the inaugural Kho Kho Women's World Cup by defeating Nepal 78-40.

In the deadliest air disaster in the US since 2001, 67 people died in a midair collision between an American Airlines jet and Army helicopter over Washington D.C., before crashing into river Potomac.

Mahakumbh Mela began at Prayagraj on 13 January. The largest public gathering of the world was held at the sangam of holy rivers, Ganga, Yamuna, and now-dried Saraswati, for 45 days, during which crores of Hindu from across the world conducted the pilgrimage.

PEOPLE METER

Donald Trump was sworn in as the 47th President of the United States on 20 January. The US Congress had earlier formally certified Trump's re-election on 6 January in a special session, presided over by then outgoing Vice-President Kamala Harris, who he defeated in the 2024 election. This came exactly four years after a mob of Trump's supporters violently besieged the US Capitol.

Rocket and spacecraft propulsion expert V Narayanan became the new chairman of Indian Space Research Organisation (Isro) on 14 January, succeeding S Somanath.

Madison Keys (29) of the US won the women's singles at 2025 Australian Open, her first major title, by defeating two-time defending champion and world no. 1, Aryna Sabalenka.

Defending champion, No.1 seed Jannik Sinner (Italy), won his second successive Australian Open title with a victory over No.2 Alexander Zverev of Germany.

Indian pacer Jasprit Bumrah was named Men's Test Cricketer of the Year in ICC awards 2024. He took 71 wickets in 13 Tests at an average of 14.92 in 2024.

India opener Smriti Mandhana was named ICC Women's ODI Cricketer of the Year 2024.

India opener Trisha Gongadi became the first cricketer to score a century in women's U-19 T20 World Cup during a match against Scotland.

Nicolás Maduro was sworn in as the Venezuelan President for a third term on 10 January.

DEATHS

Eminent physicist and scientist Rajagopala Chidambaram passed away on 4 January. The former Principal Scientific Adviser to the Government of India (2001-2018) and Chairman of the Atomic Energy Commission & Secretary of the Department of Atomic Energy (1993-2000) played a pivotal role in the country's first nuclear test at Pokhran in 1974. He was also the architect of the 1998 nuclear test in Pokhran.

Film producer and Rajya Sabha member Pritish Nandy passed away in Mumbai on 8 January at the age of 73. Born in Bihar's Bhagalpur, Nandy was also a poet, editor, TV show host and an animal rights activist.

American filmmaker and screenwriter David Lynch died on 16 January. Born 20 January 1946, at Montana in the US, Lynch directed critically acclaimed films like *The Elephant Man* (1980), which won several awards and two nominations for Academy Awards, and science-fiction *Dune* (1984).

FEBRUARY 2025

Finance Minister Nirmala Sitharaman presented the Union Budget 2025-26 on 1 February, announcing a series of major changes, including a new tax regime, making annual income of up to ₹12 lakh tax-free.

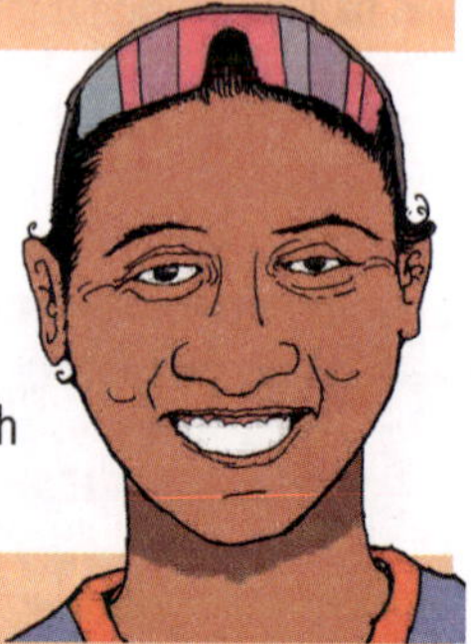

India, led by Niki Prasad, won the ICC U19 Women's T20 World Cup 2025 in Malaysia by defeating South Africa.

The BJP emerged victorious in the Delhi assembly elections, winning 48 seats out of 70 seats. Rekha Gupta, a three-time councillor, was picked as the chief minister.

US President Donald Trump signed an executive order to impose sanctions on International Criminal Court.

Manipur Chief Minister N Biren Singh resigned on 9 February, two years after an ethnic violence broke out in the state. Four days later, President's rule was imposed in Manipur.

Prime Minister Narendra Modi co-chaired AI Action Summit with French President Emmanuel Macron in Paris. During a bilateral talk between Modi and Macron, the two countries signed 10 pacts.

A Delhi court convicted former Congress MP Sajjan Kumar (80) in a double murder case during the 1984 anti-Sikh riots. Later on 25 February, the court awarded two life terms to Kumar for murdering a Sikh man and his son.

A UN report found that human rights abuses were inflicted on Bangladesh's Hindus, Ahmadiyya Muslims and indigenous communities during the anti-discrimination protests against Sheikh Hasina's government in 2024.

At least 18 people were killed in a stampede at the New Delhi railway station on 15 February. The stampede occurred due to overcrowding, with people jostling to board trains, including a special train to Maha Kumbh Mela in Prayagraj.

Central Board of Secondary Education (CBSE) decided to hold board exams for Class 10 twice a year from 2026, Union Minister of Education Dharmendra Pradhan posted on social media. It will also introduce the CBSE Global Curriculum for 260 foreign schools from 2026-2027.

Microsoft said it was retiring internet calling service Skype, which it bought in 2011. 'Starting in May 2025, Skype will no longer be available,' it said on X, directing users to sign into Microsoft's Teams platform.

PEOPLE METER

Indian-American businesswoman, philanthropist and musician Chandrika Tandon (71) won a Grammy for Best New Age, Ambient or Chant Album for Triveni, along with her collaborators Wouter Kellerman and Eru Matsumoto on 3 February.

India cricketer Shubman Gill became the fastest batter in the world to score 2,500 runs in ODIs in a match against England in Ahmedabad on 12 February. He achieved this milestone in his 50th ODI match, during which he also scored his 7th ODI century.

Tulsi Gabbard was confirmed as the director of national intelligence by the US Senate on 12 February. The senate voted 52 to 48.

British surgeon and former Paralympian John McFall (43) became the first astronaut with a physical disability to be selected for an International Space Station mission, European Space Agency announced on 14 February.

Vishvaa Rajakumar (20), a college student from Puducherry, won the Memory League World Championship 2025, an online competition, in early February by memorizing 80 digits in just 13.5 seconds and 30 images in 8.4 seconds.

Gyanesh Kumar was appointed as the chief election commissioner on 17 February.

Kash Patel became the first Indian-American and Hindu to become the Director of the FBI on 20 February. He is the 9th FBI director.

Finance Secretary Tuhin Kanta Pandey was named the new chairman of market regulator Sebi.

DEATHS

Veteran banker Victor Menezes—the first person of Indian origin to be among the top rungs of a multinational bank—passed away in the US on 3 February at 77 years of age. An alumnus of IIT-Bombay and MIT, he retired as senior vice-chairman of Citibank following a 32-year stint.

Powerlifting champion from Rajasthan's Bikaner, Yashtika Acharya (17), died after a 270 kg rod fell on her neck during a training session on 18 February. Acharya was a gold medalist at the Junior National Games.

Singer Roberta Flack, a four-time Grammy winner best known for hits like 'Killing Me Softly', died at the age of 88 on 24 February.

Oscar-winning actor Gene Hackman (95) and his wife Betsy Arakawa, a 65-year-old classical pianist, along with their dog, were found dead on 26 February at their home in the US state of New Mexico.

Prime Minister Narendra Modi chaired the seventh meeting of National Board for Wildlife in Gujarat's Gir, where he released the first-ever riverine dolphin estimation report in the country. The number of the aquatic mammal in the country was pegged at 6,327.

Modi laid the foundation stone of National Referral Centre for Wildlife at Junagadh in Gujarat and announced Centre of Excellence to deal with human-wildlife conflict at SACON, Coimbatore.

Austria's first three-party coalition government since World War-II took office, keeping Russia-friendly far-right Freedom Party out of power.

An unexploded World War II bomb found near Gare du Nord railway station in Paris was defused. Many trains to and from one of the biggest stations of Europe were cancelled.

Madhav National Park in Madhya Pradesh became the country's 58th tiger reserve. The national park is the ninth from the state to get the recognition.

After completing a mission that lasted more than nine months, NASA astronauts Butch Wilmore and Indian-American Sunita Williams returned to Earth with a splashdown in Gulf of Mexico, off the coast of Tallahassee, in Florida, US.

According to World Happiness Report 2025, Finland was ranked the happiest country, leading the nations for the eighth year in a row. Finns scored 7.73 out of 10 when asked to evaluate their lives. India ranked 118th, up from previous year's 126th.

Central Bureau of Investigation (CBI) filed a closure report in actor Sushant Singh Rajput death case, more than four years after it took over the probe.

The Centre notified a 24 per cent hike in the MPs' salaries with effect from 1 April 2023. With this, Lok Sabha and Rajya Sabha members' monthly salaries went up to ₹1.24 lakh a month, up from ₹1 lakh, and a daily allowance of ₹2,500 instead of ₹2,000 earlier. The pension for former MPs has also been increased to ₹31,000 from ₹25,000 a month.

In one of its strongest earthquakes in a century, a 7.7-magnitude earthquake rocked Myanmar, besides neighbouring Thailand, killing over 3,600 people and injuring over 3,000.

India sent an 80-member team of National Disaster Response Force to Myanmar for rescue operations. Rescue teams from China, Singapore and Thailand also joined the operations.

Hindi writer Vinod Kumar Shukla (88) was selected as a recipient of the 59th Jnanpith Award, India's highest literary honour. Known for his poetry, short stories and essays, Shukla became the first author from Chhattisgarh to receive the prestigious award.

PEOPLE METER

India's teenage chess sensation Gukesh D reached a career-high ranking of world No. 3, in the latest FIDE classical ratings released on 1 March.

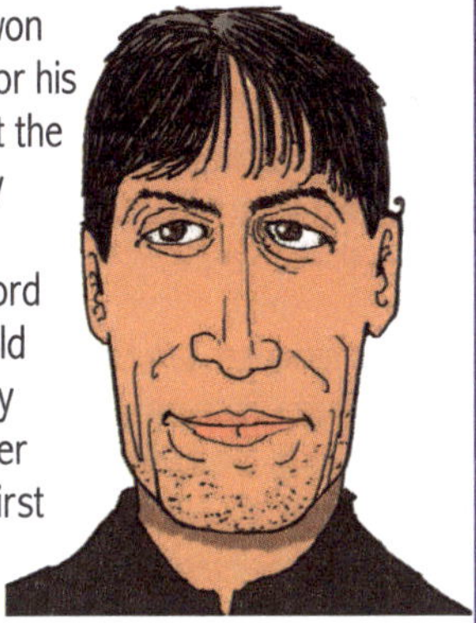

Sean Baker won four Oscars for his film 'Anora' at the 97th Academy Awards on 2 March, a record previously held by Walt Disney in 1953. Baker became the first person to win four Oscars for best picture, director, original screenplay, and film editing in the same year for the same film. Disney had won the four Oscars for four different films.

Former central banker Mark Carney was elected the leader of Canada's ruling Liberal Party on 9 March. He succeeded Justin Trudeau as Canada's prime minister.

Zimbabwe's Kirsty Coventry was elected the 10th president of International Olympic Committee (IOC) on 20 March, becoming its first woman chief. Coventry, who was elected at the 144th IOC Session in Costa Navarino, Greece, succeeded Thomas Bach, whose 12-year tenure ended on 23 June.

Indian table tennis player Achanta Sharath Kamal retired from the game after playing an international match on his home turf Chennai at WTT Star Contender, ending a career of over two decades.

DEATHS

Former India all-rounder cricketer Syed Abid Ali passed away in California, US, on 12 March, at the age of 83. He represented India in 29 Tests from 1967 to 1974.

Actor-filmmaker Deb Mukherjee passed away after a prolonged illness at his residence in suburban Mumbai on 14 March at the age of 83. He was the father of director Ayan Mukerji.

American boxer George Foreman died on 21 March, aged 76. Born 10 January 1949, at Marshall in Texas, Foreman was a two-time world heavyweight champion (1973-74 and 1994-95). He became the oldest world heavyweight champion in 1994-95 after regaining the title for the second time at the age of 45.

Indian classical vocalist and composer Garimella Balakrishna Prasad passed away on 9 March at the age of 76 years following a cardiac arrest. Prasad was renowned for his devotional compositions known as Annamacharya Sankeertanas.

Arvind Singh Mewar, a member of the erstwhile royal family of Mewar, died on 15 March in Rajasthan's Udaipur after a prolonged illness. He was the 76th custodian of the House of Mewar and was committed to the cause of heritage conservation.

APRIL 2025

US President Donald Trump imposed tariffs on various countries, including allies like India. According to Trump's Reciprocal Tariffs, US's archrival China has faced the maximum—34 per cent tariffs on its goods coming to the US. The following days saw a serious escalation in tariffs and counter-tariffs between the US and China.

The Waqf (Amendment) Act 2025 came into force on 8 April. It was passed in the Rajya Sabha with 128 members voting in favour, while 95 opposing it. In the Lok Sabha, 288 members supported the Bill, while 232 were against it.

Tahawwur Rana, one of the key conspirators in the 2008 Mumbai terrorist attacks, was extradited to India from the US. He was arrested by the National Investigation Agency (NIA) soon after he arrived in New Delhi.

Telangana became the first state in the country to implement Scheduled Caste sub-categorisation. With this, broader SC category has been divided into smaller, more specific groups to address inequalities within the group.

Manuscripts of Bhagavad Gita and Bharat Muni's Natyashastra have been added to the United Nations Educational, Scientific and Cultural Organization's (UNESCO's) Memory of the World Register.

India and France signed an Inter-Governmental Agreement (IGA) for procuring 26 Rafale-M aircraft for the Indian Navy.

US strikes on fuel port in Yemen's Hodeidah killed 74 people and injured 171. The attack was targetted at the Houthis. Days later, 68 people were killed in a US airstrike at a detention centre hosting African migrants in Yemen's Saada.

Israeli airstrikes killed at least 100 people in the Gaza Strip on 3 April, including 27 or more sheltering at a school. Days later, more than 90 people were killed in several Israeli airstrikes within a span of 48 hours in Gaza.

Twenty-six people, including 25 tourists, were gunned down by terrorists at a meadow near Pahalgam in Jammu and Kashmir on 22 April. The Resistance Front (TRF), a shadow group of terror outfit Lashkar-e-Taiba (LeT) claimed responsibility for the attack.

In a major step to normalize ties with China, India announced the resumption of Kailash Mansoravar Yatra from June this year after a gap of five years. In 2020, following the killings of 20 Indian Army soldiers after a clash with Chinese troops, the yatra was stopped.

PEOPLE METER

Vandana Katariya, first Indian woman hockey player to play 300 matches, announced her retirement. She scored 158 goals for India in 320 matches.

Chain Singh brought India its first medal, by way of a bronze in the men's 50-metre rifle 3-positions event in the ISSF World Cup in Buenos Aires, Argentina.

Rudrankksh Patil clinched the gold medal in the men's 10-metre air rifle shooting event at the ISSF World Cup 2025 in Buenos Aires, Argentina.

Abhinash Jamwal secured silver medal in the 65-kg category in the boxing world cup in Brazil. In the gold medal match, Jamwal lost 0-5 against Yuri Reis.

Suruchi Phogat, 19, clinched the gold medal in the women's 10-metre air pistol in the ISSF World Cup in Argentina.

Vijayveer Sidhu won gold medal in the men's 25-metre rapid fire event in the ISSF World Cup. This is the second medal and first gold for Sidhu in the world cup.

Simranpreet Kaur clinched the silver medal in the women's 25-metre pistol event at the ISSF World Cup in Lima, Peru.

DEATHS

Val Kilmer, American actor who was seen in movies like *Batman* and *Top Gun* died aged 65. The actor was suffering from pneumonia.

Manoj Kumar, popular actor who was known for his patriotic movies in the 1960s, passed away. He was 87.

Kumudini Lakhia, an iconic Kathak dancer, passed away at the age of 94. She was awarded Padma Shri in 1987.

Mario Vargas Llosa, eminent novelist and journalist from Peru, passed away at the age of 89. He was awarded the Nobel Prize of Literature in 2010.

Renowned author William McKay Aitken, a Scottish born Indian travel writer, passed away at the age of 90. The *Nanda Devi Affair*, 'Riding the Ranges', and 'Footloose in the Himalaya' were some of his notable works.

Pope Francis, leader of the Roman Catholic Church, passed away at the age of 88. He was the first pope from Latin America.

Former ISRO chairman Krishnaswamy Kasturirangan died at the age of 84. Under his leadership, ISRO witnessed several major milestones, including the successful launching and operationalisation of India's launch vehicle, the Polar Satellite Launch Vehicle (PSLV) and, the first successful flight testing of Geosynchronous Satellite Launch Vehicle (GSLV).

The US and Ukraine signed a deal to establish a joint investment fund for the reconstruction of Ukraine.

Prime Minister Narendra Modi inaugurated India's first deep water and container transshipment port at Vizhinjam in Kerala.

Continuing its diplomatic offensive against Pakistan, India curbed water flow through the Baglihar Dam, stopped imports, banned docking of ships from Pakistan, and suspended the exchange of all mails and parcels.

Indian Council of Agricultural Research (ICAR) has developed India's first genome-edited rice varieties—DRR Rice 100 (Kamla) and Pusa DST Rice 1.

The UK and India have agreed on a bilateral trade deal. According to the deal, UK tariffs on footwear, textiles, automobile components, electrical machinery, minerals, and base metals—currently in the range of 2-18 per cent—will be eliminated for India. Meanwhile, India will slash tariffs on whiskey and gin to 75 per cent from 150 per cent, and further to 40 per cent over 10 years. New Delhi will also cut automotive tariffs to 10 per cent from 100 per cent.

In response to the terror attack in Jammu and Kashmir in April in which 26 people were killed, India launched Operation Sindoor to target terror bases in Pakistan. India struck at nine terror sites in Pakistan's Muridke, Bahawalpur, Muzaffarabad, Sialkot, Narowal, and Pakistan-occupied Kashmir. After India's strike, 13 people were killed in India due to Pakistan's shelling near Line of Control (LoC).

After days of intense fighting following the terror attack near Pahalgam in Jammu and Kashmir, India and Pakistan on 9 May announced an end to all military action. The ceasefire was announced by Foreign Secretary Vikram Misri.

Underlining the importance of environmental conservation, the Supreme Court struck down a 2017 notification by the environment ministry that granted approval to projects ex-post facto (after the commencement of work).

The Indian Space Research Organisation's (ISRO's) earth observation satellite failed in the launch phase on 18 May. The EOS-09 satellite was aboard the PSLV-C61 (Polar Satellite Launch Vehicle) faced anomaly in the third stage of the launch.

Australian Prime Minister Anthony Albanese was re-elected to the post, becoming the first leader in decades to secure a second term in the country.

The first batch of women graduates passed out from the National Defence Academy (NDA) in Pune on 29 May.

PEOPLE METER

Indian captain Rohit Sharma and former skipper Virat Kohli retired from Test cricket.

Robert Francis Prevost was chosen as the leader of the Catholic Church. Prevost, 69, who will be known as Pope Leo XIV, is the first North American to be elected for the role.

Madhura Dhamangaonkar clinched her first individual World Cup gold in archery in Shanghai, China.

Justice Bhushan Ramkrishna Gavai has been appointed as the Chief Justice of India. He succeeded Chief Justice Sanjiv Khanna, whose tenure ended on 13 May.

Indian author Banu Mushtaq has won the International Booker Prize 2025 for her book *Heart Lamp*, a collection of short stories written in Kannada.

Jyothi Yarraji, 25, defended her gold in the 100 metres hurdles at the Asian Athletics Championships 2025, clocking 12.96 seconds to complete her race— a championship record.

Indian American Faizan Zaki (13) won the 100th US national Spelling Bee title.

Pooja (18) with a high jump of 1.89 metres secured India her first gold in the event since Bobby Aloysius's victory in 2000 at the Asian Athletics Championships.

DEATHS

Inah Canabarro Lucas, a Brazilian nun who was the world's oldest person, died just weeks before turning 117.

K V Rabiya, who rose to prominence for her role in Kerala adult literacy programme, passed away at the age of 59. In 2022, she was awarded Padma Shri for social work.

Jose Mujica, a guerilla fighter who served as the President of Uruguay, died aged 89. Nicknamed "Pepe", he led the country from 2010 to 2015.

Jayant Narlikar, eminent astrophysicist who challenged the Big Bang theory and developed an alternative model on evolution, died. He was 86.

M R Srinivasan, often regarded as the doyen of India's nuclear programme, passed away at the age of 95.

Ngũgĩ wa Thiong'o, a giant figure in modern African literature, passed away at the age of 87.

Acclaimed Indian naturalist, conservationist and writer Valmik Thapar passed away. He was 73. Thapar played a big part in India's tiger conservation efforts and wrote more than two dozen books.

JUNE 2025

Right-wing historian Karol Nawrocki was elected Poland's new president.

As many as 11 people died and 47 injured following a chaos and stampede during the celebrations of IPL victory of Royal Challengers Bengaluru at the M Chinnaswamy stadium in Bengaluru.

South Korea elected Opposition liberal candidate Lee Jae-myung its next president, six months after his predecessor's martial law bid failed.

Prime Minister Narendra Modi inaugurated the first passenger train to Srinagar. Vande Bharat Express started running from Katra to Srinagar from 7 June.

A new UN report estimated India's population for 2025 at 1.46 billion. According to the UN Population Fund's 2025 State of World Population Report, India's population is likely to grow to about 1.7 billion before it begins to fall, after about 40 years.

Amid escalation in tensions between the two countries, Israel attacked Iran's key nuclear facility. Iran responded by firing a barrage of missiles into Israel.

The Union Ministry of Home Affairs notified Census 2027, officially starting the process to count India's population. India's last census was conducted in 2011.

French Blood Establishment said the country's scientists have found a new, 'ultra rare' blood group in a Guadeloupean woman. This is the 48th known blood group system in the world.

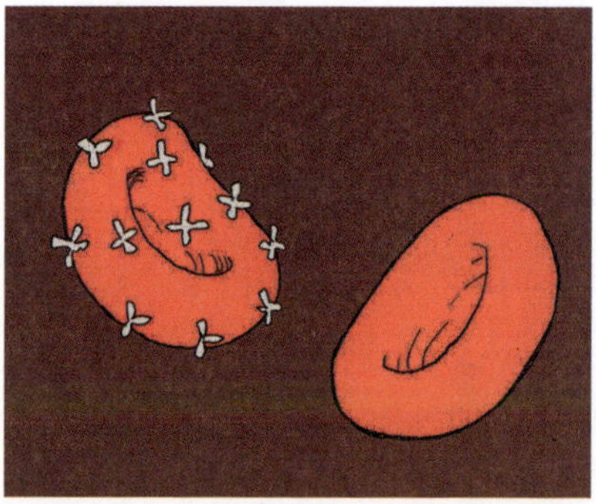

The Election Commission of India issued instructions for holding Special Intensive Revision (SIR) of the electoral rolls in Bihar.

Axiom Mission 4 (Ax-4) with Indian astronaut Shubhanshu Shukla onboard SpaceX's Dragon Crew Module was successfully launched to International Space Station. Shukla was the Ax-04 mission pilot.

A TRAGEDY IN AIR

Air India flight AI171 from Ahmedabad to London Gatwick crashed into a medical college hostel complex less than 30 seconds after takeoff from Sardar Vallabhbhai Patel International Airport around 1.39 p.m., killing 241 of the 242 people onboard and 34 on the ground. This was one of India's worst aviation disasters ever. British citizen Viswashkumar Ramesh, who was assigned seat number 11A, was the only passenger who survived the crash. Gujarat's former chief minister, Vijay Rupani, also perished in this plane crash.

PEOPLE METER

Defending champion and world No. 2 Carlos Alcaraz won the French Open by defeating Jannik Sinner in the final on 8 June.

Gymnast Pranati Nayak won her third bronze medal at Women's Artistic Gymnastics Asian Championships in vault in Jecheon, South Korea, on 14 June.

Indian javelin superstar Neeraj Chopra clinched two titles in June. Days after his Paris Diamond League win on 20 June, he won the title at Golden Spike meet in his maiden appearance on 24 June.

Nine-year-old Aarit Kapil, a Class V student, from Delhi held chess World No. 1 Magnus Carlsen to a draw in an online blitz game on 24 June.

Chess grandmaster R Praggnanandhaa became India's top-ranked player and World No. 4 in live ratings after winning UzChess Cup Masters 2025 in Tashkent on 27 June.

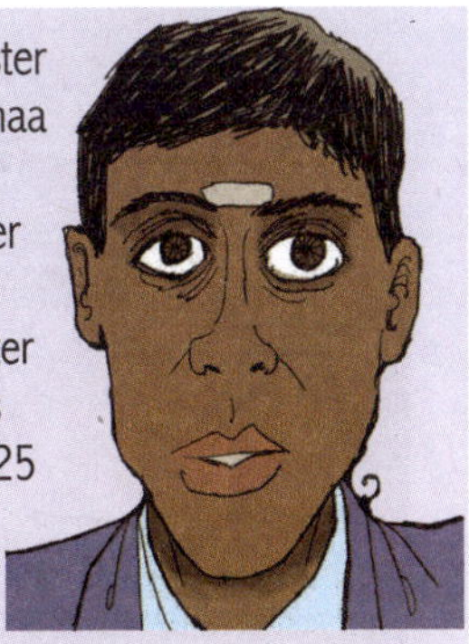

DEATHS

British novelist Frederick Forsyth died on 9 June, aged 86. A former journalist and an informant for Britain's MI6 foreign spy agency, Forsyth is known for his best-selling thrillers like *The Day of the Jackal* and *The Dogs of War*.

Gujarat's former chief minister Vijay Rupani died in the 12 June Air India crash. He was on his way to London to meet his wife and daughter.

FedEx founder Fred Smith, whose vision for shipping packages overnight led to a new sector of world economy, died at the age of 80 at Memphis in Tennessee, US, on 21 June.

Former India cricketer left-arm spinner Dilip Doshi, died at the age of 77. Doshi made his Test debut at the age of 32 in 1979. Grammy-winning composer of film *Mission: Impossible* Lalo Schifrin died of complications from pneumonia on 26 June. He was 93.

JULY 2025

A devastating flood – deadliest in the US in 100 years – hit Texas Hill Country, killing at least 134 people on 4 July. Hundreds remained missing till 15 July.

India cricket team under Shubman Gill's captaincy registered their biggest Test victory by 336 runs against England at Edgbaston.

The government released a preliminary report, submitted by Aircraft Accident Investigation Bureau, on the Air India's B787 aircraft crash in Ahmedabad on 12 June, according to which fuel supply to both its engines was cut off, three seconds after its takeoff, either by a faulty switch or manually.

Indian astronaut Group Captain Shubhanshu Shukla, along with his Axiom-4 crew members, returned to Earth on 15 July in a SpaceX Dragon spacecraft – Grace – which splashed down in Pacific Ocean off the coast of San Diego in southern California, United States.

Union Cabinet, chaired by Prime Minister Narendra Modi, approved 'Prime Minister Dhan-Dhaanya Krishi Yojana' to cover 100 districts for six years, beginning 2025-26. The scheme aims to enhance agricultural productivity, increase adoption of crop diversification and sustainable agricultural practices, augment post-harvest storage at panchayat and block levels, improve irrigation facilities and facilitate availability of long- and short-term credit.

University of Southampton opened its India campus in Gurgaon on 16 July.

At least 31 people, including the pilot, died and over 150 were injured after a Bangladesh Air Force training aircraft crashed into a school and college campus in Dhaka on 21 July.

India ranked 77th on Henley Passport Index 2025, released on 22 July, climbing eight places from 85 last year. Also, the number of countries allowing visa-free access to Indian passport holders has increased to 59 during this time.

Three terrorists, among those responsible for the Pahalgam terror attack, were killed in Operation Mahadev on 28 July.

Vice President Jagdeep Dhankhar stepped down from his post, with two years remaining of his five-year tenure, citing health concerns.

PEOPLE METER

Narendra Modi became India's second-longest serving prime minister in consecutive terms by completing 4,078 uninterrupted days in office on 25 July. He surpassed the 4,077-day tenure of Indira Gandhi, who served from January 1966 to March 1977.

1989-batch IPS officer of Punjab cadre, Parag Jain, succeeded Ravi Sinha as the incoming chief of Research & Analysis Wing (R&AW), India's external intelligence agency. His close to two-year term began on 1 July 2025, and will end on 30 June 2027.

K L Rahul became the second Indian batter to score more than one century at Lord's in London after Dilip Vengsarkar, with his ton against England on Day 3 of the 3rd test on 12 July.

Iga Swiatek won her first women's singles Wimbledon title by defeating Amanda Anisimova 6-0, 6-0 on 12 July. This was the most one-sided women's Wimbledon final in 114 years.

India-born Sabih Khan took over as the new chief operating officer of Apple in July-end, succeeding Jeff Williams.

World number one men's tennis player Jannik Sinner won his first Wimbledon championship by defeating two-time defending champion Carlos Alcaraz on 13 July.

Divya Deshmukh won the women's chess World Cup by beating Koneru Humpy in tie-breaks in the final on 28 July.

DEATHS

Telugu lyricist Siva Shakthi Datta died on 7 July. He was also the Father of 'RRR' and 'Baahubali' director S S Rajamouli.

Padma Shri and Padma Bhushan awardee south Indian actress Saroja Devi died of age-related ailments on 14 July at her residence in Bengaluru. She was 87. She acted in over 200 films.

World's oldest marathon runner 113-year-old Fauja Singh died after being struck by a vehicle on Jalandhar-Pathankot highway on 14 July.

Former Kerala chief minister V S Achuthanandan passed away on 21 July at the age 101. He was a comrade from the CPI(M)'s founding generation.

Extreme athlete Felix Baumgartner, who had jumped from the edge of space, breaking the world record for the highest skydive, died in a motorized paragliding accident in Italy on 17 July.

Musician Ozzy Osbourne, the front man of heavy metal band Black Sabbath, died in the UK on 22 July at the age of 76.

Eminent economist Meghnad Desai, who was a member of the United Kingdom's House of Lords, passed away on 23 July at the age of 85. Hailing from Gujarat, Desai served as emeritus professor of economics at London School of Economics. He taught there from 1965 to 2003.

Awards

The Padma Awards 2025

The 'Padmas'—Padma Vibhushan, Padma Bhushan and Padma Shri—are India's highest civilian awards, awarded for exceptional and distinguished service in all fields and disciplines. This year 139 awards were given.

Padma Vibhushan

- Duvvur Nageshwar Reddy - **Medicine**
- Justice (Retd.) Jagdish Singh Khehar - **Public Affairs**
- Kumudini Rajnikant Lakhia - **Art**
- Lakshminarayana Subramaniam - **Art**
- M. T. Vasudevan Nair (Posthumous) - **Literature & Education**
- Osamu Suzuki (Posthumous) - **Trade & Industry**
- Sharda Sinha (Posthumous) - **Art**

Osamu Suzuki

Padma Bhushan

- A Surya Prakash (Literature & Education-Journalism
- Anant Nag (Art)
- Bibek Debroy (Posthumous) (Literature & Education)
- Jatin Goswami (Art)
- Jose Chacko Periappuram (Medicine)
- Kailash Nath Dikshit (Archaeology)
- Manohar Joshi (Posthumous) (Public Affairs)

Bibek Debroy

- Nalli Kuppuswami Chetti (Trade & Industry)
- Nandamuri Balakrishna (Art)
- P R Sreejesh (Sports)
- Pankaj Patel (Trade & Industry)
- Pankaj Udhas (Posthumous) (Art)
- Rambahadur Rai (Literature & Education-Journalism)
- Sushil Kumar Modi (Posthumous) (Public Affairs)
- Sadhvi Ritambhara (Social Work)
- S Ajith Kumar (Art)
- Shekhar Kapur (Art)
- Shobana Chandrakumar (Art)
- Vinod Dham (Science & Engineering)

PADMA SHRI

113 people were awarded Padma Shri this year. Notable Padma Shri awardees include Gangtok folk artist Naren Gurung, Hindi and Nimadi author Jagdish Joshila, apple farmer Hariman Sharma from Bilaspur, and Dr. Neerja Bhatla, a Delhi-based gynecologist specializing in cervical cancer detection and management.

Neerja Bhatla

NOBEL PRIZE 2024

Nobel Prize for Economics: Daron Acemoglu, Simon Johnson, and James Robinson receive the prize for showing how institutional differences shape national prosperity. Their work links inequality to colonial systems and explains how institutions persist and evolve.

Nobel Prize for Peace: The Hibakusha, survivors of Hiroshima and Nagasaki, receive the Nobel Peace Prize for their fight against nuclear weapons. The extraordinary efforts of Nihon Hidankyo and other representatives of the Hibakusha have contributed greatly to the establishment of a nuclear taboo.

Nobel Prize for Literature: The 2024 Nobel Prize in Literature goes to South Korean author Han Kang for her poetic, experimental prose that explores historical trauma and the fragility of life. Her work reveals deep connections between body and soul, the living and the dead.

Han Kang

Nobel Prize in Chemistry: The 2024 Nobel Prize in Chemistry honors breakthroughs in protein science. David Baker built novel proteins, while Demis Hassabis and John Jumper used AI to predict their complex structures.

Nobel Prize in Physics: John J. Hopfield and Geoffrey Hinton used physics-based tools to shape modern machine learning. Hopfield developed a system to store and retrieve information, while Hinton created a method for uncovering patterns in data—crucial to today's large neural networks.

Nobel Prize in Physiology or Medicine: Victor Ambros and Gary Ruvkun discovered microRNA, tiny molecules that regulate genes in multicellular organisms. Their discovery in the small worm (C. elegans) revealed a new, vital principle of gene regulation.

PRADHAN MANTRI RASHTRIYA BAL PURASKAR DECEMBER 2024

The award is bestowed for different categories which include innovation, scholastic, social service, art and culture, science and technology, sports and bravery. The award was presented in December 2024 to seventeen recipients:

Art & Culture: Keya Haktar (Maharashtra), Ayan Sajad (Kashmir), Jananae Narayanan (Tamil Nadu), Vyas Om Jignesh (Gujarat), Sanchi Aggarwal (Uttar Pradesh)

Innovation: Sindhoora Raja (Karnataka), Risheek Kumar (Jammu & Kashmir)

Sports: Hembati Nag (Chhattisgarh), Priteesmita Bhoi (Odisha), Saanvi Sood (Punjab), Jessy Raj Mathrapu (Andhra Pradesh), Goldi Kumari (Bihar), Arav Bhardwaj (Delhi), Anish Sarkar (West Bengal)

Bravery: Kisen Wanniang (Meghalaya), Saurav Kumar (Bihar), Karina Thapa (Maharashtra)

THE LAUREUS WORLD SPORTS AWARDS 2025

Laureus World Sportsman of the Year: Mondo Duplantis for Athletics (Sweden)

Laureus World Sportswoman of the Year: Simone Biles for Gymnastics (USA)

Laureus World Team of the Year: Read Madrid Men's Football Team (Spain)

Laureus World Breakthrough of the Year: Lamine Yamal for Football (Spain)

Laureus World Comeback of the Year: Rebeca Andrade for Gymnastics (Brazil)

Laureus World Action Sportsperson of the Year: Tom Pidcock for Mountain Biking (UK)

Laureus World Sportsperson of the Year With a Disability: Yuyan Jiang for Para Swimming (China)

Laureus Sport for Good Award: KICK4LIFE for Football (Lesotho)

Laureus Sporting Icon: Rafael Nadal for Tennis (Spain)

Laureus Lifetime Achievement: Kelly Slater for Surfing (USA)

Mondo Duplantis

Rebeca Andrade

The Oscars 2025

Adrian Brody

Best Actor: Adrian Brody, *The Brutalist*
Best Actress: Mikey Madison, *Anora*
Best Picture: *Anora*
Best Animated Feature: *Flow*
Best Supporting Actor: Kieran Culkin, *A Real Pain*
Best Supporting Actress: Zoe Saldaña, *Emilia Pérez*
Best Documentary Feature: *No Other Land*
Best International Film: *I'm Still Here* (Brazil)
Best Documentary Short Film: *The Only Girl in the Orchestra*
Best Animated Short: *In the Shadow of the Cypress*
Best Adapted Screenplay: *Conclave*
Best Sound: *Dune: Part 2*
Best Original Song: 'El Mal' from *Emilia Pérez*
Best Editing: Sean Baker, *Anora*
Best Director: Sean Baker, *Anora*

The Grammy Awards 2025

Chappell Roan

Lady Gaga and Bruno Mars

Album of the year: *Cowboy Carter* (Beyoncé)
Best new artist: Chappell Roan
Record of the year: *'Not Like Us'* (Kendrick Lamar)
Song of the year: 'Not Like Us' (Kendrick Lamar)
Best pop solo performance: 'Espresso' (Sabrina Carpenter)
Best dance/electronic album: *BRAT* (Charli xcx)
Best pop duo/group performance: 'Die with a Smile' (Lady Gaga & Bruno Mars)
Best country album: *Cowboy Carter* (Beyoncé)
Best R&B song: 'Saturn' (SZA)
Best pop vocal album: *Short n' Sweet* (Sabrina Carpenter)
Best R&B performance: 'Made For Me' (Muni Long)
Best R&B album: *11:11* (Deluxe) (Chris Brown)
Best rap song: *"Not Like Us'* (Kendrick Lamar)

THE GOLDEN GLOBES 2025

Best Motion Picture Drama: *The Brutalist*

Best Motion Picture Musical or Comedy: *Emilia Pérez*

Best Motion Picture Non-English Language: *Emilia Pérez*

Best Motion Picture Animated: *Flow*

Best Director Motion Picture: Brady Corbet, *The Brutalist*

Best Performance by an Actor in a Motion Picture Drama: Adrian Brody, *The Brutalist*

Zoe Saldaña

Best Performance by an Actress in a Motion Picture Drama: Fernanda Torres, *I'm Still Here*

Best Performance by an Actress in a Supporting Role in any Motion Picture: Zoe Saldaña, *Emilia Pérez*

Best Performance by an Actor in a Motion Picture Musical or Comedy: Sebastian Stan, *A Different Man*

Best Performance by an Actress in a Motion Picture Musical or Comedy: Demi Moore, *The Substance*

Best Performance by an Actor in a Supporting Role in any Motion Picture: Kieran Culkin, *A Real Pain*

Best Original Score Motion Picture: Trent Reznor, *Atticus Ross Challengers*

Best Original Song Motion Picture: 'El Mal', *Emilia Pérez*

Best Television Series Drama: *Shogun*

Cinematic and Box Office Achievement: *Wicked*

Crunchyroll Anime Awards 2025

Anime of the Year: *Look Back*
Best Continuing Anime Series: *Demon Slayer*
Best Comedy Anime: *Mashle: Magic & Muscles - The Divine Visionary Candidate Exam Arc*
Best Action Anime: *Solo Leveling*
Best Slice of Life Anime: *Makeine: Too Many Losing Heroines!*
Best Anime Film: *Solo Leveling*
Best Anime Song: 'Otonoke' by Creepy Nuts *(DAN DA DAN)*

Demon Slayer

Pulitzer Prize 2025

Joseph Pulitzer was one of the most influential journalists of the late nineteenth and early twentieth centuries in America. The Pulitzer Prizes for journalism, books, music and letters were instituted at Columbia University, as per his will, in 1917.

Journalism: *ProPublica* (Public Service) for urgent reporting about pregnant women who died after doctors delayed urgently needed care for fear of violating vague 'life of the mother' exceptions in states with strict abortion laws.

Staff of Reuters (Investigative Reporting) for their bold exposé on lax global regulation making deadly fentanyl cheap and easily available in the U.S.

Declan Walsh and the Staff of the New York Times (International Reporting) for uncovering Sudan's conflict through foreign influence, gold trade links, and chilling accounts of atrocities and famine.

Fiction: *James* by Percival Everett (Doubleday)

Drama: *Purpose* by Brandon Jacob-Jenkins; a play exploring how generations of an African-American family grapple with legacy, identity, and heritage.

General Non-fiction: *To the Success of Our Hopeless Cause: The Many Lives of the Soviet Dissident Movement* by Benjamin Nathans (Princeton University Press)

International Booker Prize 2025

Banu Mushtaq and Deepa Bhasthi have won the International Booker Prize 2025 for *Heart Lamp*, the first collection of short stories to win the prize.

Written between 1990 and 2023, *Heart Lamp's* 12 stories chronicle the lives of women and girls in patriarchal communities in southern India.

It is the first book translated from Kannada, a language spoken by an estimated 65 million people, to be nominated for the prize. Deepa Bhasthi becomes the first Indian translator to win the International Booker.

INDIA
States and Union Territories
Important Office holders
Organisations and Commissions
Indian Politics
Business and Start-ups
Overview of the Economy
Landmark Judgements
Indian History Timeline

ANDHRA PRADESH

- *Capital*: Amaravati
- *Date of formation*: 1 November 1956
- *Governor*: S. Abdul Nazeer
- *Chief minister*: N. Chandrababu Naidu
- *Tourist attractions*: R K Beach, Borra Caves, Tirumala Venkateswara Temple, Thotlakonda, Horsley Hills, Kolleru Lake, Kanakadurga Temple, Dolphin House
- *Festivals*: Shivaratri, Pongal, Vinayaka Chaturthi, Jan-Makara Sankranti, Ugadi
- *Major dance and music forms*: Kuchipudi, Bhamakalpam, Dappu
- *Arts and crafts*: Kalamkari cotton, ikat handlooms, banjara embroidery
- *Languages*: Telugu, Urdu, Hindi
- *Size*: 160, 205 sq km
- *Population*: 5,31,56,000
- *Rivers*: Godavari, Krishna, Tungabhadra, Palar, Pennar
- *Forests and wildlife sanctuaries*: Rajiv Gandhi NP, Papikonda NP, Pulicat Lake and WS
- *State animal*: Blackbuck
- *State bird*: Rose-ringed parakeet
- *State flower*: Jasmine
- *State tree*: Neem
- *Major crops*: Jowar, rice, bajra, cotton

Interesting Trivia

- Sea turtles have made a nesting ground in Andhra Pradesh's east coast.
- Cured and dried goatskin is coloured with vegetable dyes to make *Tholu Bommalatta* or leather puppets.

ARUNACHAL PRADESH

- *Capital*: Itanagar
- *Date of formation*: 20 February 1987
- *Governor*: Kaiwalya Trivikram Parnaik
- *Chief minister*: Pema Khandu
- *Tourist attractions*: Tawang Gompa, Dirang, Bomdila
- *Festivals*: Losar, Si-Donyi, Reh, Mopin and Solung
- *Major dance and music forms*: Lion dance, Peacock dance, Ponung, Roppi, Wancho dance
- *Arts and crafts*: Khamptis are especially good wood carvers; women in Arunachal are expert weavers
- *Languages*: Monpa, Miki, Aka, Sherdukpen, Apatani, Adi, Hill Miri
- *Size*: 83,743 sq km
- *Population*: 17,11,947
- *Rivers*: Brahmaputra, Siang, Lohit, Kameng, Tirap, Dibang, Subansiri, Drangme Chhu, Papumpare
- *Forests and wildlife sanctuaries*: Namdapha Tiger Reserve, Mouling NP
- *State animal*: Mithun
- *State bird*: Great Indian hornbill
- *State flower*: Foxtail Orchid
- *State tree*: Hollong
- *Major crop*: Rice, maize, millet

Interesting Trivia

- Considered to be a unit of wealth, the mithun roams free till it is sacrificed on special occassions and eaten.
- Arunachal Pradesh has the lowest population density in India.

* (All population figures are merely projections for the year 2025.)

ASSAM

- *Capital*: Dispur
- *Date of formation*: 26 January 1950
- *Governor*: Lakshman Prasad Acharya
- *Chief minister*: Himanta Biswa Sarma
- *Tourist attractions*: Kamakhya temple, Umananda (Peacock Island), Navagraha Temple, Basistha Ashram
- *Festivals*: Bihu, Me-Dum-Me-Phi, Baishagu
- *Major dance and music form*: Bihu, Bagurumba, Jhumur
- *Arts and crafts*: Jappi (traditional hat), toys made of clay, cork, wood and bamboo, muga silk, masks
- *Languages*: Assamese, Bodo, Karbi, Bengali
- *Size*: 78,438 sq km
- *Population*: 3,59,98,752
- *Rivers*: Brahmaputra, Manas, Subansiri, Dhansiri
- *Forests and wildlife sanctuaries*: Kaziranga NP, Chakrashila NP, Pobitora NP
- *State animal*: One-horned rhinoceros
- *State bird*: White-winged wood duck
- *State flower*: Foxtail orchid
- *State tree*: Hollong
- *Major crops*: Rice, jute, tea

Interesting Trivia

- Its name changed to Asom in 2006.
- According to legend, Tezpur was referred to as the 'city of blood' because it was filled with blood after a mythical battle between Shiva and Vishnu.

BIHAR

- *Capital*: Patna
- *Date of formation*: 22 March 1912
- *Governor*: Arif Mohammad Khan
- *Chief minister*: Nitish Kumar
- *Tourist attractions*: Rajgir, Nalanda, Vaishali, Jalmandir, Bodh Gaya, Vikramshila, Gaya, the ancient city of Pataliputra
- *Festivals*: Chhath Puja, Sama-Chakeva, Nag Panchami
- *Major dance and music forms*: Jat-jatin dance of the Mithila region, Bidesia, Sohar, Sumangali
- *Arts and crafts*: Madhubani painting; Madhubani's marsh 'sikki' grass is used to make baskets, toys, dolls, etc.; sujani kantha embroidery is a specialization of Bihar
- *Languages*: Hindi, Bhojpuri, Maithili, Magahi
- *Size*: 94,163 sq km
- *Population*: 13,43,00,000
- *Rivers*: Ganga, Bagmati, Gandak, Ghaghra, Phalgu, Karmanasha, Kosi, Son, Mahananda, Punpun
- *Forests and wildlife sanctuaries*: Valmiki NP, Rajgir WS, Bhimbandh WS, Gautam Buddha WS, Udaypur WS
- *State animal*: Gaur/Indian Bison
- *State bird*: House sparrow
- *State flower*: Pot Marigold/Genda
- *State tree*: Peepal
- *Major crops*: Paddy, wheat, maize

Interesting Trivia

- In Bodh Gaya, a bodhi or peepal tree indicates the spot where the Budhha gained enlightenment.
- Nalanda University, a UNESCO World Heritage Site, was founded around 5th century AD.

Chhattisgarh

- *Capital*: Raipur
- *Date of formation*: 1 November 2000
- *Governor*: Ramen Deka
- *Chief minister*: Vishnu Deo Sai
- *Tourist attractions*: Bastar Royal Palace, Chitrakote Falls, Kailash and Kutumsar Caves, Bhuteshwar Shivaling

- *Festivals*: Pola, Nawakhna, Bastar Dussehra, Madai, Bhoramdeo, Goncha
- *Major dance and music forms*: Panthi, Raut Nacha and Soowa dances, Bihav and Pathoni songs
- *Arts and crafts*: Iron crafting, dhokra craft (lost wax method of metal casting), bhitti chitra or murals
- *Languages*: Hindi, Oriya, Marathi, Chhattisgarhi, Gondi, Korku

- *Size*: 1,35,190 sq km
- *Population*: 3,22,60,000
- *Rivers*: Ganga, Mahanadi, Indravati, Son, Godavari, Narmada, Sabari

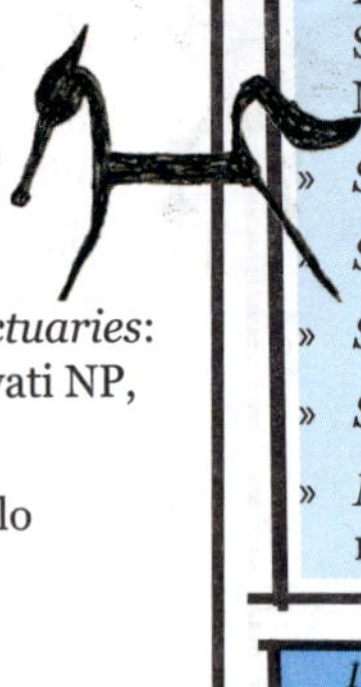

- *Forests and wildlife sanctuaries*: Barnawapara WS, Indravati NP, Kanger Valley NP
- *State animal*: Wild buffalo
- *State bird*: Hill myna
- *State tree*: Sal
- *Major crops*: Rice, wheat, soybean

Interesting Trivia

- The ancient caves of Kutumsar, Kailash and Dandak in the Kanger forest feature amazing stalagmites and stalactites.
- Around ninety languages and dialects are spoken in Chhattisgarh.

Goa

- *Capital*: Panaji
- *Date of formation*: 30 May 1987
- *Governor*: Ashok Gajapathi Raju
- *Chief minister*: Pramod Sawant
- *Tourist attractions*: Anjuna beach, Arambol beach, Basilica of Bom Jesus, Se Cathedral

- *Festivals*: Carnival, St. Francis Day, Shigmotsav
- *Major dance and music forms*: Fugdi and Dhalo dances, Mando, Durpod
- *Arts and crafts*: Terracotta or baked clay figurines, utensils, crochet tablecloths, curtains, covers, handkerchiefs, cane and bamboo fish traps, mats, baskets

- *Languages*: Konkani, Marathi
- *Size*: 3,702 sq km
- *Population*: 15,90,000
- *Rivers*: Mandovi, Zuari, Terekhol, Chapora, Sal, Talpona
- *Forests and wildlife sanctuaries*: Bondla WS, Dr Salim Ali Bird Sanctuary, Cotigao WS, Bhagwan Mahavir WS
- *State animal*: Gaur
- *State bird*: Ruby-throated bulbul
- *State flower*: Frangipani
- *State tree*: Matti
- *Major crops*: Paddy, groundnut, maize, cashew

Interesting Trivia

- The Basilica of Bom Jesus holds the tomb of St. Francis Xavier.
- Goa, Daman and Diu were liberated from Portugese rule by India in 1961.

GUJARAT

- *Capital*: Gandhinagar
- *Date of formation*: 1 May 1960
- *Governor*: Acharya Devvrat
- *Chief minister*: Bhupendrabhai Patel
- *Tourist attractions*: Rani Ki Vav, Somnath Temple, Dwarkadhish Temple, Palitana Jain Temple
- *Festivals*: Navratri, Uttarayan, Rann Utsav
- *Major dance and music forms*: Garba and Tippani dances, the music of the Charan and Gadhavi communities
- *Arts and crafts*: Bandhani or tie-and-dye fabric, woven patola fabric, rich embroidery by the Rabari tribals including Soof embroidery
- *Language*: Gujarati
- *Size*: 1,96,024 sq km
- *Population*: 7,35,13,000
- *Rivers*: Sabarmati, Mahi, Narmada, Tapti, Saraswati, Damanganga
- *Forests and wildlife sanctuaries*: Gir NP, Wild Ass Sanctuary, Nal Sarovar Bird Sanctuary, Velavadar Blackbuck NP, Vansda NP
- *State animal*: Asiatic lion
- *State bird*: Greater flamingo
- *State flower*: Marigold
- *State tree*: Banyan
- *Major crops*: Groundnut, cotton, tobacco

Interesting Trivia

- It is possible to climb down the richly carved step-wells or vavs of Gujarat.
- The ancient fort Uparkot was first built by the Mauryans.

HARYANA

- *Capital*: Chandigarh
- *Date of formation*: 1 November 1966
- *Governor*: Ashim Kumar Ghosh
- *Chief minister*: Nayab Singh Saini
- *Tourist attractions*: Karna Lake, Mata Mansa Devi temple
- *Festivals*: Gugga Naumi, Lohri, Basant Panchmi
- *Major dance and music forms*: Sarangi, Ras Leela, Phag Dance
- *Arts and crafts*: *sarkanda* (grass furniture) craft, *panja dhurries*
- *Languages*: Hindi, Punjabi, Urdu
- *Size*: 44,212 sq km
- *Population*: 3,10,57,000
- *Rivers*: Yamuna, Ghaggar-Hakra
- *Forests and wildlife sanctuaries*: Sultanpur NP, Kalesar NP
- *State animal*: Blackbuck
- *State bird*: Black francolin
- *State flower*: Lotus
- *State tree*: Peepal
- *Major crops*: Sugarcane, groundnut, paddy, wheat

Interesting Trivia

- The Huns had invaded and fought battles in Haryana.
- Gugga Naumi, a festival observed by both Hindus and Muslims, honours Gugga Pir who was known for curing snake bites.

Himachal Pradesh

- *Capital*: Shimla (summer), Dharamshala (winter)
- *Date of formation*: 25 January 1971
- *Governor*: Shiv Pratap Shukla
- *Chief minister*: Sukhvinder Singh Sukhu
- *Tourist attractions*: Shimla, Kullu, Manali, Dharamsala
- *Festivals*: Pori, Phulech
- *Major dance and music forms*: Mala dance, Chhambha or Rakshasa dance
- *Arts and crafts*: Pahari painting is done in the Chamba and Kangra styles; Kullu shawls and woollen caps are famous; the Chamba Rumal has Kangra-style paintings embroidered on cloth

- *Languages*: Hindi, Punjabi, Kinnauri, Pahari
- *Size*: 55,673 sq km
- *Population*: 75,55,000
- *Rivers*: Ravi, Beas, Chenab, Sutlej, Yamuna

- *Forests and wildlife sanctuaries*: Pin Valley NP, Great Himalayan NP, Renuka WS, Chail WS, Kalatop-Khajjiar WS
- *State animal*: Snow leopard
- *State bird*: Western tragopan
- *State flower*: Pink rhododendron
- *State tree*: Himalayan Deodar
- *Major crops*: Wheat, rice, maize, barley

Interesting Trivia

- The tiny village of Malana is believed to be the world's oldest democracy.
- During British rule, Shimla was the summer capital.

Jharkhand

- *Capital*: Ranchi
- *Date of formation*: 15 November 2000
- *Governor*: Santosh Gangwar
- *Chief minister*: Hemant Soren
- *Tourist attractions*: Dassam Falls, Sun Temple, Birsa Zoological Park, Hudco Lake
- *Festivals*: Kali Puja, Sohrai
- *Major dance and music forms*: Agni and Paika dances
- *Arts and crafts*: Deogarh's black pottery, Jadu patua painting
- *Languages*: Hindi, Urdu, Santhali
- *Size*: 79,714 sq km
- *Population*: 4,01,00,376

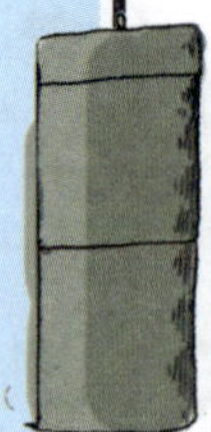

- *Rivers*: Subarnarekha, Kosi, Ganga
- *Forests and wildlife sanctuaries*: Palamau NP, Hazaribagh WS
- *State animal*: Elephant
- *State bird*: Asian koel

- *State flower*: Palash
- *State tree*: Sal
- *Major crops*: Paddy, wheat, maize

Interesting Trivia

- Dhanbad is considered to be India's coal capital.
- The adivasis of Jharkhand strongly rebelled and revolted against the British exploitation of their forests.

Karnataka

- *Capital*: Bengaluru
- *Date of formation*: 1 November 1956
- *Governor*: Thaawar Chand Gehlot
- *Chief minister*: Siddaramaiah
- *Tourist attractions*: Mysore City Palace, Chamundi Hills, Stone Chariot in Hampi
- *Festivals*: Ugadi, Ganesh Chaturthi, Kar Hunnive, Hampi Utsav
- *Major dance and music forms*: Carnatic music, Yakshagana
- *Arts and crafts*: Bidri, wood chiselling, Ganjifa (specialized card game)
- *Languages*: Kannada, Kodava, Tulu
- *Size*: 1,91,791 sq km
- *Population*: 6,86,79,000
- *Rivers*: Krishna, Tungabhadra, Kaveri, Kabini
- *Forests and wildlife sanctuaries*: Bandipur NP, Rajiv Gandhi (Nagarhole) NP, Bannerghatta NP
- *State animal*: Elephant
- *State bird*: Indian roller
- *State flower*: Lotus
- *State tree*: Sandalwood
- *Major crops*: Rice, jowar, coffee

Interesting Trivia

- Karunadu is another name for Karnataka.
- The Gol Gumbaz of Bijapur, the central dome of Muhammad Adil Shah's tomb, is the second largest in the world.

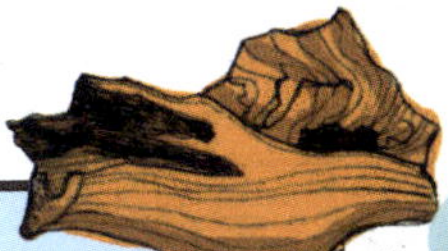

Kerala

- *Capital*: Thiruvananthapuram
- *Date of formation*: 1 November 1956
- *Governor*: Rajendra Vishwanath Arlekar
- *Chief minister*: Pinarayi Vijayan
- *Tourist attractions*: Kovalam, Wayanad, Kannur
- *Festivals*: Snake boat races, Chinakathoor, Onam
- *Major dance and music forms*: Mohiniattam, Kathakali
- *Arts and crafts*: Kalamezhuthu paintings; murals in temples using 'pure' colours such as white, red, black, green; bell metal idols, lamps, etc.
- *Language*: Malayalam
- *Size*: 38,863 sq km
- *Population*: 3,61,11,000
- *Rivers*: Periyar, Bharathappuzha
- *Forests and wildlife sanctuaries*: Periyar NP, Wayanad WS, Silent Valley NP
- *State animal*: Elephant
- *State bird*: Great Indian hornbill
- *State flower*: Golden shower tree
- *State tree*: Coconut
- *Major crops*: Coconut, rubber, tea, coffee

Interesting Trivia

- Edakkal caves in Ambukutty Mala have rock carvings believed to have been made during the Neolithic Age.
- Kalaripayattu, an ancient martial arts discipline, is derived from 'kalari' or battlefield and 'payattu' or practice.

MADHYA PRADESH

- *Capital*: Bhopal
- *Date of formation*: 1 November 1956
- *Governor*: Mangubhai Chhaganbhai Patel
- *Chief minister*: Mohan Yadav
- *Tourist attractions*: Sanchi Stupa, Gwalior Fort, Orchha Fort, Khajuraho, Ujjain

- *Festivals*: Gana-Gour, Ganga Dashami, Hareli
- *Major dance and music forms*: Karma dance, Muria dance, Relo songs
- *Arts and crafts*: Wall paintings by the Chiteras, Chippa community's hand-block printing, Battubai dolls
- *Language*: Hindi

- *Size*: 3,08,252 sq km
- *Population*: 8,89,85,000
- *Rivers*: Narmada, Tapti, Betwa, Son, Chambal
- *Forests and wildlife sanctuaries*: Bandhavgarh NP, Kanha NP, Pench NP, Kheoni WS
- *State animal*: Barasingha
- *State bird*: Indian paradise flycatcher
- *State flower*: Madonna Lily
- *State tree*: Banyan
- *Major crops*: Rice, wheat, soybean, mustard

Interesting Trivia

- Bhawani Mandi station on the Mumbai–Delhi railway line is divided between Madhya Pradesh and Rajasthan.
- Pench, Kanha and Bandhavgarh are all tiger reserves.

MAHARASHTRA

- *Capital*: Mumbai
- *Date of formation*: 1 May 1960
- *Governor*: Chandrapuram Ponnusamy Radhakrishnan
- *Chief minister*: Devendra Fadnavis
- *Tourist attractions*: Gateway of India, Murud-Janjira Fort, Elephanta Caves, Ajanta and Ellora Caves
- *Festivals*: Makar Sankranti, Ganesh Chaturthi
- *Major dance and music forms*: Vasudev dance, Lavni dance, Dhangari Gaja
- *Arts and crafts*: People of the Warli tribe create ritualistic paintings on cowdung-plastered walls; Paithani saris; Mashroo and Himroo fabrics

- *Language*: Marathi
- *Size*: 3,07,713 sq km
- *Population*: 12,86,59,000
- *Rivers*: Godavari, Painganga, Krishna, Tapti, Pravara, Mula
- *Forests and wildlife sanctuaries*: Pench NP, Tadoba NP, Nagzira WS, Nawegoan NP, Chandoli NP, Gugamal NP

- *State animal*: Giant squirrel
- *State bird*: Yellow-footed green pigeon
- *State flower*: Jarul
- *State tree*: Mango
- *Major crops*: Paddy, wheat, sugarcane, cotton

Interesting Trivia

- There are seven caves in Gharapuri with rock carvings made in 6th and 7th centuries AD.
- Kolis were among the first inhabitants of the archipelago that has now become Mumbai.

MANIPUR

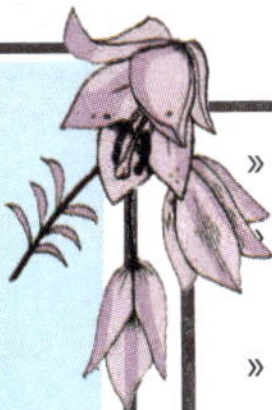

- *Capital*: Imphal
- *Date of formation*: 21 January 1972
- *Governor*: Ajay Kumar Bhalla
- *Chief minister*: Nongthombam Biren Singh
- *Tourist attractions*: Loktak Lake, Sendra Island
- *Festivals*: Heikru-Hidongba boat races, Baruni
- *Major dance and music forms*: Ras Lila, Lai Haraoba Ishei music, Nongdai Jagoi
- *Arts and crafts*: Bamboo baskets, fishing baskets, umbrellas, musical instruments, Kauna mats, etc.

- *Languages*: Manipuri, Thado, Tankhul
- *Size*: 22,327 sq km
- *Population*: 37,50,000
- *Rivers*: Manipur, Barak
- *Forests and wildlife sanctuaries*: Keibul Lamjao NP, Khonghampat Orchidarium
- *State animal*: Sangai
- *State bird*: Mrs Hume's pheasant
- *State flower*: Siroi Lily
- *State tree*: Uningthou
- *Major crops*: Paddy, wheat, maize, pulses

Interesting Trivia

- The pung is the Manipuri version of the mridanga, an ancient drum, and is played during the Ras Lila.
- Imphal's Ima Keithal is an all-women's market.

MEGHALAYA

- *Capital*: Shillong
- *Date of formation*: 21 January 1972
- *Governor*: Chandrashekhar H. Vijayashankar
- *Chief minister*: Conrad K Sangma
- *Tourist attractions*: Nohkalikai Waterfalls, Living Root Bridges, Tura, Butterfly Museum, Capt. Williamson Sangma State Museum
- *Festivals*: Wangala, Behdeinkhlam
- *Major dance and music forms*: Shad Suk Mynsiem, Shad Nongkrem and Doregata dances
- *Arts and crafts*: Eri silk is used to make colourful wraps and shawls; woven baskets known as khok, cone-shaped bamboo rain shields known as knup are also popular

- *Languages*: Khasi, Garo, Jaintia, Bengali, Assamese, English
- *Size*: 22,720 sq km
- *Population*: 39,20,000
- *Rivers*: Simsang, Someswari, Jinjiram, Kalu, Myntdu, Didram
- *Forests and wildlife sanctuaries*: Nokrek Ridge NP, Balpakram NP, Nongkhyllem WS, Siju Bird Sanctuary
- *State animal*: Clouded leopard
- *State bird*: Hill myna
- *State flower*: Lady's slipper orchid
- *State tree*: Gamhar
- *Major crops*: Potato, cotton, pineapple, orange

Interesting Trivia

- Nartiang contains a collection of megaliths and monoliths.
- Wangala, or the dance of hundred hrums, is used by the Garos to celebrate a good harvest in November.

Mizoram

- *Capital*: Aizawl
- *Date of formation*: 20 February 1987
- *Governor*: V. K. Singh
- *Chief minister*: PU Lalduhoma
- *Tourist attractions*: Phawngpui Hills, Sibuta Lung, Philpui Grave, Palak Lake
- *Festivals*: Chapchar Kut, Mim Kut, Pawl Kut
- *Major dance and music forms*: Khal Lam, Chai, Chhilam, Sawlkin
- *Arts and crafts*: Puan (traditional dress), cane and bamboo baskets, pipes, toys
- *Languages*: Mara, Mizo, Bengali, English
- *Size*: 21,081 sq km
- *Population*: 12,64,000
- *Rivers*: Tlwang, Tlau, Chhimtuipui, Tuichang, Tuirial
- *Forests and wildlife sanctuaries*: Lengteng WS, Murlen NP, Phawngpui NP, Thorangtlang WS
- *State animal*: Serow
- *State bird*: Mrs Hume's pheasant
- *State flower*:Red vanda
- *State tree*: Iron wood
- *Major crops*: Paddy, maize, sugarcane, oil palm

Interesting Trivia

- Cheraw is a popular form of dancing that uses bamboos.
- Pukzing cave, near Aizawl, stands at 25m. Legends say that Mualzavata, a very strong man, carved it out with a hair pin.

Nagaland

- *Capital*: Kohima
- *Date of formation*: 1 December 1963
- *Governor*: La. Ganesan Iyer
- *Chief minister*: Neiphiu Rio
- *Tourist attractions*: Kohima War Cemetery, Bara Basti, State Museum
- *Festivals*: Moatsu Mong, Sekrenyi, Hornbill
- *Major dance and music forms*: Zeliang, Hereileu song
- *Arts and crafts*: Naga baskets, cup violin made using bamboo and gourd, bamboo trumpet
- *Languages*: Ao, Sema, Konyak, Angami, Chakhesang, Chang, Khiamniungan, Kuki
- *Size*: 16,579 sq km
- *Population*: 45,30,000
- *Rivers*: Milak, Barak, Dhansiri, Doyang, Dikhu, Zungki, Tizu
- *Forests and wildlife sanctuaries*: Intanki NP
- *State animal*: Mithun
- *State bird*: Blyth's tragopan
- *State flower*: Rhododendron
- *State tree*: Alder
- *Major crops*: Rice, maize, millet, sugarcane

Interesting Trivia

- Nagaland is home to around 360 orchid species.
- Sekrenyi, the Angami festival, is celebrated over a period of ten days.

ODISHA

- *Capital*: Bhubaneswar
- *Date of formation*: 1 April 1936
- *Governor*: Hari Babu Kambhampati
- *Chief minister*: Mohan Charan Majhi
- *Tourist attractions*: Sun Temple, Jagannath Temple, Taptapani
- *Festivals*: Rath Yatra, Dol Jatra, Patua Jatra, Chandak Puja
- *Major dance and music forms*: Odissi, Chitrapada, Dhruvapada, Panchal music
- *Arts and crafts*: Pattachitras, palm-leaf ganjifa cards, intricate combs made using bamboo, lac and fabric, Sambalpuri double ikat
- *Language*: Oriya
- *Size*: 1,55,707 sq km
- *Population*: 46,953,000
- *Rivers*: Mahanadi, Baitarni, Brahmani, Tel, Sabari
- *Forests and wildlife sanctuaries*: Chilka Lake Sanctuary, Simlipal NP, Bhitarkanika NP
- *State animal*: Sambar
- *State bird*: Indian roller
- *State flower*: Ashoka
- *State tree*: Peepal Tree
- *Major crops*: Paddy, mustard, ragi, maize

Interesting Trivia

- The thirty-three sandstone caves on the Udaygiri and Khandagiri hills near Bhubaneshwar were probably carved during King Kharavela's reign.
- Odisha has sixty-two tribes including the Santhals, Suras, Juangs, Gonds, Bondas, etc.

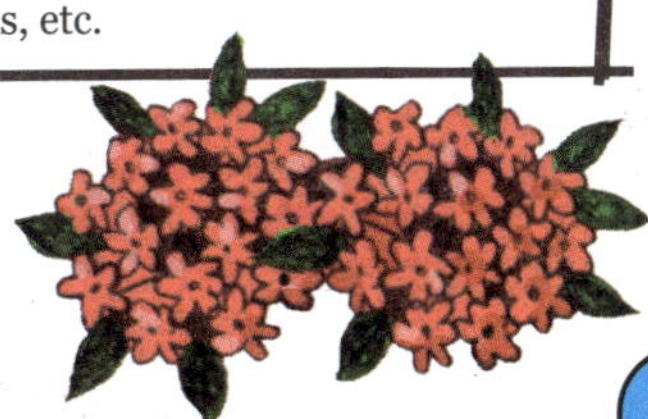

PUNJAB

- *Capital*: Chandigarh
- *Date of formation*: 1 November 1966
- *Governor*: Gulab Chand Kataria
- *Chief minister*: Bhagwant Mann
- *Tourist attractions:* Golden Temple, Jallianwalla Bagh, Anandpur Sahib Fort, Rajmahal
- *Festivals*: Lohri, Baisakhi, Gurpurab
- *Major dance and music forms*: Bhangra, Giddha
- *Arts and crafts*: Phulkari or flower embroidery, wood inlay of Hoshiarpur on black shisham wood.
- *Language*: Punjabi
- *Size*: 50,362 sq km
- *Population*: 32,110,000
- *Rivers:* Beas, Sutlej, Ravi
- *Forests and wildlife sanctuaries:* Bir Moti Bagh WS, Bir Bhunerhari WS, Bir Dosanjh WS
- *State animal:* Blackbuck
- *State bird*: Northern goshawk
- *State flower*: Gladiolus
- *State tree:* Shisham
- *Major crops*: Wheat, gram, barley, oil seeds

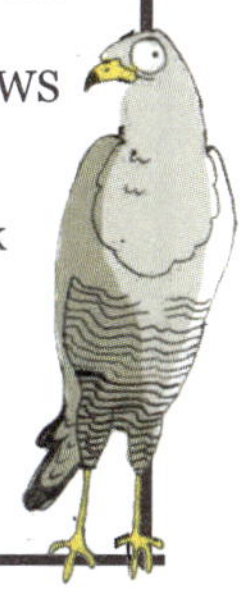

Interesting Trivia

- Sikhism, a dominant religion in Punjab, was founded by Guru Nanak. The word 'Sikh' translates to 'learner'.
- Punjab, one of India's most fertile states, is also called the 'Granary of India'.

RAJASTHAN

- *Capital*: Jaipur
- *Date of formation*: 30 March 1949
- *Governor*: Haribhau Kisanrao Bagade
- *Chief minister*: Bhajan Lal Sharma
- *Tourist attractions*: Mount Abu, City Palace Jaipur, Hawa Mahal, Jaisalmer Fort, Birla Temple, Pushkar
- *Festivals*: Teej, Gangaur, Bikaner Camel Festival, Marwar Festival
- *Major dance and music forms*: Ghoomar and Kalbeliya dances, Panihari songs, Bhopa-Bhopi songs
- *Arts and crafts*: Rajasthani miniature paintings such as Mewar, Marwar, Jaipur, etc., Pichwai paintings, hand-block printing
- *Languages*: Rajasthani, Hindi
- *Size*: 3,42,239 sq km
- *Population*: 8,30,60,000
- *Rivers*: Luni, Banas, Kali Sindh, Chambal
- *Forests and wildlife sanctuaries*: Sariska Tiger Reserve, Keoladeo Ghana NP, Ranthambore NP, Dhawa Doli WS
- *State animal*: Camel, Chinkara
- *State bird*: Great Indian bustard
- *State flower*: Rohida
- *State tree*: Khejri
- *Major crops*: Jowar, pulses, maize, gram

Interesting Trivia

- Jaipur has an Elephant Festival which includes a tug-of-war between humans and elephants.
- Rats are revered and fed in the Karni Mata temple in Bikaner.

SIKKIM

- *Capital*: Gangtok
- *Date of formation*: 16 May 1975
- *Governor*: Om Prakash Mathur
- *Chief minister*: Prem Singh Tamang (a.k.a. P S Golay)
- *Tourist attractions*: Tsuklakhang Palace, Dubdi Gompa, Gurudongmar Lake, Deorali, Orchid Sanctuary, Tathagata Tsal
- *Festivals*: Pang Lhabsol, Losoong
- *Major dance and music forms*: Enchey Chaam mask dance, Kali Topi
- *Arts and crafts*: Thangkas or religious scroll paintings, Choktse tables, hand-knotted carpets
- *Languages*: Lepcha, Bhutia, Limbu, Nepali, Hindi
- *Size*: 7,096 sq km
- *Population*: 6,98,400
- *Rivers*: Teesta, Rangeet
- *Forests and wildlife sanctuaries*: Khanchendzonga NP, Fambong Lho WS
- *State animal*: Red panda
- *State bird*: Blood pheasant
- *State tree*: Rhododendron
- *State flower*: Noble Orchid
- *Major crops*: Maize, paddy, wheat, barley

Interesting Trivia

- The red panda, which is highly endangered, is found in Sikkim.
- Sikkim is home to around 200 monasteries or gompas. The red-robed lamas chant to drums, horns and trumpets in these monasteries.

Tamil Nadu

- *Capital*: Chennai
- *Date of formation*: 1 November 1956
- *Governor*: R N Ravi
- *Chief minister*: M K Stalin
- *Tourist attractions*: Marina Beach, Mahabalipuram Beach, Ooty
- *Festivals*: Pongal, Vaikasi Visakam, Avani Moola
- *Major dance and music forms*: Bharatnatyam, Parai Attam, Naiyandi Melam
- *Arts and crafts*: Tanjore style of painting, Kanchipuram silk, Puthululi (embroidered shawls)
- *Language*: Tamil
- *Size*: 1,30,058 sq km
- *Population*: 7,73,94,000
- *Rivers*: Kaveri, Palar, Periyar, Bhavani
- *Forests and wildlife sanctuaries*: Mudumalai NP, Mukurthi NP, Indira Gandhi (Annamalai) NP, Kalakad WS
- *State animal*: Nilgiri tahr
- *State bird*: Emerald dove
- *State flower*: Glory lily or Kandhal
- *State tree*: Palmyra palm
- *Major crops*: Paddy, millets, pulses, tea

Interesting Trivia

- Mamallapuram, a group of rock-cut monuments and temples in Mahabalipuram, were carved between 7th and 8th centuries AD.
- The Pandyas built the Meenakshi temple in Madurai.

Telangana

- *Capital*: Hyderabad
- *Date of formation*: 2 June 2014
- *Governor*: Jishnu Dev Varma
- *Chief minister*: Revanth Reddy
- *Tourist attractions*: Charminar, Golconda Fort, Qutb Shahi Tombs, Chowmahalla Palace, Falaknuma Palace, Bhongir Fort
- *Festivals*: Bathukamma, Ramzan, Vinayaka Chavithi
- *Major dance and music forms*: Kuchipudi, Bhamakalpam, Dappu
- *Arts and crafts*: Kalamkari cotton; the nakashis of Cheriyal village paint vibrantly coloured scrolls.
- *Languages*: Telugu, Urdu, English
- *Size*: 1,12,077 km
- *Population*: 3,84,99,000
- *Rivers*: Godavari, Krishna, Musi, Tungabhadra, Bhima, Manjira, Pranhitha, Wardha
- *Forests and wildlife sanctuaries*: Kawal WS, Manjira WS, Nagarjunasagar-Srisailam Tiger Reserve
- *State animal*: *Spotted Deer*
- *State bird*: Indian roller
- *State flower*: Tangedu
- *State tree*: Jammi Chettu
- *Major crops*: Groundnut, rice, maize, pulses

Interesting Trivia

- Patronage by Qutb Shahi and Asafjahi rulers led to the growth of mushairas, ghazals and qawali in Hyderabad.

Tripura

- *Capital*: Agartala
- *Date of formation*:
- 21 January 1972
- *Governor*: Indrasena Reddy Nallu
- *Chief minister*: Manik Saha
- *Tourist attractions*: Ujjayanta Palace, Chaturdas Devata Temple, Neer Mahal, Jampui Hills
- *Festivals*: Kharchi Puja, Ker Puja, Garia Puja, Pous-Sankranti Mela
- *Major dance and music forms*: Bizu dance, Garia dance, Sumui music
- *Arts and crafts*: Bamboo mats, clothes with snakeskin designs known as Ponmongvom, garments called the Risa and the Rignai

- *Languages*: Kokborok, Bengali, English
- *Size*: 10,491 sq km
- *Population*: 42,80,000
- *River*: Gumti, Longai, Manu
- *Forests and wildlife sanctuaries*: Sipahijala WS, Trishna WS, Rowa WS, Rajbari NP
- *State animal*: Phayre's langur
- *State bird*: Green imperial pigeon
- *State flower*: Nageswar
- *State tree*: Agarwood
- *Major crops*: Paddy, wheat, pineapple, orange, maize

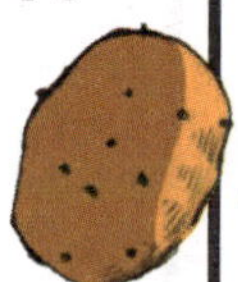

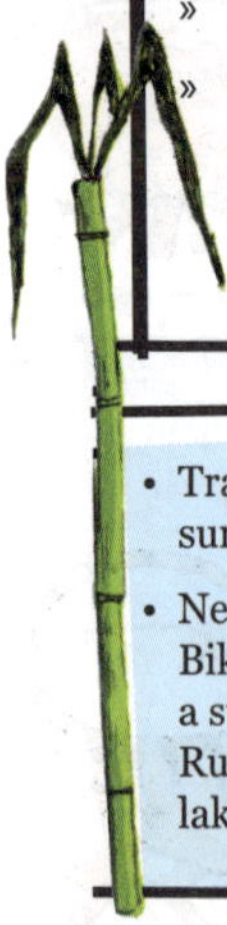

Interesting Trivia

- Traditional instruments include the sumui, sarinda and chongpreng.
- Neermahal, built by Maharaja Bir Bikram Kishore Manikya Bahadur as a summer resort, is located in Lake Rudrasagar. It is the only palace in a lake in eastern India.

Uttar Pradesh

- *Capital*: Lucknow
- *Date of formation*: 24 January 1950
- *Governor*: Anandiben Patel
- *Chief minister*: Yogi Adityanath
- *Tourist attractions*: Taj Mahal, Sangam, Varanasi
- *Festivals*: Karva Chauth, Annakoot, Sheetala Ashtami, Eid

- *Major dance and music forms*: Kathak, Lucknow and Benares Gharanas of music
- *Arts and crafts*: Chikankari or shadow-work embroidery, Baranasi brocades, Sanjhi (the art of paper-cutting)

- *Languages*: Hindi, Urdu
- *Size*: 2,40,928 sq km
- *Population*: 24,12,65,000
- *Rivers*: Ganga, Yamuna, Gomti, Ghaghra, Ramganga, Betwa
- *Forests and wildlife sanctuaries*: Dudhwa NP, Ranipur WS
- *State animal*: Swamp deer
- *State bird*: Sarus crane
- *State flower*: Palash
- *State tree*: Ashoka
- *Major crops*: Wheat, rice, potato, sugarcane

Interesting Trivia

- The ancient Dhamek Stupa in Sarnath is the spot where Buddha gave his first sermon.
- The Taj Mahal took about twenty-two years to build.

UTTARAKHAND

- *Capital*: Dehradun (winter), Bhararisain (summer)
- *Date of formation*: 9 November 2000
- *Governor*: Gurmit Singh
- *Chief minister*: Pushkar Singh Dhami
- *Tourist attractions*: Rishikesh, Nainital, Almora, Mussoorie, Nanda Devi
- *Festivals*: Bagwal Mela, Nanda Devi Mela, Purnagiri Mela
- *Major dance and music forms*: Bhotia dance, Barada Nati dance, Chancheri dance
- *Arts and crafts*: Kholi woodcarving, Aipan (rangoli)
- *Languages*: Hindi, Garhwali, Kumaoni
- *Size*: 53,483 sq km
- *Population*: 1,19,13,000
- *Rivers*: Ganga, Yamuna, Ramganga, Kali
- *Forests and wildlife sanctuaries*: Nanda Devi NP, Rajaji NP, Corbett NP
- *State animal*: White-bellied musk deer
- *State bird*: Monal
- *State flower*: Brahma kamal
- *State tree*: Burans
- *Major crops*: Rice, wheat, soyabean, pulses, oilseed

Interesting Trivia

- Kedarnath temple is situated at a height of 3,584m above sea level.
- Rock-paintings dating back to the Mesolithic period have been found here.

WEST BENGAL

- *Capital*: Kolkata
- *Date of formation*: 26 January 1950
- *Governor*: CV Ananda Bose
- *Chief minister*: Mamata Banerjee
- *Tourist attractions*: Victoria Memorial, Vidyasagar Setu, Shantiniketan, Darjeeling
- *Festivals*: Durga Puja, Rabindra Jayanti
- *Major dance and music forms*: Gaudiya Nritya, Baul, Rabindrasangeet
- *Arts and crafts*: Terracotta Bankura horses, Kalighat style of painting, hand-woven Baluchari silk textiles
- *Languages*: Bengali, Hindi
- *Size*: 88,752 sq km
- *Population*: 10,02,02,000
- *Rivers*: Hooghly, Teesta, Torsa, Subarnarekha, Damodar
- *Forests and wildlife sanctuaries*: Sunderbans NP, Jaldapara NP
- *State animal*: Fishing cat
- *State bird*: White-breasted kingfisher
- *State flower*: Shiuli
- *State tree*: Devil tree or Chatim
- *Major crops*: Rice, potato, jute, tea

Interesting Trivia

- Bengali literature developed early thanks to the cultural awakening brought about by the Brahmo Samaj.
- Rabindranath Tagore, the first Asian to win the Nobel Prize for Literature, was from Bengal.

Andaman and Nicobar Islands

- *Capital*: Port Blair
- *Date of formation*: 1 November 1956
- *Lieutenant Governor*: Admiral Devendra Kumar Joshi
- *Tourist attractions*: Cellular Jail, Ross Island, Havelock Island, Samudrika Museum
- *Festivals*: Island Tourism Festival, Janamashtami
- *Languages*: Hindi, Nicobarese, Bengali, Tamil, Malayalam, Telugu
- *Size*: 8,249 sq km
- *Population*: 4,13,000
- *Rivers*: Kalpong, Galathea, Dagmar
- *State animal*: Dugong (Sea Cow)
- *State bird*: Andaman wood pigeon
- *State flower*: Andaman pyinma
- *State tree*: Andaman Padauk
- *Major crops*: Paddy, coconut, nuts, banana, mango

Interesting Trivia

- It is located in the Bay of Bengal.
- It is composed of 572 islands.

Chandigarh

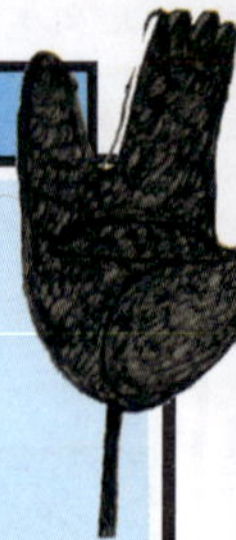

- *Capital*: Chandigarh
- *Date of formation*: 1 November 1966
- *Administrator*: Gulab Chand Kataria
- *Tourist attractions*: Rock Garden, Sukhna Lake, Open-hand monument in Capitol Complex, Rose Garden
- *Festivals*: Festival of Gardens, Mango Festival, Teej
- *Languages*: Hindi, Punjabi, English
- *Size*: 114 sq km
- *Population*: 12,66,000
- *State animal*: Indian grey mongoose
- *State bird*: Indian grey hornbill
- *State tree*: Mango
- *State flower*: Dhak
- *Major crops*: Wheat, maize, paddy

Interesting Trivia

- Chandigarh derives its name from the goddess Chandi.
- Swiss-born architect Le Corbusier (Charles-Edouard Jeanneret) planned the city.

Delhi

- *Capital*: New Delhi
- *Date of formation*: 1 November 1956
- *Lieutenant Governor*: Vinai Kumar Saxena
- *Chief minister*: Rekha Gupta
- *Tourist attractions*: Qutub Minar, Humayun's Tomb, Jantar Mantar, Red Fort, India Gate
- *Festivals*: Diwali, Holi, Eid
- *Languages*: Hindi, English, Urdu, Punjabi
- *Size*: 1,484 sq km
- *Population*: 2,39,19,000
- *River*: Yamuna
- *State animal*: Nilgai
- *State bird*: House sparrow
- *State flower*: Alfalfa
- *State tree:* Gulmohar
- *Major crops*: Rice,
- millet, mustard

Interesting Trivia

- The National Capital Region or NCR is believed to be one of the world's biggest urban clusters.
- It is believed that Delhi was destroyed and rebuilt many times.

DAMAN AND DIU, AND DADRA AND NAGAR HAVELI

- *Capital*: Daman
- *Date of formation*: 26 January 2020
- *Administrator*: Praful Patel
- *Tourist attractions*: Somnath Mahadev Temple, Devka Beach, Diu Fort, Pani Kotha, Nagoa Beach, Tadkeshwar Temple, Van Vihar Tourist Complex, Silvassa Vasona Lion Safari, Dudhani Lake

- *Festivals*: Gangaji Fair, Holi, Diwali, Garba Festival, Folk Dance Festival, Barash (Diwali), Ivaso, Bhawada
- *Languages*: Gujarati, Hindi, Marathi, Konkani
- *Size*: 603 sq km
- *Population*: 5,75,300
- *Rivers*: Damanganga, Kolak, Kalai, Silvassa, Khanvel
- *Major crops*: Paddy, ragi, millet, pulses, jowar, groundnut, pulses

Interesting Trivia

- Daman is believed to have belonged to the Mauryan Empire.
- The ancient river Damanganga is possibly the source of the name of the region of Daman.

Interesting Trivia

- The Koknas are known for their body and forehead tattoos.
- The ghangal, a musical instrument that is part of Warli religious rituals, is made from bamboo, a gourd and iron strings.

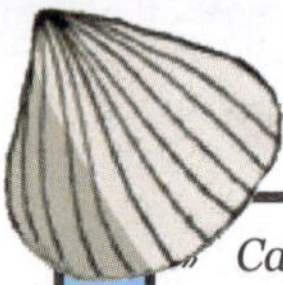

Lakshadweep

- *Capital*: Kavaratti
- *Date of formation*: 1 November 1956
- *Administrator*: Praful Patel
- *Tourist attractions*: Kavaratti Kadamat, Kalpeni, Minicoy Lighthouse, Bangaram islands
- *Festivals*: Muharram, Eid
- *Languages*: Malayalam, Mahl, Hindi, Tamil
- *Size*: 32 sq km
- *Population*: 68,900
- *State animal*: Butterfly fish
- *State bird*: Sooty tern
- *State tree*: Breadfruit
- *Major crop*: Coconut

Interesting Trivia

- Lakshadweep has been ruled by Kerala dynasties such as the Kulashekharas and the Kolathiris.
- Mahi or Mahl (a dialect of Dhiveli—the national language of Maldives) is only spoken on the island of Minicoy.

Puducherry

- *Capital*: Puducherry
- *Date of formation*: 1 July 1963
- *Lieutenant Governor*: K. Kailashnathan
- *Chief minister*: N Rangaswamy
- *Tourist attractions*: Serenity Beach, Paradiso Beach, Karaikal Beach, Place du Gouvernement, Aurobindo Ashram
- *Festivals*: Fire-Walk festival, Sedal, Mascarade festival
- *Languages*: Tamil, Telugu, Malayalam, English and French
- *Size*: 479 sq km
- *Population*: 17,32,000
- *Rivers*: Gingee, Guduvaiyar, Malattar, Pambaiyar, Pennaiyar
- *State animal*: Indian Palm Squirrel
- *State bird*: Asian koel
- *State tree*: Bael
- *State flower*: Cannonball
- *Major crops*: Paddy, pulses, coconut, areca nut, spices

Interesting Trivia

- Mahe is also known as Mayyazhi or the 'sea's eyebrow'.
- The ancient town of Arikamedu traded terracotta objects, beads, precious stones and spices with the Romans in exchange for wine, cups and other ceramic items

Jammu and Kashmir

- *Capital*: Srinagar (summer), Jammu (winter)
- *Date of Formation*: 31 October 2019
- *Lieutenant Governor*: Manoj Sinha
- *Chief Minister:* Omar Abdullah
- *Tourist attractions*: Dal Lake, Shalimar Bagh, Pahalgam, Gulmarg, Vaishno Devi
- *Festivals*: Makar Sankranti, Eid, Shab-e-Miraj
- *Languages*: Urdu, Hindi, Punjabi, Kashmiri, Dogri, Gojri
- *Population:* 1,37,58,000
- *Rivers*: Chenab, Jhelum, Tawi, Ravi
- *State animal*: Hangul
- *State bird*: Kalij pheasant
- *State flower*: Rhododendron
- *State tree*: Chinar
- *Major crops*: Rice, maize, barley, wheat

Interesting Trivia

- The erstwhile state of Jammu and Kashmir has been divided into two union territories: Jammu & Kashmir and Ladakh.
- While Jammu and Kashmir will have a legislature, Ladakh will not.

Ladakh

- *Capital*: Leh
- *Date of Formation*: 31 October 2019
- *Lieutenant Governor*: Kavinder Gupta
- *Tourist attractions*: Lamayuru, Pangong Lake, Nubra, Zanskar, Drass, Suru Valley
- *Festivals*: Hemis, Saka Dawa, Losar, Ladakh
- *Languages*: Bhoti, Ladakhi, Tibetan, Urdu, Balti, Purig, Hindi
- *Population:* 3,03,000
- *Rivers*: Zanskar, Indus, Shyok, Nubra, Suru
- *State animal*: Snow Leopard
- *State bird*: Black-necked crane
- *Major crops*: Wheat, barley

Interesting Trivia

- The Indian Astronomical Observatory at Hanle is the second-highest optical telescope in the world. It is set up at a height 4,500m.
- The rare two-humped camel or Bactrian camel are found only in Ladakh in India.

Presidents (past and present)

Dr Rajendra Prasad: 1950–1962
Dr Sarvepalli Radhakrishnan: 1962–1967
Dr Zakir Hussain: 1967–1969
Varahagiri Venkata Giri: May–July 1969 (Acting)
Justice Mohammad Hidayatullah: July–Aug 1969 (Acting)
Varahagiri Venkata Giri: 1969–1974
Fakhruddin Ali Ahmed: 1974–1977
B D Jatti: Feb–July 1977 (Acting)
Neelam Sanjiva Reddy: 1977–1982
Giani Zail Singh: 1982–1987
R Venkataraman: 1987–1992
Dr Shankar Dayal Sharma: 1992–1997
K R Narayanan: 1997–2002
Dr A P J Abdul Kalam: 2002–2007
Pratibha Patil: 2007–2012
Pranab Mukherjee: 2012–2017
Ram Nath Kovind: 2017–2022
Droupadi Murmu: 2022—present

Prime Ministers (past and present)

Jawaharlal Nehru: 1947–1964
Gulzari Lal Nanda: May–June 1964 (Acting)
Lal Bahadur Shastri: 1964–1966
Gulzari Lal Nanda: 11–24 Jan 1966 (Acting)
Indira Gandhi: 1966–1977
Morarji Desai: 1977–1979
Charan Singh: 1979–1980
Indira Gandhi: 1980–1984
Rajiv Gandhi: 1984–1989
Vishwanath Pratap Singh: 1989–1990
Chandrasekhar: 1990–1991
P V Narasimha Rao: 1991–1996
Atal Bihari Vajpayee: May–June 1996
H D Deve Gowda: June 1996–April 1997
Inder Kumar Gujral: April 1997–March 1998
Atal Bihari Vajpayee: 1998–2004
Dr Manmohan Singh: 2004–2014
Narendra Modi: May 2014–present

Important Indian Office Holders

Chief Justice: B. R. Gavai
Chief of Defence Staff: General Anil Chauhan
Chief of the Army Staff: General Upendra Dwivedi
Chief of the Naval Staff: Admiral Dinesh K Tripathi
Chief of the Air Staff: Air Chief Marshal Amar Preet Singh
Attorney General: R. Venkataramani
Chief Election Commissioner: Gyanesh Kumar
Comptroller and Auditor-General: K. Sanjay Murthy
Foreign Secretary: Vikram Misri
Speaker of the Lok Sabha: Om Birla
RBI Governor: Sanjay Malhotra
Finance Secretary: Ajay Seth
R&AW Chief: Parag Jain
NCC Director General: Lt. Gen. Gurbirpal Singh

Important Industrialists

Mukesh D Ambani *(Reliance Industries Limited)*
Dilip Shanghvi *(Sun Pharmaceuticals)*
Azim H Premji *(Wipro Limited)*
Lakshmi N Mittal *(Arcelor Mittal)*
Srichand P Hinduja *(Hinduja Group)*
Shiv Nadar *(HCL Technologies)*
Adi B Godrej *(Godrej Group)*
Kumar Mangalam Birla *(Aditya Birla Group)*
Sunil Mittal *(Bharti Enterprises)*
Cyrus Poonawalla *(Poonawalla Group)*
Anil D Ambani *(Reliance ADA Group)*
Rahul Bajaj *(Bajaj Group)*
Nandan Nilekani *(Infosys Technologies)*
Gautam Adani (*Adani Enterprises Limited*)
Natarajan Chandrasekaran *(Tata Group)*

Important Organisations

- Anthropological Survey of India
- Archaeological Survey of India
- Department of Public Enterprises
- Central Board of Film Certification
- Comptroller and Auditor-General
- Council of Scientific and Industrial Research
- Defence Research and Development Organisation
- Dental Council of India
- Film and Television Institute of India
- Forest Survey of India
- Geological Survey of India
- Indian Council of Agricultural Research
- Indian Council for Cultural Relations
- Indian Council of Historical Research
- Indian Council of Medical Research
- Indian Council of Philosophical Research
- Indian Council of Social Science Research
- Indian Farmers Fertilizers Cooperative Ltd.
- Indian Institute of Advanced Study
- Indian Institute of Forest Management
- Indian Institute of Mass Communication
- Indian Space Research Organisation
- Indira Gandhi National Centre for the Arts
- Indira Gandhi National Open University
- Industrial Development Bank of India
- Industrial Investment Bank of India
- National Archives of India
- National Bank for Agriculture and
- Rural Development
- National Book Trust
- National Council of Educational Research and Training
- National Development Council
- National Film Festival
- National Informatics Centre
- National Sample Survey Organisation
- National School of Drama
- Press Council of India
- Press Information Bureau
- Reserve Bank of India
- Zoological Survey of India

Important Commissions

- Atomic Energy Commission
- Commission for Agricultural Costs and Prices
- Census Commission
- National Forest Commission
- Central Information Commission
- Central Water Commission
- Earth Commission
- Election Commission
- Finance Commission
- Indo-Bangladesh Joint Rivers Commission
- Khadi and Village Industries Commission
- Law Commission
- Mandal Commission
- National Commission on Farmers
- National Commission to Review the Working of the Constitution
- National Knowledge Commission
- National Statistical Commission
- NITI Aayog
- Staff Selection Commission
- Union Public Service Commission
- University Grants Commission
- Venkataswami Commission
- National Commission for Protection of Child Rights
- Digital Communications Commission

INDIA-PAKISTAN CONFLICT: PAHALGAM TERROR ATTACK AND OPERATION SINDOOR

Twenty-six civilians, mostly tourists, were killed in a dastardly terror attack in Jammu & Kashmir's Pahalgam on 22 April 2025. Pakistan-based terrorist group—The Resistance Front (a proxy of Lashkar-e-Taiba)—claimed responsibility for the ghastly incident, considered one of the worst terror strikes on civilians since the 2008 Mumbai terror attacks. On 7 May, India launched 'Operation Sindoor'—a series of precision strikes by the Indian Air Force, reducing nine militant-linked sites in Pakistan and Pakistanadministered Kashmir into rubble. Pakistan retaliated with drone and missile attacks on Indian military targets, but they were thwarted by India's air defence systems with pinpoint accuracy. During this period, both countries suspended all diplomatic ties, with India even indefinitely putting the Indus Waters Treaty in abeyance. The conflict, which lasted four days amid apprehensions of it escalating into a full-blown war, eventually ended in a ceasefire on 10 May 2025, after India accepted Pakistan's request for de-escalation. The Indian government has maintained that 'Operation Sindoor' continues to be in effect till Pakistan-sponsored terrorism ceases to exist. However, on 28 July 2025, the Indian Army, CRPF and J&K Police in a joint operation killed all the terrorists behind the incident, bringing closure to the horrific incident that took place over three months ago.

DELHI GETS A NEW CM

After the BJP's sweeping victory in the Delhi Assembly elections held on 5 February, Rekha Gupta was appointed Chief Minister of Delhi, becoming the fourth woman to hold the post in the National Capital Territory after Sushma Swaraj, Sheila Dikshit, and Atishi. A 50-year-old first-time MLA from Shalimar Bagh, Gupta was elected Leader of the House at the BJP legislature party meeting on 19 February, 2025. Her appointment ended AAP's decade-long governance and marked BJP's return to power in Delhi after 27 years, with the party winning 48 of 70 Assembly seats.

US, INDIA TARIFF WAR

On 2 April 2025, President Donald Trump of the the United States imposed new tariffs on India as part of a broader trade strategy targeting nations with sizable trade surpluses. India was hit with a 27 per cent 'reciprocal' tariff on top of a 10 per cent base tariff that took effect on 5 April at 12.01 a.m. EDT. The U.S. cited India's current tariff regime as justification, while India argued its policies protected domestic industry. Key Indian exports—chemicals, auto parts, steel, and aluminum derivatives—were impacted, threatening jobs in vital sectors. With bilateral trade at US$124 billion and India holding a US$37 billion surplus, the move risked straining economic ties. Choosing diplomacy over retaliation, India announced on 6 April it would pursue negotiations instead of counter-tariffs. Trump responded by pausing the reciprocal tariffs for 90 days on 9 April, enabling talks. This pause was later extended to 1 August, allowing continued engagement to resolve the issue.

INDIA, CHINA LAC AGREEMENT: OCTOBER 2024

On 21 October 2024, India and China announced a landmark agreement on patrolling protocols along the Line of Actual Control (LAC) in eastern Ladakh, effectively ending a military standoff that had lingered for over four years since the deadly Galwan Valley clash in June 2020. Foreign Secretary Vikram Misri stated the deal resulted in 'disengagement and resolution of the issues that had emerged in these areas in 2020'. It specifically addressed the key flashpoints—Depsang Plains and Demchok—where Chinese forces had obstructed Indian patrols since May 2020. The pact allowed Indian troops renewed access to patrol points 10 to 13 in Depsang, while in Demchok, patrolling resumed up to the Charding Nullah. Disengagement commenced on 25 October 2024, with both sides gradually withdrawing troops and dismantling barricades in these strategic zones. Both militaries agreed to revert to pre-May 2020 patrolling patterns along the LAC. By December 2024, full disengagement was declared, paving the way for renewed bilateral dialogue. The breakthrough represented a major diplomatic success for both countries, easing tensions between Asia's two largest nations and nuclear-armed neighbours.

UNIFORM CIVIL CODE IN UTTARAKHAND

On 27 January 2025, Uttarakhand made history as the first Indian state to implement the Uniform Civil Code (UCC), marking a major shift in the country's legal structure. Chief Minister Pushkar Singh Dhami inaugurated the UCC and its official online portal at 12.30 p.m., replacing religion-based personal laws with a single legal system for all residents. The UCC governs matters like marriage, divorce, inheritance, adoption, and succession uniformly for all citizens of Uttarakhand, excluding Scheduled Tribes. The law was drafted by a five-member panel led by former Supreme Court judge Ranjana Prakash Desai and approved by the state assembly in February 2024.

WAQF AMENDMENT ACT

The Waqf (Amendment) Act, 2025—also known as the UMEED Act—was enacted by the Indian Parliament on 3–4 April, 2025, following the Rajya Sabha's approval. It introduced sweeping reforms to the governance of Waqf properties across India by amending the Waqf Act of 1995. The Act addresses longstanding controversies, including high-profile corruption cases like the Karnataka Waqf Board Land Scam. Key reforms include mandating non-Muslim representation on the Central Waqf Council and state Waqf Boards, aiming to establish a more secular, transparent, and accountable system. The role of Survey Commissioner has been replaced with the District Collector, now empowered to survey Waqf assets. Additionally, government land previously classified as Waqf will no longer retain that status. The law also abolishes the 'Waqf by user' concept for new properties and expands government oversight in the resolution of Waqf-related disputes. Minority Affairs Minister Kiren Rijiju defended the law in Parliament, asserting that it would uplift millions of poor Muslims without disadvantaging any individual.

FORMER BANGLADESH PM SHEIKH HASINA GIVEN REFUGE IN INDIA

On 5 August 2024, then Bangladesh's prime minister Sheikh Hasina fled to India after weeks of deadly, student-led protests forced her resignation, ending her 15-year tenure since 2009. Escaping Dhaka by military helicopter, she landed at Ghaziabad's Hindon airbase near New Delhi, where India's National Security Adviser Ajit Doval received her.

MAHA KUMBH 2025

The Maha Kumbh Mela 2025 was observed from 13 January to 26 February, 2025, at the Triveni Sangam in Uttar Pradesh's Prayagraj—the confluence of the Ganga, Yamuna, and Saraswati rivers. Over 630 million (63 crore) devotees attended the event, making it the largest human gathering in history. On main auspicious days such as the Mauni Amavasya, Maghi Purnima, and Maha Shivratri, around 7–10 million people took the holy dip every single day. The Maha Kumbh this year was significant because it was the rare 'Purna Kumbh' which is celebrated every 12 years, during which people believe that bathing in the confluence of the sacred rivers purifies sins and invites spiritual blessings.

ASSEMBLY ELECTIONS IN MAHARASHTRA, JHARKHAND, JAMMU & KASHMIR

Between September and November 2024, three key assembly elections were held in Maharashtra, Jharkhand, and Jammu & Kashmir. The Jammu & Kashmir Legislative Assembly election for 90 seats was conducted in three phases from 18 September to 1 October, with results declared on 8 October. The INDIA alliance, led by the National Conference (NC) and Congress, won 48 seats, including 42 by NC, making Omar Abdullah the chief minister after victories in Budgam and Ganderbal. Jharkhand held elections in two phases on 13 November and 20, with the JMM-led coalition defeating the BJP-led NDA when results were announced on 23 November. Maharashtra's 288-seat election took place on 20 November, registering a 66.05 per cent turnout—its highest since 1995. The BJP-led Maha Yuti alliance won a landslide 235-seat majority, defeating the opposition decisively. These elections were significant, marking the return of democratic governance in Jammu & Kashmir after several years, while also showcasing the evolving political landscape and electoral preferences in Maharashtra and Jharkhand—two economically vital Indian states.

DELHI EXCISE POLICY CASE: KEJRIWAL, SISODIA, KAVITHA RELEASED FROM PRISON

Former Delhi chief minister Arvind Kejriwal, deputy chief minister Manish Sisodia, and Bharat Rashtra Samithi leader K. Kavitha were released from prison after being in police custody in connection with the alleged Delhi liquor excise policy scam. Alongside several businessmen and middlemen, the trio face investigation by the CBI and ED, both of which have accused Kejriwal of being the key conspirator, allegedly involving crores in kickbacks. Although Kejriwal was granted temporary bail during the final phase of the parliamentary elections, his campaign failed, with the AAP drawing a blank in Delhi's Lok Sabha seats in 2024 and losing the 2025 Delhi Assembly elections to the BJP.

RESERVATION FOR SC/ST STAFF IN SUPREME COURT

In a historic move, the Supreme Court of India introduced an official reservation policy for Scheduled Caste (SC) and Scheduled Tribe (ST) employees, covering both direct recruitment and promotional opportunities. Implemented from 23 June 2025, this landmark step marks a major shift in the internal workings of the apex court, which has long been considered cautious in adopting affirmative action measures within its own administrative framework. The decision reflects a growing commitment to inclusivity and social justice, aligning the institution with broader constitutional principles and government policies aimed at uplifting historically marginalized communities within India's judicial system.

MANIPUR CONFLICT

It was a year of turmoil in Manipur. The divide between the Meitei community in the valley and the Kuki tribes in the hills deepened in 2024, causing heavy human casualties, widespread violence, mob attacks and drone strikes on civilian areas. Once known for its cultural harmony, the state now faces deepening divisions, with thousands displaced and communities living in constant fear, as tensions show no signs of easing and peace remained a far cry in the years gone by.

By **MURUKESH KRISHNAN**

BUDGET FOR THE MIDDLE CLASS

Finance Minister Nirmala Sitharaman, who, on 1 February, presented her record eighth straight Budget, announced sweeping changes to the new Income Tax regime to provide relief to the middle class. In the new tax slabs announced in the 2025-26 Union Budget, Sitharaman said citizens with income of up to ₹12 lakh will have to pay zero tax. Further, 36 more life-saving medicines have been exempted from customs duty. She said the government will develop 50 tourism sites and announced the creation of Makhana Board in Bihar. She further announced a new Income Tax Bill.

NEW TAX CODE

Union Finance Minister Nirmala Sitharaman on 13 February introduced the Income Tax Bill, 2025, in the Lok Sabha. The Bill replaces the Income Tax Act, 1961 with a simplified and abridged new code. The Bill will replace terminologies such as 'assessment year' and 'previous year' with the easier-to-understand 'tax year'. The old Income Tax Act was enacted in 1961 and came into existence with effect from 1 April 1962. It has been amended nearly 65 times with more than 4,000 amendments. The new Bill has a word count of 2.6 lakh compared to 5.12 lakh in the existing I-T Act. The number of sections is 536, as against 819 effective sections in the existing law. Sitharaman had announced changing the over six-decade-old Income Tax Act while presenting the Union Budget.

TRADE TALKS

A) THE BIG TRUMP TARIFFS

US President Donald Trump announced sweeping reciprocal tariffs, or import duties, on a number of countries, including India and China, on 2 April. India faced a 26 per cent tariff from the US. The tariffs were in response to duties and taxes imposed by countries on imports of US goods.

However, on 9 April, Trump announced a 90-day suspension of these tariffs until 9 July, except for those on China and Hong Kong. In July, the US further postponed the tariffs on several countries, including India, until 1 August.

As the tariff war escalated, the US pushed up rates on up to 245 per cent duty on Chinese goods entering America. China, too, didn't back down, and kept hiking their rates on US goods entering their country. After a month of back and forth, both countries rolled back most of their hikes.

B) HISTORIC INDIA-UK TRADE DEAL

India and the UK on 4 May sealed a landmark deal to double trade between the two economies from USD 60 billion to USD 120 billion by 2030. The free trade agreement will lower tariffs on 99 per cent of Indian exports to zero and would make it easier for

British firms to export whisky, cars and other products to India. The deal is aimed at boosting the overall trade basket.

JIO, AIRTEL LOG INTO STARLINK

Bharti Airtel and Reliance Jio have entered into agreements with SpaceX to offer Starlink's satellite internet services in India. As part of the deals, Jio and Airtel will distribute Starlink's equipment through their retail networks, with Jio also handling customer service, installation, and activation support. The partnership will primarily aim to provide high-speed internet access to businesses, schools, healthcare centres, and remote communities throughout India. In May, Airtel signed an agreement with Starlink to offer the latter's services in Africa. On 6 June 2025, Starlink received a licence from India's telecom department for providing satellite internet services in India, taking it closer to launching commercial operations in the country.

TOUCHING NEW LEVELS

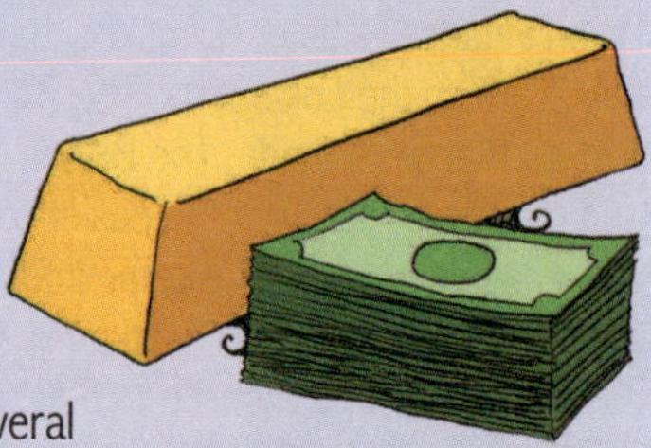

A) 10 GM GOLD AT ₹1 LAKH!

On 22 April, gold did the unimaginable. 10 grams of the yellow metal crossed the ₹1 lakh barrier for the very first time. The precious metal had been hovering around the ₹90,000-99,500-mark for several weeks, and it eventually crossed the ₹1 lakh barrier on 22 April. Gold is considered among the safest investment instruments, and the ongoing geopolitical strifes, and the trade war between the US and China triggered the surge in prices.

B) FOREX RESERVES PAST USD 700 BN

India's forex reserves breached the USD 700-billion mark for the first time to reach a new all-time high of USD 704.885 billion in September 2025. In the last week of September, the forex reserves surged USD 12.588 billion, which was one of the highest rises ever. Having more foreign reserves allows a country to better manage its economy and gives it a protection during an economic crisis.

C) RECORD GST REVENUES

Goods and Services Tax (GST) collection reached an all time high of about ₹2.37 lakh crore in April 2025. Higher GST collections reflect strong economic activity. The previous highest GST collections was in April 2024 at ₹2.10 lakh crore. Annual collections for the 2024-25 financial year also touched a record ₹22.08 lakh crore. GST was rolled out on 1 July 2017.

MERGER IN THE SKIES

Air India and Vistara officially merged into one entity on 12 November 2024 in a big consolidation in the Indian aviation space. According to reports, the merged entity will fly over 1,20,000 passengers daily and connect more than 90 destinations.

Ten-year-old Vistara was a joint venture between the Tatas and Singapore Airlines. The merger was announced in November 2022. Only six weeks earlier, Air India Express and AIX Connect had integrated into one unit.

THE BIG APPOINTMENTS

A) A NEW RBI GOVERNOR AFTER 6 YEARS

Former Revenue Secretary Sanjay Malhotra took charge as the 26th governor of the Reserve Bank of India (RBI) in December 2024 after the incumbent Shaktikanta Das retired. Das, who held the office for six years, was made the principal secretary to the Prime Minister.

B) NEW SEBI CHIEF

Tuhin Kanta Pandey took over as the Chairman of the Securities and Exchange Board of India (Sebi) on 1 March. Pandey took over from Madhabi Puri Buch, whose tenure ended on 28 February. Pandey had earlier served as the finance secretary and the revenue secretary, besides holding a host of top positions in the government.

HINDENBURG SHUTS SHOP

Hindenburg Research, known for its high-profile campaigns against the likes of Adani Group, decided to close operations in January 2025 about eight years after it was founded. Activist short-seller Nathan Anderson-led Hindenburg Research had made it to headlines across India in January 2023 for its report accusing the Adani Group of rampant corruption, calling it 'the largest con in corporate history'. The Adani group had repeatedly denied all allegations.

DID YOU KNOW?

- The number of Unified Payments Interface (UPI) transactions reached a record high of 18.68 billion in May 2025, while the total transaction value was ₹25.14 trillion, also the highest ever. UPI transactions, which started in India in April 2016, have seen a steep rise over the past few years both in value and volume terms and is now the most-favoured mode of payment in many parts of the country.
- India is set to overtake Japan to become the world's fourth-largest economy by the end of the 2025-26 financial year. The International Monetary Fund (IMF) made the observation in its World Economic Outlook (WEO) report in April. A few years ago, India overtook the United Kingdom to become the fifth largest economy. The US, China, and Germany are the top three economies of the world.

By Thirumoy Banerjee

NATIONAL CENTRE OF EXCELLENCE FOR ANIMATION, VISUAL EFFECTS, GAMING, COMICS, AND EXTENDED REALITY

The National Centre of Excellence for Animation, Visual Effects, Gaming, Comics, and Extended Reality (AVGC-XR) is a premier institution established by the Indian government to promote innovation, education, and industry growth in the AVGC sector. Set up in Mumbai through a collaboration between the Ministry of Information and Broadcasting and the Indian Institute of Mass Communication, it serves as a hub for world-class training, research, and content creation, aligning with India's vision to become a global leader in digital media. The centre promotes collaboration between academia and industry, empowering youth with cutting-edge skills and boosting employment in the creative economy.

BABY GROK CHATBOT FOR KIDS

Baby Grok is a kid-friendly chatbot created to offer children a safe and engaging way to interact with Artificial Intelligence. Using age-appropriate language and strong content filters, it provides fun and educational conversations suited to young users. Baby Grok can answer basic questions, share stories, and spark curiosity, all within a secure digital space. It supports children's learning and communication development, making it a helpful resource for parents and educators guiding kids through the digital world responsibly.

HUMANOIDS SUMMIT IN CALIFORNIA AND LONDON

The Humanoids Summit is a flagship global event spotlighting the future of humanoid (having an appearance or character resembling that of a human) robotics and embodied Artificial Intelligence. Debuting in December 2024 at the Computer History Museum in Mountain View, California (United States), it convened leading technologists, investors, and innovators to push the boundaries of commercial humanoid tech. Building on its success, the summit expanded to Europe with its first London edition on 30 May, 2025. Held at Novotel London West, the event drew 1,000+ attendees and featured live demos of humanoids and expert insights.

TECHKRITI FESTIVAL IN KANPUR FOR STUDENT INVENTORS

Techkriti, Asia's premier tech and entrepreneurship festival, was held at IIT Kanpur from 27-30 March, 2025. Aimed at student innovators, it provides an exciting platform to showcase advancements in robotics (Robowars), machine learning (ML Hackathon), electronics (ECDC), aerospace ('Take Off'), and ideation (Techkriti Innovation Challenge). With over ₹1 crore in prizes, global participation, and workshops by experts, Techkriti encourages young minds to innovate, collaborate, and transform ambitious technological concepts into impactful real-world solutions.

INDIA'S UPI EXTENDS GLOBAL EXPANSION

India's Unified Payments Interface (UPI) continues its global expansion with its integration into Sri Lanka's LankaPay network, enabling seamless cross-border digital payments. This move enhances financial connectivity and supports tourism, remittances, and business transactions between the two nations. UPI is now operational in the United Arab Emirates, Singapore, Bhutan, Nepal, France, and Mauritius. The growing international reach of UPI highlights India's leadership in digital payments and aims to offer faster, secure, and more convenient transactions for Indian travelers and diaspora abroad.

SKINNOVATION: SKIING AND START-UPS IN THE ALPS

Skinnovation is a distinctive startup and innovation festival that merges alpine skiing with entrepreneurship in the Austrian Alps. Held in March 2025 at Axamer Lizum near Innsbruck in Austria, it welcomed over 800 participants, featuring 100+ startups and 90 tech investors. Highlights included the famous Ski Lift Pitch—where founders pitch to investors inside gondolas (the seating compartment in a ski lift)—along with ski-hut sessions, pitch contests, ski races, and a sunset celebration. This adventurous setting offered a dynamic environment for business networking, idea sharing, and building meaningful connections.

FROM SHARK TANK

GOOD GOOD PIGGY BANK

Good Good Piggy Bank, founded in 2021 by Purva Aggarwal, is an Indian Ed-FinTech startup that helps children build smart money habits through a digital piggy bank. The platform features gamified incentives, real-money tasks, and parental controls to teach financial literacy early. Featured in Season 1, Episode 14 of Shark Tank India, the startup pitched for ₹45 lakhs in exchange for 5 per cent equity at a ₹9 crore valuation. Though no deal was secured, it gained traction through media buzz and new funding. Since appearing on the show, Good Good Piggy Bank has secured follow-on funding from both angel and venture capital investors, grown its early access waitlist to over 3,500 users, and established collaborations with schools and ed-tech platforms. The startup is steadily expanding across India, with a focus on reaching Tier 2 and Tier 3 cities. It also has ambitions to enter international markets, including the United Arab Emirates, Indonesia, and others, aiming to make financial literacy accessible to children globally.

COGRAD

CoGrad, established in 2019 under the company Supervision Educare Pvt. Ltd., is an education management startup headquartered in Prayagraj, Uttar Pradesh. It transforms underutilised rural schools by integrating Artificial Intelligence, coding, and STEM (Science, Technology, Engineering, and Mathematics) learning via its core offering—the Medha AI teacher-assist platform. Guided by mentors from Indian Institutes of Technology and National Institutes of Technology, CoGrad has reached over 8,000 students in 16+ schools and trained more than 5,000 youth in skill development. Featured in Season 4 of Shark Tank India, it champions AI-powered rural education aligned with National Education Policy 2020 goals.

BAMBINOS.LIVE

Bambinos.live is an online English communication platform for kids, delivering engaging, gamified, and customised lessons to develop spoken English and creative writing skills. Since its founding, it has earned the trust of more than 10,000 parents and consistently receives ratings between 4.6 and 4.7 stars out of 5. The platform features live, interactive classes with qualified instructors, flexible learning schedules, and strong community support. In March 2025, it raised US $114.8K to further its mission of shaping confident, articulate young learners worldwide.

By Murukesh Krishnan

CONSTITUTIONAL ISSUES

A. In the landmark judgment of 'State of Tamil Nadu vs. Governor of Tamil Nadu', the Supreme Court held withholding of 10 state legislative bills by the Governor of State of Tamil Nadu as "illegal" and "erroneous" and clarified the exercise of power vested to the Governor under Article 200 of Constitution of India, 1950. It stated that when a Governor receives a bill, it only has three options- it can either (i) grant assent, (ii) withhold assent, leading to applicability of the first proviso of Article 200, send back the bill to the State legislature for reconsideration. However, if the bill returns to the Governor, then the Governor cannot withhold assent. (iii) If the Governor believes that the bill derogates the powers of the High Courts, he may reserve it for the president under the second proviso of Article 200. The president then would accordingly grant or withhold assent as per Article 201 of the Constitution of India.

B. The Supreme Court in the matter of 'Pragya Prasun vs. Union of India' tagged with 'Amar Jain vs. Union of India' held 'Right to Digital Access' as an intrinsic component of the right to life and liberty as enshrined in Article 21 of the Constitution of India. In light of Article 21, read in conjunction with Articles 14, 15, and 38, it directed States to ensure that digital infrastructure, government portals, online learning platforms, and financial technologies are universally accessible, inclusive, and responsive to the needs of all vulnerable and marginalized populations, especially persons with disabilities.

C. The Supreme Court in 'Rajeeb Kalita vs. Union of India', a PIL, emphasized that toilet facilities are not merely a matter of convenience, but a facet of human rights, and access to proper sanitation is recognized as a fundamental right under Article 21 (right to life or personal liberty) of the Constitution of India, 1950. This right inherently includes ensuring a safe and hygienic environment for all individuals. The Court further issued directions to the State Governments/UTs while also making it clear that they will allocate sufficient funds for construction, maintenance, and cleanliness. Additionally, these facilities shall be periodically reviewed in consultation with the committee constituted by the High Courts.

D. In a significant judgment, the 3 judge bench of the Supreme Court in the matter of *All India Judges Association vs Union of India (Minimum Practice & LDCE issue),* restored the condition that a minimum practice of three years as an advocate is necessary for a candidate to apply for entry-level posts in judicial service, with the period of practice could be reckoned from the date of provisional

LANDMARK JUDGEMENTS

enrollment. The said condition, however will apply only to future recruitments. The apex court opined that allowing fresh graduates to enter the judicial services without having any prior practice in the courts has led to problems, as the fresh graduate is not exposed to the workings of the court and how the lawyers as well as judges function in the court. Previously, there was a condition in most States that only lawyers with a minimum practice of three years could apply for judicial service, which was subsequently removed by the Supreme Court, allowing fresh law graduates to apply for Munsiff-Magistrate posts. However, the same has been brought back in the year 2025 and will apply to recruitments made in future.

E. The Hon'ble Supreme Court in the matter of *Harinagar Sugar Mills Ltd. (Biscuit Division) & Anr. vs. State of Maharashtra* held that the right under Article 19(1)(g) of the Constitution to carry on any trade or business includes the right to shut down that business. However, this right is not absolute and is subject to reasonable restrictions aimed at protecting workers and ensuring compliance with statutory procedures. In the present matter, Harinagar Sugar Mills Ltd. (HSML) had operated a biscuit manufacturing division exclusively for Britannia Industries Limited (BIL) for over three decades under Job Work Agreements (JWAs). In 2019, BIL terminated this agreement, triggering HSML to seek closure of its business under the Industrial Disputes Act. HSML filed its closure application but the application was rejected, as incomplete, demanding resubmission. Despite HSML's efforts to provide additional information, the closure application was delayed. Workers' unions moved the Industrial Tribunal seeking to restrain closure, which was granted. HSML's petitions challenging this were dismissed by the High Court, leading to appeals before the Supreme Court. Ultimately, the Supreme Court acknowledged the balance between the constitutional right to conduct business and the need for reasonable restrictions to protect employees. It held that the application was complete.

WOMEN'S RIGHTS

A. The Supreme Court in the matter of 'Rinku Baheti vs. Sandesh Sharda' emphasized for requirement of parity and consistency in approach in terms of seeking and granting alimony, irrespective of the financial status or wealth of the parties in hand. The Court held that the factors, while determining permanent alimony (not limited or exhaustive) are- status of the parties, social and financial, reasonable needs of the wife and dependent children, etc. The court held that the wife, i.e., the Petitioner, simply cannot claim an amount equivalent to what the ex-wife of the husband, i.e., the Respondent, had received or based on the Respondent's income. Her entitlement to maintenance has to be decided based on the factors applicable to her.

B. The Division Bench of the Supreme Court in the case of 'Pinky Meena vs. High Court of Judicature for Rajasthan at Jodhpur' emphasized '...that a greater representation of women in the judiciary, would greatly improve the overall quality of judicial decision making and this impacts generally and also specifically in cases affecting women…' In this case, the allegations against Appellant, who happened to be a Scheduled Tribe (ST) woman, were that while in service of the Education Department of the State of Rajasthan, she obtained LL.B. and B.Ed degree in the same year, obtained LL.M. degree while being in service as a teacher showing her attendance as a regular student, and did not obtain No Objection Certification from the State Government while participating in the RJS examination. It was also alleged that she concealed her resignation from government service while joining as a Civil Judge. The court set aside a show cause notice and the discharge order issued against the Appellant, Pinky Meena, and reinstated her to her original post, Civil Judge and Judicial Magistrate.

C. The Supreme Court, in the matter of *K. Umadevi v. Government of Tamil Nadu,* while setting aside the order of Madras High Court which stated that maternity leave was not a fundamental right but a statutory right or a right flowing from service conditions, and categorically held that the maternity benefits are part of reproductive rights and that maternity leave is integral to those benefits, further the apex court held that the reproductive rights are now recognized as part of several intersecting domains of international human rights law viz. the right to health, right to privacy, right to equality and non-discrimination and the right to dignity.

D. In a significant judgment of *Ravish Singh Rana vs. State of Uttarakhand,* the Supreme Court stated that when a couple continues their live-in relationship for a long period, there is a presumption that they did not want marriage. When two adults reside together as a live-in couple for many years, an allegation that the relationship was entered into based on a false promise of marriage is untenable. In the present case, the couple lived together for over two years. On 19 November 2023, they also executed a settlement deed, affirming their love for each other and stating that they will get married. The FIR was lodged by the woman alleging that the man had forced sex with her. After the Uttarakhand High Court refused to quash the FIR, the man approached the Supreme Court, and the apex court noted that there was no allegation in the FIR that a physical relationship was established only because there was a promise of marriage.

PROTECTION & SAFEGUARDING OF CHILDREN

A. To provide protection and safeguard the interests of children, the Supreme Court in the matter of 'Just Rights for Children Alliance vs. S. Harish' have specifically criminalized the viewing, storage, and possession of 'child pornography', and substituting the word 'child pornography' with 'child sexual abuse and exploitative material', or 'CSEAM'. The court, under Section 15 of the POCSO Act, has made it vehemently clear that both possessing the material and failing to delete and destroy it, as well as possessing it with the purpose to distribute, are punishable crimes. Furthermore, if intermediaries do not "expeditiously" remove such content when the government notifies them, their safe harbor status given under the Information Technology Act, 2000 shall expire.

B. In the judgment of 'Ramji Lal Bairwa vs. State of Rajasthan', the Supreme Court held that the criminal proceedings for offences under POCSO Act cannot be quashed merely based on a compromise between the offender and the victim's family. The judgment emphasized such offences being non-compoundable and underscored the State's paramount role in prosecuting offences that have broader societal implications.

C. The Supreme Court in the matter of *In Re Alarming Rise In The Number Of Reported Child Rape Incidents*, while closing the suo moto proceedings initiated in 2019 regarding systemic flaws under the Protection of Children from Sexual Offences (POCSO) Act, 2012, has given directions to the Union and State Governments to set up special POCSO courts on top priority basis, take appropriate steps to sensitize the officials who are involved or associated with the investigation of POCSO cases, ensure charge-sheets are filed within mandatory time-period as stipulated in the Act and trial proceedings are completed within time frame contemplated in the Act.

ENVIRONMENT / FOREST CONCERNS

A. 'In Re: The Solid Waste Management Rules, 2016 & In Re: Dumping Of Solid Waste', the Supreme Court found that in the Municipal Corporation of Delhi (MCD) area, 11,000 tonnes of municipal solid waste was being generated daily, leading to a processing gap of 3000 tonnes per day, as well as 800 tonnes of solid waste per day being dumped at Ghazipur and Bhalsawa, all posing grave threats of environmental degradation, frequent fires and overall public health risk. Therefore, it directed the Delhi Government as well as MCD to file affidavits to address the issue of solid waste by coming up with innovative means and measures to bridge the gap, along with an additional affidavit to be filed by the Delhi Government stating detailed measures implemented to prevent fire mishaps at the dumping sites.

B. 'In Re: Ban On The Use Of Firecrackers', the Supreme Court while taking note of the ban imposed on the use of firecrackers by the Government of Delhi and the State of Rajasthan, directed the governments of Uttar Pradesh and Haryana to impose a similar ban till 17th January 2025 to their respective NCR regions.

C. In a significant judgment of 'In Re: T.N. Godavarman Thirumulpad vs. Union Of India', the Supreme Court recognized Oran (derivative of Sanskrit word 'Aranya' meaning undisturbed forest, also known as Dev-vans/Rundhs), being sacred groves as Forests under the Forest Conservation Act, 1980, holding deep cultural and spiritual significance for local communities in Rajasthan. It issued directions to the effect of carrying out on-ground mapping and satellite mapping of each sacred grove, survey and notification of all sacred groves in each district, recommendation of grant of protection of sacred groves under the Wildlife Protection Act, 1972 among others.

BAIL MATTERS

A. The Supreme Court in the matter of 'Manish Sisodia vs. Directorate of Enforcement', while hearing and allowing the bail plea of the former Deputy Chief Minister of Delhi Manish Sisodia in the liquor policy case, lamented that the Trial Courts and High Courts in the country have forgotten the principle 'Bail is rule, jail an exception' and attempt to play safe and held bail cannot be withheld as a punishment.

B. The Supreme Court in the matter of 'Jitendra Paswan vs. State of Bihar', ruled that once a court concludes that an accused is entitled to bail, it cannot delay the implementation of the bail order, as doing so may violate the rights guaranteed under Article 21 of the Constitution of India, 1950. The court deleted the condition while granting bail to an accused that the bail order will be executed after six months, as the Patna High Court in the impugned judgment did not provide any reason for imposing such a condition.

C. The Supreme Court in the matter of 'Rup Bahadur Magar @ Sanki @ Rabin vs. State of West Bengal' emphasized that bail cannot be rejected merely on the ground that the trial will be expedited. In the present circumstances, the Court held that since the trial at the trial court had been delayed considerably, the Appellant(s) herein are entitled to be enlarged on bail till the final disposal of the trial.

STRANGE BUT TRUE PILS

- A rather unusual PIL came to be filed in May 2025 wherein the Petitioner in 'Narender Kumar Malhotra vs. Union of India' pleaded before the Supreme Court for the enforcement of 'Karva Chauth' festival for all women regardless of their status (marital), the issuance of mandamus by High Court to the Union and the State to enact a law, and if the women do not follow it, the inaction should be punishable. The Petitioner had first approached the Hon'ble Punjab & Haryana High Court, which allowed the withdrawal of PIL only after issuance of a symbolic cost of ₹ 1000. The Supreme Court dismissed the PIL and upheld the High Court's order, refusing to interfere with the same.
- A PIL was filed in the matter of 'Omanakuttan KG vs. Whatsapp Applications Services Private Ltd.' seeking directions to the Central Government to ban the operation of WhatsApp for alleged violation of the orders of the legal authorities in the country. The Petitioner claimed the Kerala High Court had dismissed his PIL prematurely. The SC refused to entertain his plea and dismissed the PIL.

By **Karan Audichya**

INDIAN HISTORY TIMELINE

3000 BC
The Indus Valley Civilization is established.

543 BC
Bimbisara, later a follower of Gautama Budhha, conquers and becomes the king of Magadha (modern Bihar).

800 – 300 BC
The Upanishads, cornerstone philosophical texts of Hinduism, composed around this time.

400 – 200 BC
Mahabharata, the great Sanskrit epic, composed.

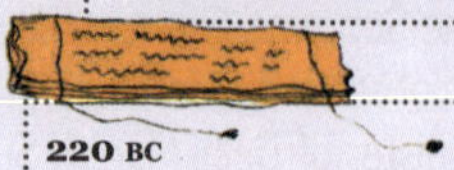

220 BC
Mauryan dynasty expands to almost all of India.

265 BC
After the bloodbath at the battle of Kalinga, Emperor Ashoka embraces Buddhism.

273 BC
Ashoka is the new Mauryan Emperor.

1500 BC
The Aryans arrive from Europe and a unique Indo-Aryan culture develops.

2000 BC
The Indus Valley Civilization begins to decline.

1200 BC
Indo-Aryans start using iron tools. This is dubbed the Iron Age.

500 BC
Prince Mahavira establishes Jainism in northern India.

3000 BC — 1500 BC — 500 BC — 0 BC

1500 BC
One of the oldest books in Sanskrit or any Indo-Eurpoean language, the Rig Veda, is composed.

527 BC
Prince Siddhartha Gautama establishes Buddhism and is known as the Buddha.

326 BC
Alexander the Great of Macedonia wins the famous battle against Porus, a ruler in Eastern Punjab.

73 BC
Sunga dynasty declines.

322 BC
Mauryan Empire founded by Chandragupta Maurya.

185 BC
Mauryan dynasty collapses; Sunga dynasty established.

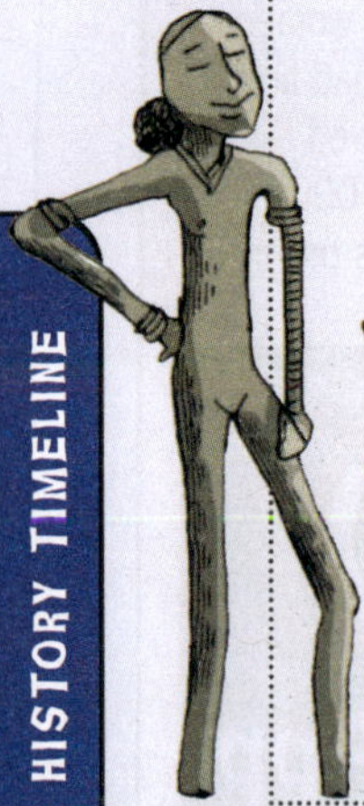

2500 BC
Cities of Harappa and Mohenjo-Daro in the Indus Valley start flourishing.

304 BC
Ramayana, the famous Sanskrit epic, is composed.

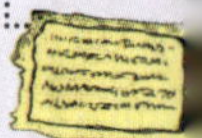

200 BC
Bhagavad Gita is composed.

300 BC
Chola dynasty establishes one of the earliest South Indian kingdoms with its capital at Uraiyur

50 AD
First Buddha stupa constructed at Sanchi.

300 AD
Pallava dynasty established in Kanchi.

350AD
Sangam compiled in Tamil in the kingdom of Madurai, and the Puranas composed.

390 AD
Chandra Gupta II extends Gupta kingdom to Gujarat.

655 AD
Pallavas of Kanchipuram are defeated by the Chalukyas.

985 AD
Rajaraja Chola extends the Chola Empire to all of South India. He would go on to construct the temple of Thanjavur.

888 AD
Cholas put an end to the Pallava dynasty.

850 AD
Cholas get back their independence from the Pallavas.

753 AD
Rashtrakutas overthrow the Chalukyas.

0 AD — 500 AD — 750 AD — 1000 AD

402 AD
Chinese scholar Fa-Hsien reaches India.

427 AD
Monastic university of Nalanda is built.

499 AD
Aryabhatta writes the *Aryabhatiya*, a compendium of mathematics and astronomy.

500 AD
Beginning of Bhakti cult in Tamil Nadu.

550 AD
Downfall of Gupta Empire due to continuous barbaric invasions.

606 AD
Harshavardhana, a Buddhist king, unites the kingdoms of Thanesar and Kanauj.

600 AD
Pallavan dynasty governs southern India from Kanchi.

788 AD
Birth of Shankaracharya.

543 AD
Chalukyan kingdom established in central India with Badami as the capital.

1010 AD
Chola king Rajaraja builds the Brihadeshvara Temple in Thanjavur.

1001 AD
Mahmud of Ghazni raids northern India.

Not to scale.

1017 AD
Al-Biruni, Persian mathematician, travels to India.

1556 AD
Humayun dies and his son Akbar becomes one of the greatest rulers of India.

1555 AD
Humayun fights Sher Shah and regains India.

1100 AD
Chandelas, Cholas, Kadambas and Rashtrakutas reign in different parts of India.

1540 AD
Humayun loses the empire to Afghan leader Sher Shah and goes into exile.

1530 AD
Babur dies and his son Humayun is the next Mughal emperor.

1192 AD
Mohammad of Ghori captures Delhi and establishes a Muslim Sultanate at Delhi.

1490 AD
Guru Nanak Dev Ji establishes Sikhism.

1526 AD
Babur, an Afghan ruler, establishes the Mughal dynasty in India.

1010 AD — 1250 AD — 1450 AD — 1600 AD

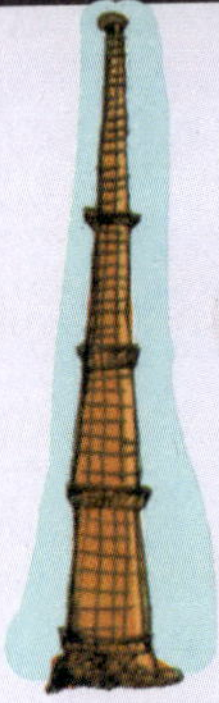

1190 AD
Chalukya Empire is split among Hoysalas, Yadavas and Kakatiyas.

1336–1565 AD
Vijayanagar Empire is established.

1371 AD
Vijayanagar kingdom takes over the Muslim Sultanate of Madura in Tamil Nadu.

1206 AD
Qutub-ud-din Aibak becomes the first Sultan of Delhi.

1347 AD
Bahmani kingdom established in the Deccan.

1279 AD
Chola dynasty comes to an end.

1325 AD
Turks invade and Muhammad bin Tughlaq becomes Sultan of Delhi.

1290 AD
Establishment of the Khilji Sultanate at Delhi.

1292 AD
Marco Polo comes to India.

1605 AD
Jahangir succeeds his father Akbar.

1611 AD
East India Company is established in India by the British.

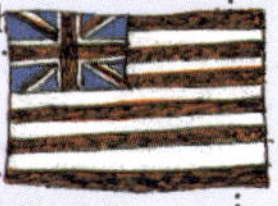

1628 AD
Shah Jahan succeeds Jahangir.

1707 AD
Aurangzeb dies, Mughal Empire destabilized, Bahadur Shah I comes to the throne.

1757 AD
British defeat Siraj-ud-daulah at the Battle of Plassey in Bengal.

1793 AD
Permanent Settlement of Bengal—reorganisation of the tax laws by the British.

1799 AD
British defeat Tipu Sultan.

1818 AD
End of the Maratha Empire—British control extends over most of India.

1829 AD
Prohibition of Sati by law.

1848 AD
Lord Dalhousie becomes the Governor-General of India.

1851-1853 AD
Railway, postal services and telegraph line introduced in India.

1650 AD — 1700 AD — 1800 AD — 1899 AD

1618–1656 AD
Shah Jahan builds Taj Mahal, Jama Masjid and Red Fort.

1658 AD
Shah Jahan's son Aurangzeb seizes power.

1674 AD
Shivaji's coronation takes place and Maratha Empire established.

1761 AD
Marathas rule over most of northern India.

1769 AD
A famine kills ten million people in Bengal and the East India Company is ineffectual.

1773 AD
Warren Hastings, Governor of Bengal, establishes a monopoly on the sale of opium.

1831 AD
Administration of Mysore is taken over by East India Company.

1857 AD
First War of Indian Independence also known as Revolt of 1857 or Sepoy Mutiny.

1877 AD
Queen of England is proclaimed the Empress of India.

1885 AD
Formation of the Indian National Congress.

1899 AD
Lord Curzon becomes Governor-General and Viceroy of India.

SIMON GO BACK
1900 AD
1920 AD
1935 AD
1905 AD
The Partition of Bengal takes place.
1906 AD
Muslim League is formed.
1912 AD
The Imperial capital shifts from Calcutta to Delhi.
1919 AD
The Jallianwalla Bagh massacre takes place due to protests against the Rowlatt Act.
1920 AD
Non-cooperation Movement formally launched.
1928 AD
Lala Lajpat Rai killed by the British during a peaceful protest.
1928 AD
Simon Commission comes to India and is boycotted by all parties.
1930 AD
Salt Satyagraha is launched as an agitation against salt tax.
1930–31 AD
First Round Table Conference in London to discuss constitutional reforms for India.
1931 AD
Second Round Table Conference takes place and Irwin–Gandhi Pact is signed.
1934 AD
Civil Disobedience Movement is called off.

1942 AD
Quit India Movement is launched.

1942 AD
Cripps Mission deputed by British Parliament to contain political crisis in India.

1942 AD
Indian National Army is formed with Netaji Subhash Chandra Bose spearheading the movement.

1947 AD
Partition of India and Independence from British rule.

1951 AD
First General Elections and Jawaharlal Nehru of the Congress Party elected prime minister.

1965 AD
Second war with Pakistan over Kashmir.

1966 AD
Indira Gandhi, Nehru's daughter, elected prime minister.

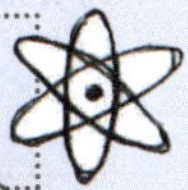

1971 AD
Third war with Pakistan over creation of Bangladesh.

1971 AD
Soviet Union and India sign twenty-year treaty of friendship.

1974 AD
India's first underground nuclear test is carried out.

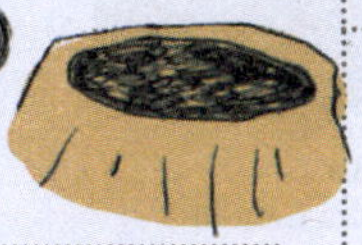

1962 AD
The main pretext for the India–China War is a disputed Himalayan border.

1948 AD
First war over Kashmir with Pakistan.

1948 AD
Mahatma Gandhi assassinated by Nathuram Godse.

1947 – 48 AD
Widespread communal riots during and after the Partition into two nations: India and Pakistan.

1975 AD
Indira Gandhi declares Emergency—considered the darkest hour of Indian democracy.

1964 AD
Lal Bahadur Shastri becomes prime minister after Nehru's death.

1977 AD
Indira Gandhi loses the General Elections.

1980 AD
Indira Gandhi returns to power.

1991 AD
Rajiv Gandhi assassinated by suicide bomber.

1991 AD
Economic reform begun by Prime Minister P V Narasimha Rao and Finance Minister Manmohan Singh.

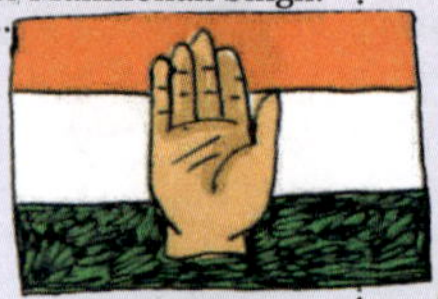

1992 AD
Hindu extremists demolish Babri mosque in Ayodhya, triggering widespread Hindu–Muslim violence.

1989 AD
Congress defeated in General Elections. V P Singh is prime minister.

1987 AD
India sends troops for peacekeeping operations in Sri Lanka's civil conflict with the LTTE.

1998 AD
India conducts five nuclear tests, closely followed by Pakistan.

1980 AD ---------- 1990 AD ---------- 1998 AD

1984 AD
Gas leak at Union Carbide pesticides plant in Bhopal. Thousands are killed.

1984 AD
Indira Gandhi assassinated by bodyguards, sparking off anti-Sikh riots in Delhi.

1984 AD
Troops storm Golden Temple in Amritsar, the hide-out of Sikh militants demanding self-rule.

1983 AD
India wins the cricket Prudential World Cup under the captaincy of Kapil Dev.

1996 AD
Congress suffers worst ever electoral defeat as the BJP emerges as single largest party.

2001 AD
Massive earthquakes hit Gujarat, leaving at least 30,000 dead.

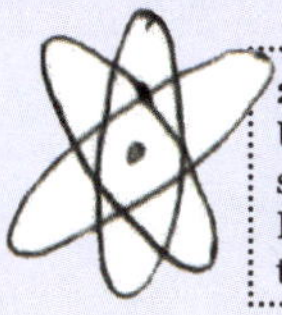

2006 AD
US president George W Bush signs agreement with Indian PM for sharing nuclear technology with India.

2007 AD
Pratibha Patil becomes India's first woman president.

2001 AD
US lifts sanctions imposed on India and Pakistan after they staged nuclear tests in 1998.

2008 AD
Terrorists of Pakistani origin execute large-scale attack on various busy spots in Mumbai.

2000 AD
The billionth Indian citizen is born.

2002 AD
Retired scientist and architect of India's nuclear programme, A P J Abdul Kalam is elected president of India.

2010 AD
The largest ever multi-sport event to be staged in India, the 2010 Commonwealth Games, are held in New Delhi from 3–14 October.

2003 AD
India and Pakistan agree to resume air links, banned for years.

2011 AD
India wins the Cricket World Cup again after twenty-eight years, beating Sri Lanka by six wickets. The last World Cup victory came in 1983.

2000 AD — 2005 AD — 2011 AD

1999 AD
Cyclone devastates Odisha, leaving at least 10,000 dead.

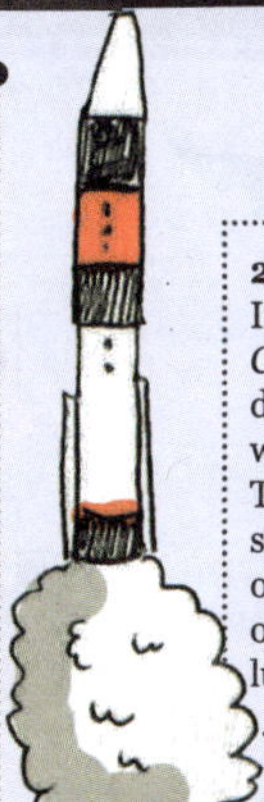

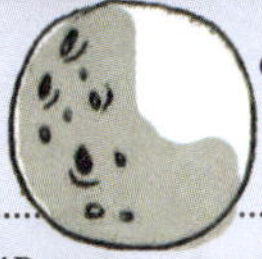

2009 AD
India's lunar mission, *Chandrayaan-I*, discovers traces of water on the moon. This is India's greatest space discovery so far, opening the possibility of setting up future lunar colonies.

2009 AD
The world's cheapest car, Nano, manufactured in India, hits the roads.

1999 AD
War with Pakistan-backed forces in the Kargil region of India-held Kashmir.

2004 AD
Whole islands and tribes in the Andaman and Nicobar Islands disappear due to tsunami.

2005 AD
At least 1,000 people are killed in floods and mudslides in Maharashtra.

1999 AD
Prime Minister Vajpayee takes the bus to Pakistan to sign bilateral Lahore peace declaration.

2004 AD
Manmohan Singh becomes prime minister.

2004 AD
A huge earthquake in Indonesia triggers a tsunami. India's southern coast severely affected.

2012 AD
Former finance minister Pranab Mukherjee becomes new president of India.

2013 AD
The 163-year-old telegram service breathed its last, marking the end of an era.

2014
India's low-cost Mars Mission, *Mangalyaan*, successfully entered the Mars orbit on its maiden attempt.

2016 AD
The government announced a 'Demonitisation Drive' to eradicate black money, corruption and fake currency from the country.

2017 AD
Ram Nath Kovind becomes the 14th president of India.

2019 AD
The state of Jammu and Kashmir is divided into two union territories: Jammu & Kashmir and Ladakh.

2020 AD
Covid-19 pandemic hits India with the first case emerging in Kerala on January 30.

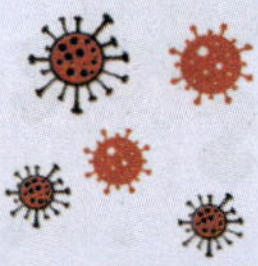

2012 AD — 2015 AD — 2020 AD

2011–2012 AD
Widespread corruption in government exposed in 2G scam and Coalgate.

2014 AD
The 29th Indian state—Telangana—came into being, with the division of Andhra Pradesh.

2013 AD
India's cricketing god, Sachin Tendulkar, announced retirement from all forms of cricket.

2017 AD
GST, a universal taxation system for the country, was rolled out on 1 July 2017.

2016 AD
Mother Teresa canonized at a ceremony at the Vatican by Pope Francis. She will now be called Saint Teresa.

2015 AD
The people's president, A P J Abdul Kalam, also called the Missile Man of India, died on 27 July.

2021 AD
Covid-19 vaccine rollout begins on 16 January with Covishield and Covaxin.

2021 AD
Indian hockey team bags an Olympic medal in Tokyo breaking a 41-year jinx.

2023 AD
Chandrayaan-3 makes history with soft landing on the Moon's south pole on August 23rd 2023.

2023 AD — 2025 AD

2024 AD
Arvind Kejriwal becomes the first sitting Chief Minister of India to be placed under arrest. He was arrested by the ED in the Delhi liquor policy case.

2025 AD
Air India Flight 171 crashes 32 seconds after take-off.

WORLD

- Countries of the World*
- International Organizations
- Important Office Holders
- World Round-up
- World History Timeline
- Top Ten

ALGERIA

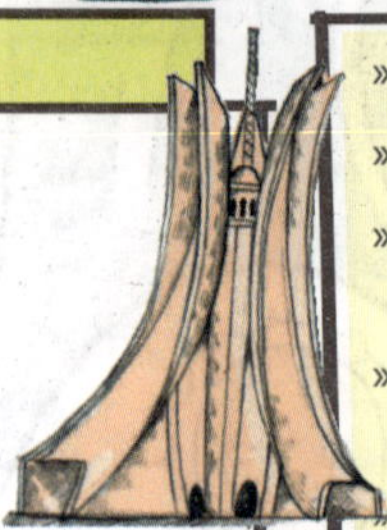

- *Location*: Northern Africa
- *Capital*: Algiers
- *Languages*: Arabic, French, Berber
- *Dominant religion*: Islam
- *Time zone*: +1
- *Currency*: Algerian Dinar
- *Current head of state*: Abdelmadjid Tebboune
- *Type of government*: Presidential Republic

ANGOLA

- *Location*: Southern Africa
- *Capital*: Luanda
- *Languages*: Portuguese, Umbundu, Kimbundu
- *Dominant religions*: Christianity, indigenous beliefs
- *Time zone*: +1
- *Currency*: Angolan Kwanza
- *Current head of state and government*: João Lourenço
- *Type of government*: Presidential Republic

BENIN

- *Location*: Western Africa
- *Capital*: Porto-Novo (constitutional capital); Cotonou (seat of government)
- *Languages*: French, Fon, Yoruba
- *Dominant religions*: Christianity, Islam, Vodoun
- *Time zone*: +1
- *Currency*: West African CFA Franc
- *Current head of state and government*: Patrice Talon
- *Type of government*: Presidential Republic

BOTSWANA

- *Location*: Southern Africa
- *Capital*: Gaborone
- *Languages*: English, Setswana, Sekalanga
- *Dominant religion*: Christianity
- *Time zone*: +2
- *Currency*: Botswana Pula
- *Current head of state and government*: Mokgweetsi Eric Masisi
- *Type of government*: Parliamentary Republic

BURUNDI

- *Location*: Central Africa
- *Capital*: Gitega (political capital), Bujumbura (commercial capital)
- *Languages*: Kirundi, French, English
- *Dominant religion*: Christianity
- *Time zone*: +2
- *Currency*: Burundian Franc
- *Current head of state and government*: Evariste Ndayishimiye
- *Type of government*: Presidential Republic

BURKINA FASO

- *Location*: Western Africa
- *Capital*: Ouagadougou
- *Languages*: French, Moore
- *Dominant religions*: Islam, Catholicism, Animism
- *Time zone*: GMT
- *Currency*: West African CFA Franc
- *Current head of state*: Ibrahim Traoré
- *Current head of government*: Joachim Kyélem de Tambèla
- *Type of government*: Presidential Republic

CAMEROON

- *Location*: Central Africa
- *Capital*: Yaoundé
- *Languages*: French, English, African languages
- *Dominant religions*: Indigenous beliefs, Christianity, Islam
- *Time zone*: +1
- *Currency*: Central African CFA Franc
- *Current head of state*: Paul Biya
- *Current head of government*: Joseph Dion Ngute
- *Type of government*: Presidential Republic

CENTRAL AFRICAN REPUBLIC

- *Location*: Central Africa
- *Capital*: Bangui
- *Languages*: French, Sangho
- *Dominant religions*: Indigenous beliefs, Christianity, Islam
- *Time zone*: +1
- *Currency*: Central African CFA Franc
- *Current head of state*: Faustin Archange Touadéra
- *Current head of government*: Félix Moloua
- *Type of government*: Presidential Republic

CABO VERDE

- *Location*: Western Africa
- *Capital*: Praia
- *Languages*: Portuguese, Crioulo
- *Dominant religion*: Roman Catholicism
- *Time zone*: -1
- *Currency*: Cape Verdean Escudo
- *Current head of state*: José Maria Pereira Neves
- *Current head of government*: José Ulisses de Pina Correia e Silva
- *Type of government*: Parliamentary Republic

CHAD

- *Location*: Central Africa
- *Capital*: N'Djamena
- *Languages*: Arabic, French
- *Dominant religions*: Islam, Christianity
- *Time zone*: +1
- *Currency*: Central African CFA Franc
- *Current head of state and government*: Mahamat Idriss Déby Itno
- *Type of government*: Presidential Republic

COMOROS

- *Location*: Southern Africa
- *Capital*: Moroni
- *Languages*: Arabic, French, Shikomoro
- *Dominant religion*: Islam
- *Time zone*: +3
- *Currency*: Comorian Franc
- *Current head of state and government*: Azali Assoumani
- *Type of government*: Federal Presidential Republic

REPUBLIC OF THE CONGO

- *Location*: Central Africa
- *Capital*: Brazzaville
- *Languages*: French
- *Dominant religion*: Christianity
- *Time zone*: +1
- *Currency*: Central African CFA Franc
- *Current head of state*: Denis Sassou Nguesso
- *Current head of government*: Anatole Collinet Makosso
- *Type of government*: Presidential Republic

DEMOCRATIC REPUBLIC OF THE CONGO

- *Location*: Central Africa
- *Capital*: Kinshasa
- *Languages*: French, Lingala
- *Dominant religion*: Christianity
- *Time zone*: +1, +2
- *Currency*: Congolese Franc
- *Current head of state*: Félix Tshisekedi
- *Current head of government*: Sama Lukonde Kyenge
- *Type of government*: Semi-Presidential Republic

EGYPT

- *Location*: Northern Africa
- *Capital*: Cairo
- *Languages*: Arabic, English
- *Dominant religion*: Islam
- *Time zone*: +2
- *Currency*: Egyptian Pound
- *Current head of state*: Abdel Fattah Saeed Hussein Khalil Al-Sisi
- *Current head of government*: Mostafa Madbouly
- *Type of government*: Semi-Presidential Republic

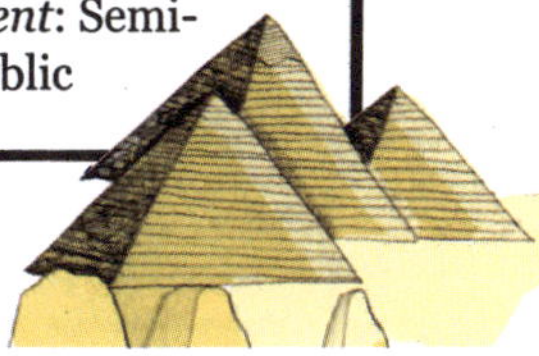

DJIBOUTI

- *Location*: Eastern Africa
- *Capital*: Djibouti
- *Languages*: French, Arabic
- *Dominant religion*: Islam
- *Time zone*: +3
- *Currency*: Djiboutian Franc
- *Current head of state*: Ismaïl Omar Guelleh
- *Current head of government*: Abdoulkader Kamil Mohamed
- *Type of government*: Semi-Presidential Republic

EQUATORIAL GUINEA

- *Location*: Central Africa
- *Capital*: Malabo
- *Languages*: Spanish, French
- *Dominant religion*: Roman Catholicism
- *Time zone*: +1
- *Currency*: Central African CFA Franc
- *Current head of state*: Teodoro Obiang Nguema Mbasogo
- *Current head of government*: Manuela Roka Botey
- *Type of government*: Presidential Republic

ERITREA

- *Location*: Eastern Africa
- *Capital*: Asmara
- *Language*: Arabic, Tigrinya, English
- *Dominant religion*: Islam
- *Time zone*: +3
- *Currency*: Eritrean Nakfa
- *Current head of state and government*: Isaias Afwerki
- *Type of government*: Presidential Republic

ETHIOPIA

- *Location*: Eastern Africa
- *Capital*: Addis Ababa
- *Languages*: Oromo, Amharic, Somali, Tigrigna, Afar, English
- *Dominant religion*: Christianity
- *Time zone*: +3
- *Currency*: Ethiopian Birr
- *Current head of state*: Sahle-Work Zewde
- *Current head of government*: Abiy Ahmed
- *Type of government*: Federal Parliamentary Republic

ESWATINI

- *Location*: Southern Africa
- *Capital*: Mbabane (administrative capital); Lobamba (royal and legislative capital)
- *Languages*: English, SiSwati
- *Dominant religion*: Christianity
- *Time zone*: +2
- *Currency*: Swazi Lilangeni
- *Current head of state*: King Msawti III
- *Current head of government*: Russell Mmemo Dlamini
- *Type of government*: Absolute Monarchy

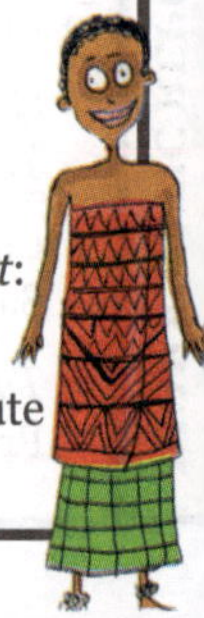

GABON

- *Location*: Central Africa
- *Capital*: Libreville
- *Languages*: French, Fang
- *Dominant religions*: Christianity, Islam
- *Time zone*: +1
- *Currency*: Central African CFA Franc
- *Current head of state*: Brice Clotaire Oligui Nguema
- *Current head of government*: Raymond Ndong Sima
- *Type of government*: Presidential Republic

GHANA

- *Location*: Western Africa
- *Capital*: Accra
- *Languages*: Asante, Ewe, Fante
- *Dominant religion*: Christianity
- *Time zone*: GMT
- *Currency*: Ghanaian Cedi
- *Current head of state and government*: Nana Addo Dankwa Akufo-Addo
- *Type of government*: Presidential Republic

THE GAMBIA

- *Location*: Western Africa
- *Capital*: Banjul
- *Languages*: English, indigenous languages
- *Dominant religion*: Islam
- *Time zone*: GMT
- *Currency*: Gambian Dalasi
- *Current head of state and government*: Adama Barrow
- *Type of government*: Presidential Republic

GUINEA

- *Location*: Western Africa
- *Capital*: Conakry
- *Language*: French
- *Dominant religion*: Islam
- *Time zone*: GMT
- *Currency*: Guinean Franc
- *Current head of state*: Mamady Doumbouya
- *Current head of government*: Mamadou Oury Bah
- *Type of government*: Presidential Republic

GUINEA-BISSAU

- *Location*: Western Africa
- *Capital*: Bissau
- *Languages*: Portuguese, Criuolo
- *Dominant religions*: Islam, Christianity
- *Time zone*: GMT
- *Currency*: West African CFA Franc
- *Current head of state*: Umaro Sissoco Embaló
- *Current head of government*: Rui Duarte De Barros
- *Type of government*: Semi-Presidential Republic

CÔTE D'IVOIRE

- *Location*: Western Africa
- *Capital*: Yamoussoukro (legislative capital), Abidjan (administrative capital)
- *Languages*: French, Dioula
- *Dominant religions*: Islam, Christianity, indigenous beliefs
- *Time zone*: GMT
- *Currency*: West African CFA Franc
- *Current head of state*: Alassane Dramane Ouattara
- *Current head of government*: Robert Beujre Mambe
- *Type of government*: Presidential Republic

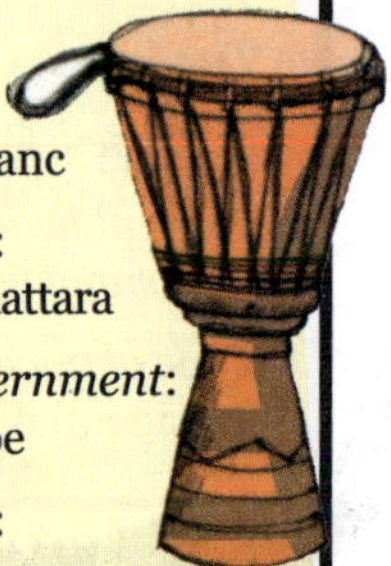

KENYA

- *Location*: Eastern Africa
- *Capital*: Nairobi
- *Languages*: English, Kiswahili
- *Dominant religion*: Christianity
- *Time zone*: +3
- *Currency*: Kenyan Shilling
- *Current head of state and government*: William Ruto
- *Type of government*: Presidential Republic

LIBERIA

- *Location*: Western Africa
- *Capital*: Monrovia
- *Languages*: English, ethnic languages
- *Dominant religions*: Christianity, Islam, indigenous beliefs
- *Time zone*: GMT
- *Currency*: Liberian Dollar
- *Current head of state and government*: Joseph Boakai
- *Type of government*: Presidential Constitutional Republic

LESOTHO

- *Location*: Southern Africa
- *Capital*: Maseru
- *Languages*: Sesotho, English
- *Dominant religion*: Christianity
- *Time zone*: +2
- *Currency*: Lesotho Loti
- *Current head of state*: King Letsie III
- *Current head of government*: Ntsokoane Samuel Matekane
- *Type of government*: Parliamentary Constitutional Monarchy

LIBYA

- *Location*: Northern Africa
- *Capital*: Tripoli
- *Area*: 17,59,540 sq km
- *Dominant religion*: Islam
- *Time zone*: +2
- *Currency*: Libyan Dinar
- *Current head of state*: Mohamed al-Menfi
- *Current head of government:* Abdul Hamid Dbeibeh
- *Type of government*: In transition

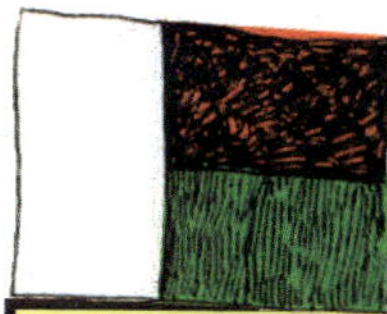

MADAGASCAR

- *Location*: Southern Africa
- *Capital*: Antananarivo
- *Languages*: Malagasy, English, French
- *Dominant religions*: Indigenous faiths, Christianity
- *Time zone*: +3
- *Currency*: Malagasy Ariary
- *Current head of state*: Andry Rajoelina
- *Current head of government*: Christian Ntsay
- *Type of government*: Semi-Presidential Republic

MALAWI

- *Location*: Southern Africa
- *Capital*: Lilongwe
- *Languages*: English, Chichewa
- *Dominant religion*: Christianity
- *Time zone*: +2
- *Currency*: Malawian Kwacha
- *Current head of state and government*: Lazarus McCarthy Chakwera
- *Type of government*: Presidential Republic

MALI

- *Location*: Western Africa
- *Capital*: Bamako
- *Languages*: Bambara, French
- *Dominant religion*: Islam
- *Time zone*: GMT
- *Currency*: West African CFA Franc
- *Current head of state*: Assimi Goita
- *Current head of government:* Choguel Kokalla Maïga
- *Type of government*: Semi-Presidential Republic

MAURITANIA

- *Location*: Western Africa
- *Capital*: Nouakchott
- *Languages*: Arabic, Pulaar, Soninke, Wolof
- *Dominant religion*: Islam
- *Time zone*: GMT
- *Currency*: Ouguyia
- *Current head of state*: Mohamed Ould Ghazouani
- *Current head of government*: Mohamed Ould Bilal
- *Type of government*: Presidential Republic

MAURITIUS

- *Location*: Southern Africa
- *Capital*: Port Louis
- *Languages*: Creole, French, Bhojpuri, English
- *Dominant religions*: Hinduism, Christianity
- *Time zone*: +4
- *Currency*: Mauritian Rupee
- *Current head of state*: Prithvirajsing Roopun
- *Current head of government*: Pravind Kumar Jugnauth
- *Type of government*: Parliamentary Republic

MOROCCO

- *Location*: Northern Africa
- *Capital*: Rabat
- *Language*: Arabic, Tamazight
- *Dominant religion*: Islam
- *Time zone*: +1
- *Currency*: Moroccan Dirham
- *Current head of state*: King Mohammed VI
- *Current head of government*: Aziz Akhannouch
- *Type of government*: Parliamentary Constitutional Monarchy

MOZAMBIQUE

- *Location*: Southeastern Africa
- *Capital*: Maputo
- *Languages*: Portuguese, Emakhuwa, Tsonga
- *Dominant religions*: Christianity, Islam
- *Time zone*: +2
- *Currency*: Mozambican Metical
- *Current head of state and government*: Filipe Jacinto Nyusi
- *Type of government*: Presidential Republic

NAMIBIA

- *Location*: Southern Africa
- *Capital*: Windhoek
- *Languages*: English, Oshiwambo languages
- *Dominant religion*: Christianity
- *Time zone*: +2
- *Currency*: Namibian Dollar
- *Current head of state and government*: Nangolo Mbumba
- *Type of government*: Presidential Republic

NIGER

- *Location*: Western Africa
- *Capital*: Niamey
- *Languages*: French, Hausa, Djerma
- *Dominant religion*: Islam
- *Time zone*: +1
- *Currency*: West African CFA Franc
- *Current head of state*: Abdourahame Tiani
- *Current head of government*: Ali Mahaman Lamine Zeine
- *Type of government*: Semi-Presidential Republic

NIGERIA

- *Location*: Western Africa
- *Capital*: Abuja
- *Languages*: English, Hausa
- *Dominant religions*: Islam, Christianity
- *Time zone*: +1
- *Currency*: Nigerian Naira
- *Current head of state and government*: Bola Ahmed Adekunle Tinubu
- *Type of government*: Federal Presidential Republic

RWANDA

- *Location*: Central Africa
- *Capital*: Kigali
- *Languages*: Kinyarwanda, French, English, Swahili
- *Dominant religion*: Christianity
- *Time zone*: +2
- *Currency*: Rwandan Franc
- *Current head of state*: Paul Kagame
- *Current head of government*: Édouard Ngirente
- *Type of government*: Presidential Republic

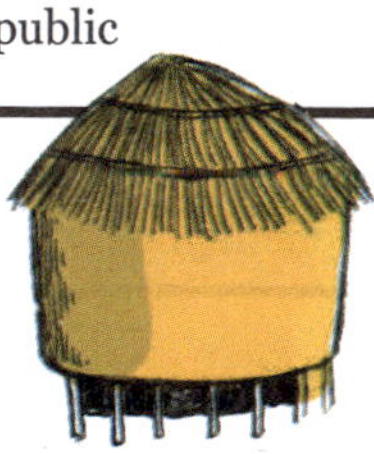

SÃO TOMÉ AND PRÍNCIPE

- *Location*: Central Africa
- *Capital*: São Tomé
- *Language*: Portuguese
- *Dominant religion*: Christianity
- *Time zone*: GMT
- *Currency*: São Tomé and Príncipe Dobra
- *Current head of state*: Carlos Manuel Vila Nova
- *Current head of government*: Patrice Trovoada
- *Type of government*: Semi-Presidential Republic

SENEGAL

- *Location*: Western Africa
- *Capital*: Dakar
- *Languages*: French, Wolof
- *Dominant religion*: Islam
- *Time zone*: GMT
- *Currency*: West African CFA Franc
- *Current head of state*: Bassirou Diomaye Faye
- *Current head of government*: Ousmane Sonko
- *Type of government*: Presidential Republic

SEYCHELLES

- *Location*: Indian Ocean
- *Capital*: Victoria
- *Languages*: Creole, English, French
- *Dominant religion*: Christianity
- *Time zone*: +4
- *Currency*: Seychellois Rupee
- *Current head of state and government*: Wavel Ramkalawan
- *Type of government*: Presidential Republic

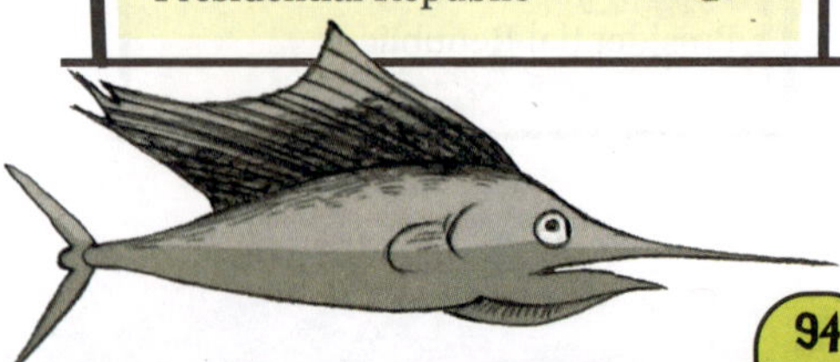

SIERRA LEONE

- *Location*: Western Africa
- *Capital*: Freetown
- *Languages*: English, Mende, Temne
- *Dominant religions*: Islam, Christianity
- *Time zone*: GMT
- *Currency*: Sierra Leonean Leone
- *Current head of state and government*: Julius Maada Bio
- *Type of government*: Presidential Republic

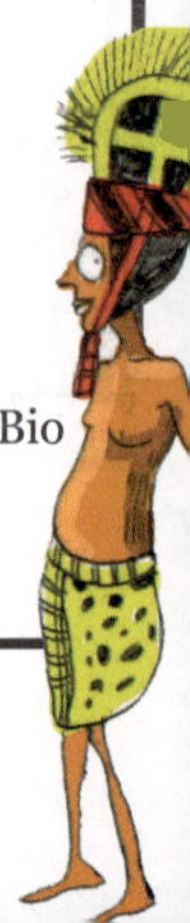

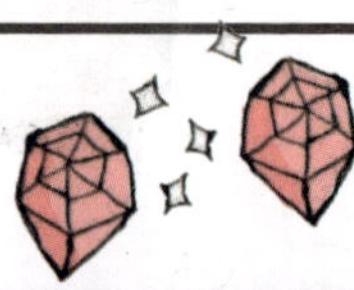

SOMALIA

» *Location*: Eastern Africa

» *Capital*: Mogadishu

» *Languages*: Somali, Arabic

» *Dominant religion*: Islam

» *Time zone*: +3

» *Currency*: Somali Shilling

» *Current head of state*: Hassan Sheikh Mohamud

» *Current head of government*: Hamza Abdi Barre

» *Type of government*: Federal Parliamentary Republic

SOUTH AFRICA

» *Location*: Southern Africa

» *Capital*: Pretoria (administrative capital); Cape Town (legislative capital); Bloemfontein (judicial capital)

» *Languages*: English, isiZulu and ten other official languages

» *Dominant religion*: Christianity

» *Time zone*: +2

» *Currency*: South African Rand

» *Current head of state and government*: Cyril Ramaphosa

» *Type of government*: Parliamentary Republic

SUDAN

» *Location*: Northeastern Africa

» *Capital*: Khartoum

» *Languages*: Arabic, English

» *Dominant religion*: Islam

» *Time zone*: +2

» *Currency*: Sudanese Pound

» *Current head of state*: Abdel Fattah al-Burhan

» *Current head of government*: Osman Hussein

» *Type of government*: Presidential Republic

SOUTH SUDAN

» *Location*: East Central Africa

» *Capital*: Juba

» *Languages*: English, Arabic, indigenous languages

» *Dominant religions*: Christianity, indigenous beliefs

» *Time zone*: +3

» *Currency*: South Sudanese Pound

» *Current head of state and government*: Salva Kiir Mayardit

» *Type of government*: Presidential Republic

UNITED REPUBLIC OF TANZANIA

- *Location*: Eastern Africa
- *Capital*: Dodoma
- *Languages*: Swahili, English, Arabic
- *Dominant religions*: Islam, indigenous beliefs, Christianity
- *Time zone*: +3
- *Currency*: Tanzanian Shilling
- *Current head of state and government*: Samia Suluhu Hassan
- *Type of government*: Presidential Republic

TOGO

- *Location*: Western Africa
- *Capital*: Lomé
- *Languages*: French, Ewe, Mina, Kabye, Dagbani
- *Dominant religions*: Indigenous beliefs, Christianity, Islam
- *Time zone*: GMT
- *Currency*: West African CFA Franc
- *Current head of state*: Faure Essozimna Gnassingbé
- *Current head of government*: Victoire Tomégah Dogbé
- *Type of government*: Presidential Republic

TUNISIA

- *Location*: Northern Africa
- *Capital*: Tunis
- *Languages*: Arabic, French, Berber
- *Dominant religion*: Islam
- *Time zone*: +1
- *Currency*: Tunisian Dinar
- *Current head of state*: Kais Saied
- *Current head of government*: Ahmed Hachani
- *Type of government*: Parliamentary Republic

UGANDA

- *Location*: East Central Africa
- *Capital*: Kampala
- *Languages*: English, Ganda, Swahili
- *Dominant religions*: Christianity, Islam
- *Time zone*: +3
- *Currency*: Ugandan Shilling
- *Current head of state*: Yoweri Kaguta Museveni
- *Current head of government*: Robinah Nabbanja
- *Type of government*: Presidential Republic

ZAMBIA

- *Location*: Southern Africa
- *Capital*: Lusaka
- *Languages*: English, Bembe, Nyanja, Tonga
- *Dominant religion*: Christianity
- *Time zone*: +2
- *Currency*: Zambian Kwacha
- *Current head of state and government*: Hakainde Hichilema
- *Type of government*: Presidential Republic

ZIMBABWE

- *Location*: Southern Africa
- *Capital*: Harare
- *Languages*: Shona, Ndebele, English and thirteen other official languages
- *Dominant religions*: Christianity, indigenous faiths
- *Time zone*: +2
- *Currency*: Zimbabwean Dollar
- *Current head of state and government*: Emmerson Dambudzo Mnangagwa
- *Type of government*: Presidential Republic

AFGHANISTAN

- *Location*: Southern Asia
- *Capital*: Kabul
- *Languages*: Pashto, Dari
- *Dominant religion*: Islam
- *Time zone*: +4:30
- *Currency*: Afghan Afghani
- *Current head of state and government*: Taliban Leader Haybatullah Akhundzada
- *Type of government*: Theocratic

BANGLADESH

- *Location*: Southern Asia
- *Capital*: Dhaka
- *Languages*: Bengali, English
- *Dominant religion*: Islam
- *Time zone*: +6
- *Currency*: Bangladeshi Taka
- *Current head of state*: Mohammad Shahabuddin Chuppi
- *Current head of goverment*: Sheikh Hasina
- *Type of government*: Parliamentary Republic

BAHRAIN

- *Location*: Middle East
- *Capital*: Manama
- *Languages*: Arabic, English, Farsi
- *Dominant religion*: Islam
- *Time zone*: +3
- *Currency*: Bahraini Dinar
- *Current head of state*: Sheikh Hamad bin Isa Al Khalifa
- *Current head of government*: Salman bin Hamad Al Khalifa
- *Type of government*: Constitutional Monarchy

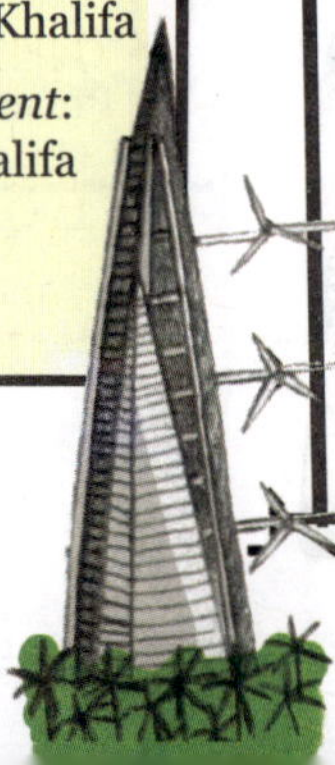

BHUTAN

- *Location*: Southern Asia
- *Capital*: Thimphu
- *Language*: Dzongkha, Sharchopka
- *Dominant religion*: Buddhism
- *Time zone*: +6
- *Currency*: Ngultrum
- *Current head of state*: King Jigme Khesar Namgyel Wangchuck
- *Current head of government*: Tshering Tobgay
- *Type of government*: Constitutional Monarchy

BRUNEI DARUSSALAM

- *Location*: Southeastern Asia
- *Capital*: Bandar Seri Begawan
- *Languages*: Malay, Chinese
- *Dominant religion*: Islam
- *Time zone*: +8
- *Currency*: Brunei Dollar
- *Current head of state and government*: Sultan Hassanal Bolkiah Mu'izzaddin Waddaulah
- *Type of government*: Absolute Monarchy

BURMA (MYANMAR)

- *Location*: Southeastern Asia
- *Capital*: Nai Pyi Taw
- *Language*: Burmese
- *Dominant religion*: Buddhism
- *Time zone*: +6:30
- *Currency*: Kyat
- *Current head of state and government*: Min Aung Hlaing
- *Type of government*: Military regime

CAMBODIA

- *Location*: Southeastern Asia
- *Capital*: Phnom Penh
- *Language*: Khmer
- *Dominant religion*: Buddhism
- *Time zone*: +7
- *Currency*: Riel
- *Current head of state*: King Norodom Sihamoni
- *Current head of government*: Samdech Moha Bovorthipadi Hun Manet
- *Type of government*: Parliamentary Constitutional Monarchy

PEOPLE'S REPUBLIC OF CHINA

- *Location*: Eastern Asia
- *Capital*: Beijing
- *Languages*: Mandarin, various Chinese dialects
- *Dominant religions*: Atheism (official), Buddhism
- *Time zone*: +8
- *Currency*: Yuan/Renminbi
- *Current head of state*: Xi Jinping
- *Current head of government*: Li Qiang
- *Type of government*: Communist Party-led State

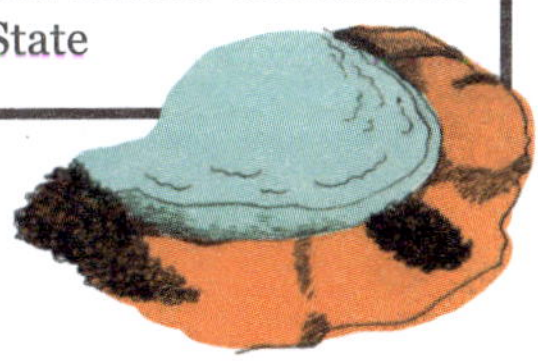

INDIA

- *Location*: Southern Asia
- *Capital*: New Delhi
- *Languages*: Hindi, English and twenty-one other official languages
- *Dominant religions*: Hinduism, Islam, Sikhism, Christianity
- *Time zone*: +5:30
- *Currency*: Indian Rupee
- *Current head of state*: Droupadi Murmu
- *Current head of government*: Narendra Modi
- *Type of government*: Federal Parliamentary Republic

INDONESIA

- *Location*: Southeastern Asia
- *Capital*: Jakarta
- *Language*: Bahasa Indonesia
- *Dominant religion*: Islam
- *Time zone*: +7
- *Currency*: Indonesian Rupiah
- *Current head of state and government*: Joko Widodo
- *Type of government*: Presidential Republic

IRAN

- *Location*: Middle East
- *Capital*: Tehran
- *Languages*: Persian, Azeri Turkic and Turkic dialects
- *Dominant religion*: Islam
- *Time zone*: +3:30
- *Currency*: Iranian Rial
- *Supreme Leader*: Sayyid Ali Hosseini Khamenei
- *Current head of state*: Ebrahim Raisi
- *Type of government*: Islamic Republic

IRAQ

- *Location*: Middle East
- *Capital*: Baghdad
- *Languages*: Arabic, Kurdish
- *Dominant religion*: Islam
- *Time zone*: +3
- *Currency*: Iraqi Dinar
- *Current head of state*: Abdul Latif Rashid
- *Current head of government*: Mohammed Shia' Al Sudani
- *Type of government*: Federal Parliamentary Republic

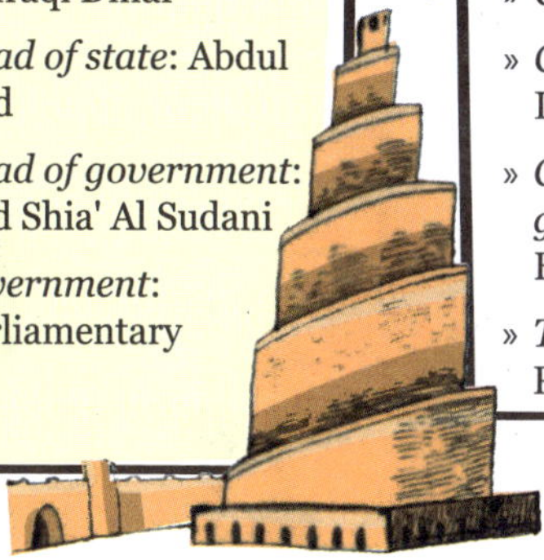

ISRAEL

- *Location*: Middle East
- *Capital*: Jerusalem
- *Languages*: Hebrew, Arabic, English
- *Dominant religion*: Judaism
- *Time zone*: +2
- *Currency*: Israeli Shekel
- *Current head of state*: Isaac Herzog
- *Current head of government*: Benjamin Netanyahu
- *Type of government*: Parliamentary Democracy

JAPAN

- *Location*: Eastern Asia
- *Capital*: Tokyo
- *Language*: Japanese
- *Dominant religions*: Shinto, Buddhism
- *Time zone*: +9
- *Currency*: Japanese Yen
- *Current head of state*: Emperor Naruhito
- *Current head of government*: Fumio Kishida
- *Type of government*: Parliamentary Constitutional Monarchy

JORDAN

- *Location*: Middle East
- *Capital*: Amman
- *Languages*: Arabic, English
- *Dominant religion*: Islam
- *Time zone*: +3
- *Currency*: Jordanian Dinar
- *Current head of state*: King Abdullah II ibn Al-Hussein
- *Current head of government*: Bishr al-Khasawneh
- *Type of government*: Parliamentary Constitutional Monarchy

KAZAKHSTAN

- *Location*: Central Asia
- *Capital*: Nur-Sultan
- *Languages*: Kazakh, Russian
- *Dominant religions*: Islam, Christianity
- *Time zone*: +6
- *Currency*: Tenge
- *Current head of state*: Kassym-Jomart Tokayev
- *Current head of government*: Oljas Bektenov
- *Type of government*: Presidential Republic

KOREA (NORTH)

- *Location*: Eastern Asia
- *Capital*: Pyongyang
- *Language*: Korean
- *Dominant religions*: Buddhism, Chondogyo
- *Time zone*: +8:30
- *Currency*: North Korean Won
- *Current head of state and government*: Kim Jong-Un
- *Type of government*: Dictatorship

KOREA (SOUTH)

- *Location*: Eastern Asia
- *Population*: 51,741,963
- *Language*: Korean
- *Dominant religions*: Christianity, Buddhism
- *Time zone*: +9
- *Currency*: South Korean Won
- *Current head of state and government*: Yoon Suk-yeol
- *Type of government*: Presidential Republic

KUWAIT

- *Location*: Middle East
- *Capital*: Kuwait City
- *Languages*: Arabic, English
- *Dominant religion*: Islam
- *Time zone*: +3
- *Currency*: Kuwaiti Dinar
- *Current head of state*: Sheikh Mishal Al-Ahmad Al-Jaber Al-Sabah
- *Current head of government*: Sheikh Ahmad Abdullah Al-Sabah
- *Type of government*: Constitutional Monarchy

KYRGYZSTAN

- *Location*: Central Asia
- *Capital*: Bishkek
- *Languages*: Kyrgyz, Russian, Uzbek
- *Dominant religion*: Islam
- *Time zone*: +6
- *Currency*: Kyrgyzstani Som
- *Current head of state*: Sadyr Japarov
- *Current head of government*: Japarov Üsönbek uulu Aqılbek
- *Type of government*: Parliamentary Republic

LEBANON

- *Location*: Middle East
- *Capital*: Beirut
- *Languages*: Arabic, French
- *Dominant religions*: Islam, Christianity
- *Time zone*: +2
- *Currency*: Lebanese Pound
- *Current head of state*: Vacant
- *Current head of government*: Najib Mikati
- *Type of government*: Parliamentary Republic

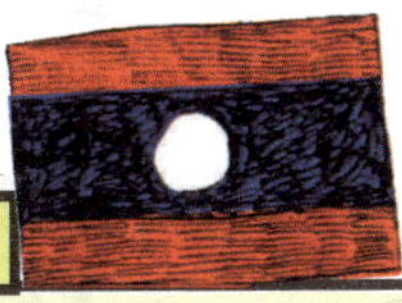

LAOS

- *Location*: Southeastern Asia
- *Capital*: Vientiane
- *Languages*: Lao, French
- *Dominant religion*: Buddhism
- *Time zone*: +7
- *Currency*: Kip
- *Current head of state*: Thongloun Sisoulith
- *Current head of government*: nexay Siphandone
- *Type of government*: Communist State

MALAYSIA

- *Location*: Southeastern Asia
- *Capital*: Kuala Lumpur
- *Languages*: Bahasa Malaysia, English, Tamil, Cantonese
- *Dominant religions*: Islam, Buddhism
- *Time zone*: +8
- *Currency*: Ringgit
- *Current head of state*: King Sultan Ibrahim ibni Sultan Iskandar (known as Yang di-Pertuan Agong)
- *Current head of government*: Anwar Ibrahim
- *Type of government*: Federal Parliamentary Constitutional Monarchy

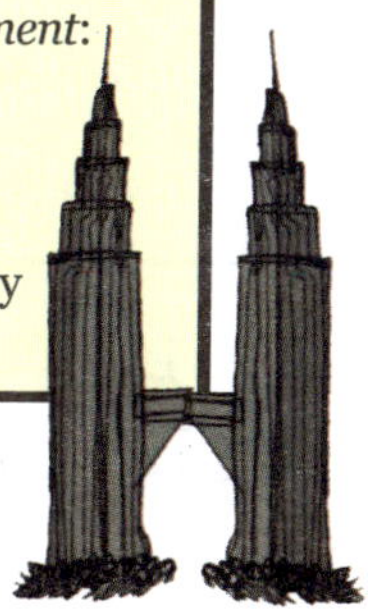

MALDIVES

- *Location*: Southern Asia
- *Capital*: Malé
- *Languages*: Maldivian Dhivehi, English
- *Dominant religion*: Islam
- *Time zone*: +5
- *Currency*: Rufiyaa
- *Current head of state and government*: Mohamed Muizzu
- *Type of government*: Presidential Republic

NEPAL

- *Location*: Southern Asia
- *Capital*: Kathmandu
- *Language*: Nepali
- *Dominant religion*: Hinduism
- *Time zone*: +5:45
- *Currency*: Nepalese Rupee
- *Current head of state*: Ram Chandra Poudel
- *Current head of government*: Pushpa Kamal Dahal
- *Type of government*: Federal Parliamentary Republic

MONGOLIA

- *Location*: Northern Asia
- *Capital*: Ulaanbaatar
- *Language*: Khalkha
- *Dominant religion*: Buddhism
- *Time zone*: +7, +8
- *Currency*: Tögrög
- *Current head of state*: Ukhnaagiin Khürelsükh
- *Current head of government*: Luvsannamsrain Oyun-Erdene
- *Type of government*: Semi-Presidential Republic

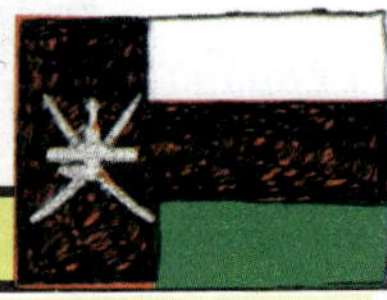

OMAN

- *Location*: Middle East
- *Capital*: Muscat
- *Language*: Arabic
- *Dominant religion*: Islam
- *Time zone*: +4
- *Currency*: Omani Rial
- *Current head of state and government*: Sultan Haitham bin Tariq al-Said
- *Type of government*: Absolute Monarchy

PAKISTAN

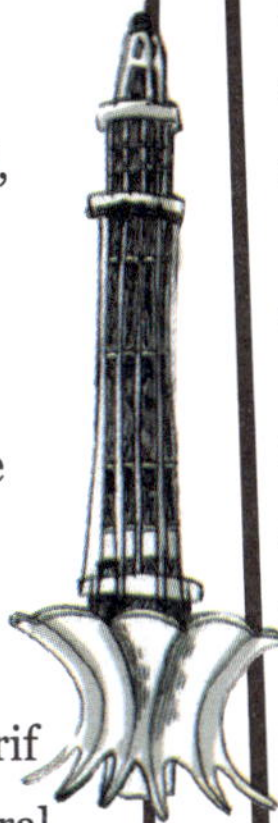

- *Location*: Southern Asia
- *Capital*: Islamabad
- *Languages*: Urdu, Punjabi, English
- *Dominant religion*: Islam
- *Time zone*: +5
- *Currency*: Pakistani Rupee
- *Current head of state*: Asif Ali Zardari
- *Current head of government*: Shehbaz Sharif
- *Type of government*: Federal Parliamentary Republic

PHILIPPINES

- *Location*: Southeastern Asia
- *Capital*: Manila
- *Languages*: Filipino, English
- *Dominant religion*: Catholicism
- *Time zone*: +8
- *Currency*: Philippines Peso
- *Current head of state and government*: Bongbong Marcos
- *Type of government*: Presidential Republic

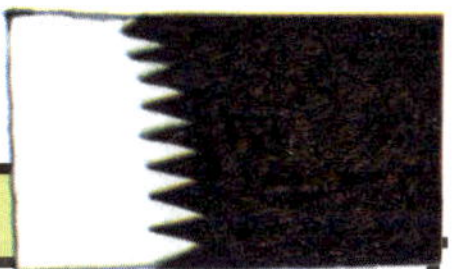

QATAR

- *Location*: Middle East
- *Capital*: Doha
- *Languages*: Arabic, English
- *Dominant religion*: Islam
- *Time zone*: +3
- *Currency*: Qatari Rial
- *Current head of state*: Sheikh Tamim bin Hamad Al-Thani
- *Current head of government*: Sheikh Mohammed bin Abdulrahman bin Jassim Al Thani
- *Type of government*: Absolute Monarchy

RUSSIAN FEDERATION

- *Location*: Eurasia
- *Capital*: Moscow
- *Language*: Russian
- *Dominant religion*: Russian Orthodox, Islam
- *Time zone*: + 3 to + 12
- *Currency*: Ruble
- *Current head of state*: Vladimir Vladimirovich Putin
- *Current head of government*: Mikhail Mishustin
- *Type of government*: Semi-Presidential Federation

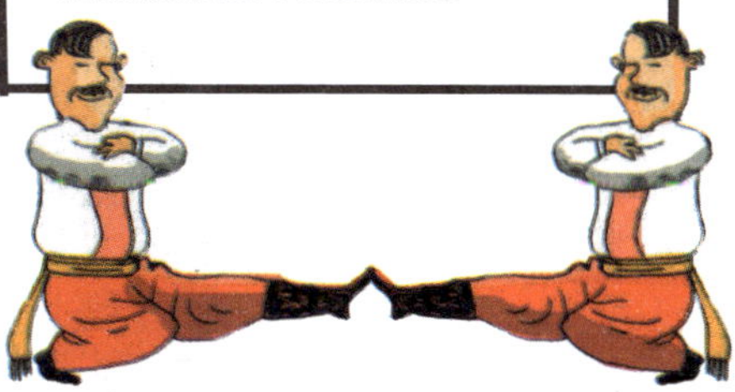

SAUDI ARABIA

- *Location*: Middle East
- *Capital*: Riyadh
- *Language*: Arabic
- *Dominant religion*: Islam
- *Time zone*: +3
- *Currency*: Saudi Rial
- *Current head of state*: King Salman bin Abdulaziz Al-Saud
- *Current head of government*: Prince Mohammed bin Salman bin Abdulaziz Al Saud
- *Type of government*: Absolute Monarchy

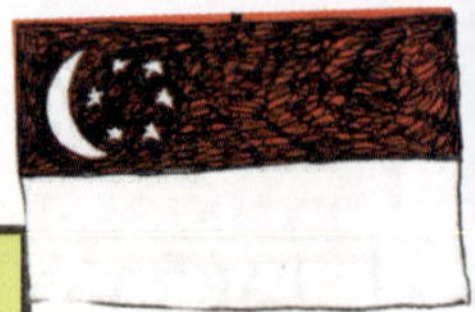

SINGAPORE

- *Location*: Southeastern Asia
- *Capital*: Singapore
- *Languages*: English, Malay, Mandarin, Tamil
- *Dominant religions*: Buddhism, Islam, Christianity
- *Time zone*: +8
- *Currency*: Singapore Dollar
- *Current head of state*: Tharman Shanmugaratnam
- *Current head of government*: Lawrence Wong
- *Type of government*: Parliamentary Republic

SRI LANKA

- *Location*: Southern Asia
- *Capital*: Colombo (commercial capital); Sri Jayewardenepura Kotte (legislative capital)
- *Languages*: Sinhala, Tamil
- *Dominant religions*: Buddhism, Christianity
- *Time zone*: +5:30
- *Currency*: Sri Lankan Rupee
- *Current head of state and government*: Ranil Wickremesinghe
- *Type of government*: Presidential Republic

SYRIA

- *Location*: Middle East
- *Capital*: Damascus
- *Language*: Arabic
- *Dominant religion*: Islam
- *Time zone*: +2
- *Currency*: Syrian Pound
- *Current head of state*: Bashar al-Assad
- *Current head of government*: Hussein Arnous
- *Type of government*: Presidential Republic

TAJIKISTAN

- *Location*: Central Asia
- *Capital*: Dushanbe
- *Languages*: Tajik, Russian
- *Dominant religion*: Islam
- *Time zone*: +5
- *Currency*: Somoni
- *Current head of state*: Emomali Rahmon
- *Current head of government*: Kokhir Rasulzoda
- *Type of government*: Presidential Republic

THAILAND

- *Location*: Southeastern Asia
- *Capital*: Bangkok
- *Language*: Thai
- *Dominant religion*: Buddhism
- *Time zone*: +7
- *Currency*: Baht
- *Current head of state*: Maha Vajiralongkorn
- *Current head of government*: Srettha Thavisin
- *Type of government*: Constitutional Monarchy

TIMOR-LESTE

- *Location*: Southeastern Asia
- *Capital*: Dili
- *Languages*: Tetun Prasa, Mambai, Makasai
- *Dominant religion*: Roman Catholicism
- *Time zone*: +9
- *Currency*: US Dollar
- *Current head of state*: José Manuel Ramos-Horta
- *Current head of government*: Xanana Gusmão
- *Type of government*: Semi-Presidential Republic

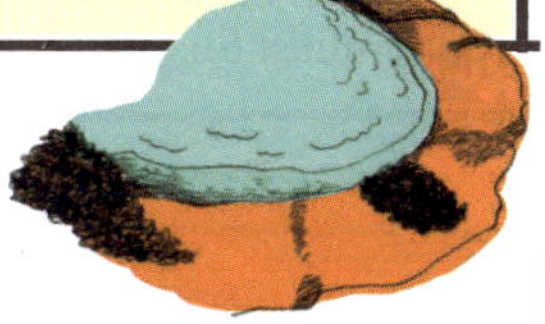

TURKMENISTAN

- *Location*: Central Asia
- *Capital*: Ashgabat
- *Language*: Turkmen
- *Dominant religion*: Islam
- *Time zone*: +5
- *Currency*: Turkmen Manat
- *Current head of state and government*: Serdar Berdimuhamedow
- *Type of government*: Presidential Republic

TURKEY

- *Location*: Eurasia
- *Capital*: Ankara
- *Language*: Turkish
- *Dominant religion*: Islam
- *Time zone*: +2
- *Currency*: Lira
- *Current head of state and government*: Recep Tayyip Erdoğan
- *Type of government*: Presidential Republic

UNITED ARAB EMIRATES

- *Location*: Middle East
- *Capital*: Abu Dhabi
- *Language*: Arabic
- *Dominant religion*: Islam
- *Time zone*: +4
- *Currency*: UAE Dirham
- *Current head of state*: Sheikh Khalifa Bin Zayed Al Nahyan
- *Current head of government*: Sheikh Mohammed Bin Rashid Al Maktoum
- *Type of government*: Federation of Monarchies

UZBEKISTAN

- *Location*: Central Asia
- *Capital*: Tashkent
- *Language*: Uzbek
- *Dominant religion*: Islam
- *Time zone*: +5
- *Currency*: Uzbekistan Som
- *Current head of state*: Shavkat Mirziyoyev
- *Current head of government*: Abdulla Aripov
- *Type of government*: Presidential Republic

VIETNAM

- *Location*: Southeastern Asia
- *Capital*: Hanoi
- *Languages*: Vietnamese, English
- *Dominant religions*: Buddhism, Christianity
- *Time zone*: +7
- *Currency*: Dong
- *Current head of state*: Tô Lâm
- *Current head of government*: Pham Minh Chinh
- *Type of government*: Communist State

YEMEN

- *Location*: Middle East
- *Capital*: Sana'a
- *Language*: Arabic
- *Dominant religion*: Islam
- *Time zone*: +3
- *Currency*: Yemeni Rial
- *Current head of state*: Rashad al-Alimi
- *Current head of government*: Ahmed Awad bin Mubarak
- *Type of government*: In transition

ALBANIA

- *Location*: Southeastern Europe
- *Capital*: Tirana
- *Language*: Albanian
- *Dominant religions*: Islam
- *Time zone*: +1
- *Currency*: Lek
- *Current head of state*: Bajram Begaj
- *Current head of government*: Edi Rama
- *Type of government*: Parliamentary Republic

ANDORRA

- *Location*: Southwestern Europe
- *Capital*: Andorra la Vella
- *Language*: Catalan
- *Dominant religion*: Roman Catholicism
- *Time zone*: +1
- *Currency*: Euro
- *Current heads of state*: Co-Prince Emmanuel Macron and Co-Prince Archbishop Joan-Enric Vives i Sicília
- *Current head of government*: Xaviar Espot Zamora
- *Type of government*: Parliamentary Democracy

ARMENIA

- *Location*: Eurasia
- *Capital*: Yerevan
- *Language*: Armenian
- *Dominant religion*: Armenian Apostolic
- *Time zone*: +4
- *Currency*: Dram
- *Current head of state*: Vahagn Khachaturyan
- *Current head of government*: Nikol Pashinyan
- *Type of government*: Parliamentary Democracy

AUSTRIA

- *Location*: Central Europe
- *Capital*: Vienna
- *Language*: German
- *Dominant religion*: Roman Catholicism
- *Time zone*: +1
- *Currency*: Euro
- *Current head of state*: Alexander Van der Bellen
- *Current head of government*: Karl Nehammer
- *Type of government*: Federal Parliamentary Republic

AZERBAIJAN

- *Location*: Eurasia
- *Capital*: Baku
- *Languages*: Azerbaijani, Russian, Armenian
- *Dominant religion*: Islam
- *Time zone*: +4
- *Currency*: Manat
- *Current head of state*: Ilham Heydar oglu Aliyev
- *Current head of government*: Ali Asadov
- *Type of government*: Presidential Republic

BELARUS

- *Location*: Eastern Europe
- *Capital*: Minsk
- *Languages*: Belarusian, Russian
- *Dominant religion*: Eastern Orthodox Church
- *Time zone*: +3
- *Currency*: Belarusian Ruble
- *Current head of state*: Aleksandr Grigoryevich Lukashenko
- *Current head of government*: Roman Golovchenko
- *Type of government*: Presidential Republic

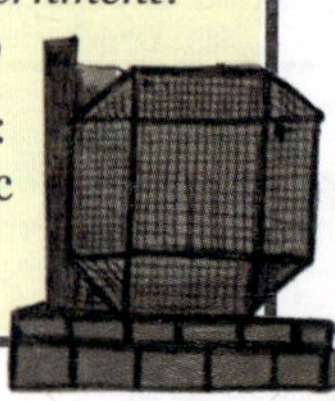

BELGIUM

- *Location*: Western Europe
- *Capital*: Brussels
- *Languages*: Dutch, French, German
- *Dominant religion*: Roman Catholicism
- *Time zone*: +1
- *Currency*: Euro
- *Current head of state*: King Philippe
- *Current head of government*: Alexander De Croo
- *Type of government*: Federal Parliamentary Democracy under a Constitutional Monarchy

BOSNIA AND HERZEGOVINA

- *Location*: Southeastern Europe
- *Capital*: Sarajevo
- *Languages*: Serbian, Croatian, Bosnian
- *Dominant religions*: Christianity, Islam
- *Time zone*: +1
- *Currency*: Convertible Mark
- *Current heads of state*: Denis Bećirović, Zeljka Cvijanovic and Željko Komšić
- *Current head of government*: Borjana Krišto
- *Type of government*: Parliamentary Republic

CROATIA

- *Location*: Southeastern Europe
- *Capital*: Zagreb
- *Language*: Croatian
- *Dominant religion*: Roman Catholicism
- *Time zone*: +1
- *Currency*: Kuna
- *Current head of state*: Zoran Milanović
- *Current head of government*: Andrej Plenković
- *Type of government*: Parliamentary Republic

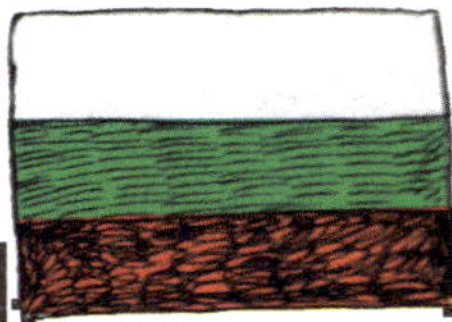

BULGARIA

- *Location*: Southeastern Europe
- *Capital*: Sofia
- *Language*: Bulgarian
- *Dominant religion*: Eastern Orthodox Church
- *Time zone*: +2
- *Currency*: Lev
- *Current head of state*: Rumen Radev
- *Current head of government*: Dimitar Glavchev
- *Type of government*: Parliamentary Republic

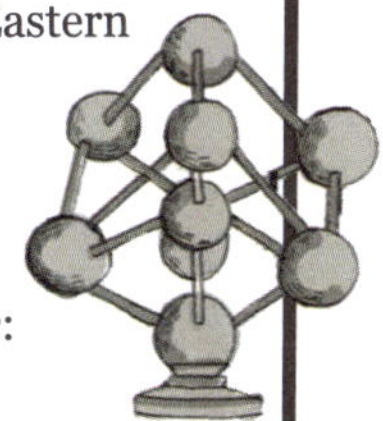

CYPRUS

- *Location*: Mediterranean
- *Capital*: Nicosia
- *Languages*: Greek, Turkish
- *Dominant religion*: Greek Orthodox Church
- *Time zone*: +2
- *Currency*: Euro
- *Current head of state and government*: Nikos Christodoulides
- *Type of government*: Unitary Presidential Republic

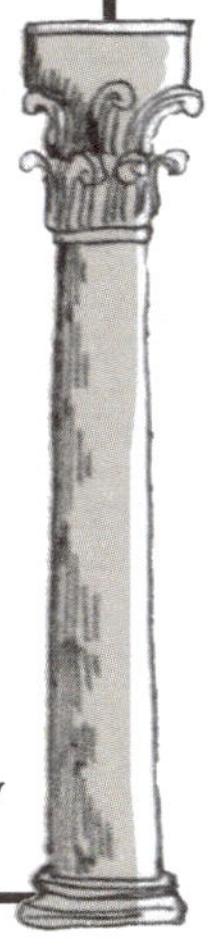

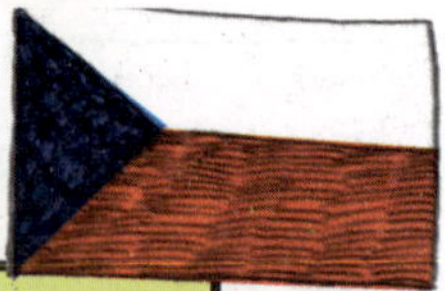

CZECH REPUBLIC

- *Location*: Central Europe
- *Capital*: Prague
- *Language*: Czech
- *Dominant religion*: Roman Catholicism
- *Time zone*: +1
- *Currency*: Koruna
- *Current head of state*: Petr Pavel
- *Current head of government*: Petr Fiala
- *Type of government*: Parliamentary Republic

DENMARK

- *Location*: Northern Europe
- *Capital*: Copenhagen
- *Languages*: Danish, English
- *Dominant religion*: Evangelical Lutheran Church
- *Time zone*: +1
- *Currency*: Krone
- *Current head of state*: King Frederik X
- *Current head of government*: Mette Frederiksen
- *Type of government*: Parliamentary Constitutional Monarchy

ESTONIA

- *Location*: Eastern Europe
- *Capital*: Tallinn
- *Languages*: Estonian, Russian
- *Dominant religion*: Orthodox Church of Estonia, Lutheran
- *Time zone*: +2
- *Currency*: Euro
- *Current head of state*: Alar Karis
- *Current head of government*: Kaja Kallas
- *Type of government*: Parliamentary Republic

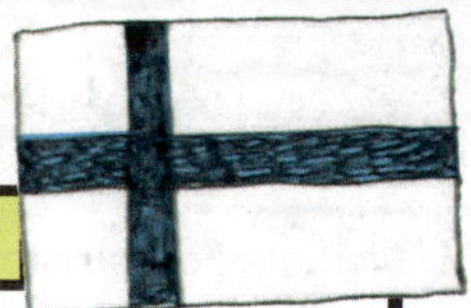

FINLAND

- *Location*: Northern Europe
- *Capital*: Helsinki
- *Languages*: Finnish, Swedish
- *Dominant religion*: Lutheran
- *Time zone*: +2
- *Currency*: Euro
- *Current head of state*: Alexander Stubb
- *Current head of government*: Petteri Orpo
- *Type of government*: Parliamentary Republic

FRANCE

- *Location*: Western Europe
- *Capital*: Paris
- *Language*: French
- *Dominant religion*: Roman Catholicism
- *Time zone*: +1
- *Currency*: Euro
- *Current head of state*: Emmanuel Jean-Michel Frédéric Macron
- *Current head of government*: Gabriel Attal
- *Type of government*: Semi-Presidential Republic

GEORGIA

- *Location*: Southwestern Asia/ Eastern Europe
- *Capital*: Tbilisi
- *Languages*: Georgian, Azeri, Armenian
- *Dominant religion*: Orthodox Christian
- *Time zone*: +4
- *Currency*: Lari
- *Current head of state*: Salome Zourabichvili
- *Current head of government*: Irakli Kobakhidze
- *Type of government*: Semi-Presidential

GERMANY

- *Location*: Central Europe
- *Capital*: Berlin
- *Language*: German
- *Dominant religion*: Roman Catholicism, Protestantism
- *Time zone*: +1
- *Currency*: Euro
- *Current head of state*: Frank-Walter Steinmeier
- *Current head of government*: Olaf Scholz
- *Type of government*: Federal Parliamentary Republic

GREECE

- *Location*: Southern Europe
- *Capital*: Athens
- *Language*: Greek
- *Dominant religion*: Greek Orthodox Church
- *Time zone*: +2
- *Currency*: Euro
- *Current head of state*: Katerina Sakellaropoulou
- *Current head of government*: Kyriakos Mitsotakis
- *Type of government*: Parliamentary Republic

HUNGARY

- *Location*: Central Europe
- *Capital*: Budapest
- *Language*: Hungarian
- *Dominant religion*: Roman Catholicism
- *Time zone*: +1
- *Currency*: Forint
- *Current head of state*: Tamás Sulyok
- *Current head of government*: Viktor Orbán
- *Type of government*: Parliamentary Republic

ICELAND

- *Location*: Northern Europe
- *Capital*: Reykjavik
- *Languages*: Icelandic, English
- *Dominant religion*: Evangelical Lutheran Church of Iceland
- *Time zone*: GMT
- *Currency*: Icelandic Króna
- *Current head of state*: Halla Tómasdóttir
- *Current head of government*: Bjarni Benediktsson
- *Type of government*: Unitary Parliamentary Republic

IRELAND

- *Location*: Western Europe
- *Capital*: Dublin
- *Languages*: Irish, English
- *Dominant religion*: Roman Catholicism
- *Time zone*: +1
- *Currency*: Euro
- *Current head of state*: Michael D Higgins
- *Current head of government*: Simon Harris
- *Type of government*: Parliamentary Republic

ITALY

- *Location*: Southern Europe
- *Capital*: Rome
- *Language*: Italian
- *Dominant religion*: Roman Catholicism
- *Time zone*: +1
- *Currency*: Euro
- *Current head of state*: Sergio Mattarella
- *Current head of government*: Giorgia Meloni
- *Type of government*: Parliamentary Republic

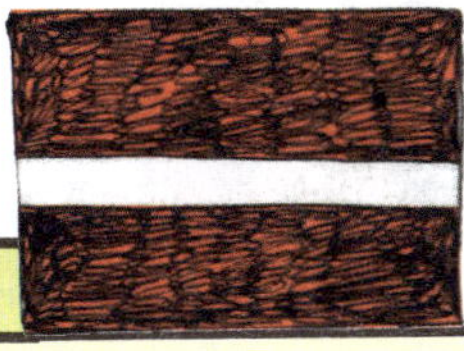

LATVIA

» *Location*: Eastern Europe

» *Capital*: Riga

» *Language*: Latvian

» *Dominant religion*: Lutheran

» *Time zone*: +2

» *Currency*: Euro

» *Current head of state*: Edgars Rinkēvičs

» *Current head of government*: Evika Siliņa

» *Type of government*: Parliamentary Republic

LIECHTENSTEIN

» *Location*: Central Europe

» *Capital*: Vaduz

» *Language*: German

» *Dominant religion*: Roman Catholicism

» *Time zone*: +1

» *Currency*: Swiss Franc

» *Current head of state*: Prince Hans-Adam II

» *Current head of government*: Daniel Risch

» *Type of government*: Constitutional Monarchy

LITHUANIA

» *Location*: Eastern Europe

» *Capital*: Vilnius

» *Language*: Lithuanian

» *Dominant religion*: Roman Catholicism

» *Time zone*: +2

» *Currency*: Euro

» *Current head of state*: Gitanas Nauṡda

» *Current head of government*: Ingrida Šimonytė

» *Type of government*: Semi-Presidential Republic

LUXEMBOURG

» *Location*: Western Europe

» *Capital*: Luxembourg

» *Languages*: Luxembourgish, French, German

» *Dominant religion*: Roman Catholicism

» *Time zone*: +1

» *Currency*: Euro

» *Current head of state*: Grand Duke Henri

» *Current head of government*: Luc Frieden

» *Type of government*: Constitutional Monarchy

MALTA

- *Location*: Southern Europe
- *Capital*: Valletta
- *Languages*: Maltese, English
- *Dominant religion*: Roman Catholicism
- *Time zone*: +1
- *Currency*: Euro
- *Current head of state*: Myriam Spiteri Debono
- *Current head of government*: Robert Abela
- *Type of government*: Parliamentary Republic

MOLDOVA

- *Location*: Eastern Europe
- *Capital*: Chisinau
- *Languages*: Moldovan, Romanian, Russian
- *Dominant religion*: Moldovan Orthodox Church
- *Time zone*: +2
- *Currency*: Moldovan Leu
- *Current head of state*: Maia Sandu
- *Current head of government*: Dorin Recean
- *Type of government*: Parliamentary Republic

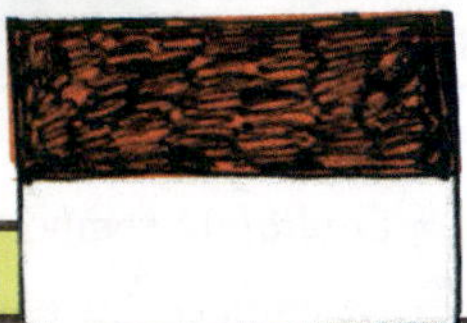

MONACO

- *Location*: Western Europe
- *Capital*: Monaco
- *Languages*: French, English
- *Dominant religion*: Roman Catholicism
- *Time zone*: +1
- *Currency*: Euro
- *Current head of state*: Prince Albert II
- *Current head of government*: Pierre Dartout
- *Type of government*: Constitutional Monarchy

MONTENEGRO

- *Location*: Southeastern Europe
- *Capital*: Podgorica
- *Languages*: Montenegrin, Serbian
- *Dominant religion*: Christian Orthodox
- *Time zone*: +1
- *Currency*: Euro
- *Current head of state*: Jakov Milatović
- *Current head of government*: Milojko Spajić
- *Type of government*: Parliamentary Republic

NORTH MACEDONIA

- *Location*: Southeastern Europe
- *Capital*: Skopje
- *Languages*: Macedonian, Albanian
- *Dominant religions*: Macedonian Orthodox, Islam
- *Time zone*: +1
- *Currency*: Macedonian Denar
- *Current head of state*: Gordana Siljanovska-Davkova
- *Current head of government*: Talat Xhaferi
- *Type of government*: Parliamentary Republic

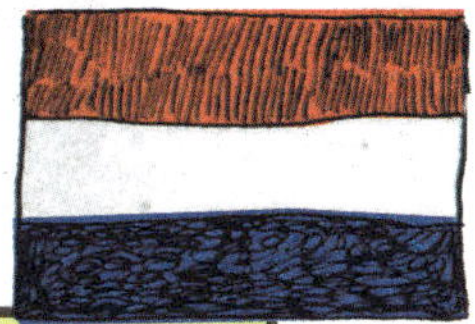

THE NETHERLANDS

- *Location*: Western Europe
- *Capital*: Amsterdam
- *Language*: Dutch
- *Dominant religion*: Roman Catholicism
- *Time zone*: +1
- *Currency*: Euro
- *Current head of state*: King Willem-Alexander
- *Current head of government*: Mark Rutte
- *Type of government*: Parliamentary Constitutional Monarchy

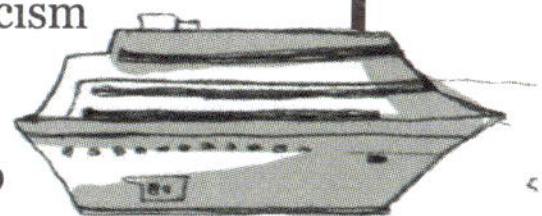

NORWAY

- *Location*: Northern Europe
- *Capital*: Oslo
- *Languages*: Bokmal Norwegian, Nynorsk Norwegian
- *Dominant religion*: Evangelical Lutheran
- *Time zone*: +1
- *Currency*: Norwegian Krone
- *Current head of state*: King Harald V
- *Current head of government*: Jonas Gahr Støre
- *Type of government*: Parliamentary Constitutional Monarchy

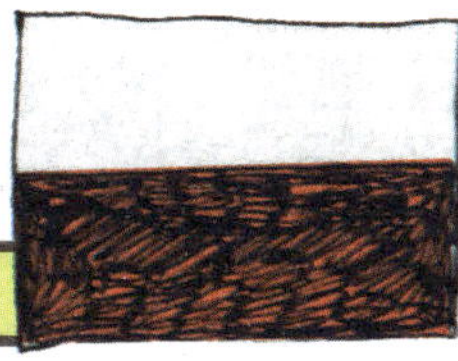

POLAND

- *Location*: Central Europe
- *Capital*: Warsaw
- *Language*: Polish
- *Dominant religion*: Catholicism
- *Time zone*: +1
- *Currency*: Zloty
- *Current head of state*: Andrzej Duda
- *Current head of government*: Donald Tusk
- *Type of government*: Parliamentary Republic

PORTUGAL

- *Location*: Southwestern Europe
- *Capital*: Lisbon
- *Language*: Portuguese
- *Dominant religion*: Roman Catholicism
- *Time zone*: +1
- *Currency*: Euro
- *Current head of state*: Marcelo Rebelo de Sousa
- *Current head of government*: Luís Montenegro
- *Type of government*: Semi-Presidential Republic

ROMANIA

- *Location*: Southeastern Europe
- *Capital*: Bucharest
- *Languages*: Romanian, Hungarian
- *Dominant religion*: Eastern Orthodox
- *Time zone*: +2
- *Currency*: Leu
- *Current head of state*: Klaus Werner Iohannis
- *Current head of government*: Marcel Ciolacu
- *Type of government*: Semi-Presidential Republic

SAN MARINO

- *Location*: Southern Europe
- *Capital*: San Marino
- *Language*: Italian
- *Dominant religion*: Roman Catholicism
- *Time zone*: +1
- *Currency*: Euro
- *Current head state and head of government*: Alessandro Rossi and Milena GasperoniI
- *Type of government*: Parliamentary Republic

SERBIA

- *Location*: Southeastern Europe
- *Capital*: Belgrade
- *Language*: Serbian
- *Dominant religion*: Serbian Orthodox
- *Time zone*: +1
- *Currency*: Serbian Dinar
- *Current head of state*: Aleksandar Vučić
- *Current head of government*: Milos Vucevic
- *Type of government*: Parliamentary Republic

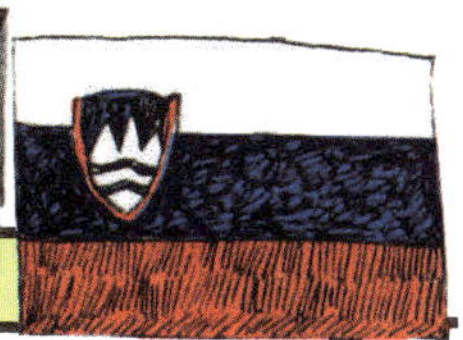

SLOVAKIA

- *Location*: Central Europe
- *Capital*: Bratislava
- *Language*: Slovak
- *Dominant religion*: Roman Catholicism
- *Time zone*: +1
- *Currency*: Euro
- *Current head of state*: Zuzana Čaputová
- *Current head of government*: Robert Fico
- *Type of government*: Parliamentary Republic

SLOVENIA

- *Location*: South Central Europe
- *Capital*: Ljubljana
- *Language*: Slovenian
- *Dominant religion*: Catholicism
- *Time zone*: +1
- *Currency*: Euro
- *Current head of state*: Nataša Pirc Musar
- *Current head of government*: Robert Golob
- *Type of government*: Parlimentary Republic

SPAIN

- *Location*: Southwestern Europe
- *Capital*: Madrid
- *Languages*: Castilian Spanish, Catalan
- *Dominant religion*: Roman Catholicism
- *Time zone*: +1
- *Currency*: Euro
- *Current head of state*: King Felipe VI
- *Current head of government*: Pedro Sánchez
- *Type of government*: Parliamentary Constitutional Monarchy

SWEDEN

- *Location*: Northern Europe
- *Capital*: Stockholm
- *Language*: Swedish
- *Dominant religion*: Church of Sweden (Lutheran)
- *Time zone*: +1
- *Currency*: Swedish Krona
- *Current head of state*: King Carl XVI Gustaf
- *Current head of government*: Ulf Kristersson
- *Type of government*: Parliamentary Constitutional Monarchy

SWITZERLAND

- *Location*: Central Europe
- *Capital*: Bern
- *Languages*: German, French, Italian
- *Dominant religion*: Roman Catholicism
- *Time zone*: +1
- *Currency*: Swiss Franc
- *Current head of state and government*: Viola Amherd
- *Type of government*: Confederation (Federal Republic)

UKRAINE

- *Location*: Eastern Europe
- *Capital*: Kyiv
- *Languages*: Ukranian, Russian
- *Dominant religion*: Ukranian Orthodox Church
- *Time zone*: +2
- *Currency*: Hryvnia
- *Current head of state*: Volodymyr Zelenskyy
- *Current head of government*: Denys Shmyhal
- *Type of government*: Semi-Presidential Republic

UNITED KINGDOM

- *Location*: Western Europe
- *Capital*: London
- *Language*: English
- *Dominant religion*: Christianity
- *Time zone*: GMT
- *Currency*: British Pound
- *Current head of state*: King Charles III
- *Current head of government*: Rishi Sunak
- *Type of government*: Parliamentary Constitutional Monarchy

VATICAN CITY (HOLY SEE)

- *Location*: Southern Europe (a city-state in Rome, Italy)
- *Capital*: Vatican City
- *Languages*: Italian, Latin
- *Dominant religion*: Roman Catholicism
- *Time zone*: +1
- *Currency*: Euro
- *Current head of state*: Pope Francis
- *Current head of government*: Fernando Vérgez Alzaga
- *Type of government*: Ecclesiastical Elective Monarchy

ANTIGUA AND BARBUDA

» *Location*: Caribbean

» *Capital*: Saint John's

» *Language*: English

» *Dominant religion*: Protestantism

» *Time zone*: -4

» *Currency*: East Caribbean Dollar

» *Current head of state*: King Charles III and Sir Rodney Williams

» *Current head of government*: Gaston Alphonso Browne

» *Type of government*: Parliamentary Democracy under a Constitutional Monarchy

BARBADOS

» *Location*: Caribbean

» *Capital*: Bridgetown

» *Languages*: English, Bajan

» *Dominant religion*: Protestantism

» *Time zone*: -4

» *Currency*: Bajan Dollar

» *Current head of state*: Dame Sandra Prunella Mason

» *Current head of government*: Mia Mottley

» *Type of government*: Parliamentary Democracy under a Constitutional Monarchy

BAHAMAS

» *Location*: North Atlantic Ocean

» *Capital*: Nassau

» *Languages*: English, Creole

» *Dominant religion*: Protestantism

» *Time zone*: -4

» *Currency*: Bahamian Dollar

» *Current head of state*: King Charles III and Cynthia A. Pratt

» *Current head of government*: Philip Edward Davis

» *Type of government*: Parliamentary Democracy under a Constitutional Monarchy

NORTH AMERICA

BELIZE

- *Location*: Central America
- *Capital*: Belmopan
- *Languages*: English, Creole, Spanish
- *Dominant religion*: Roman Catholicism
- *Time zone*: -6
- *Currency*: Belizean Dollar
- *Current head of state*: King Charles III and Dame Froyla Tzalam
- *Current head of government*: Johnny Briceño
- *Type of government*: Parliamentary Democracy under a Constitutional Monarchy

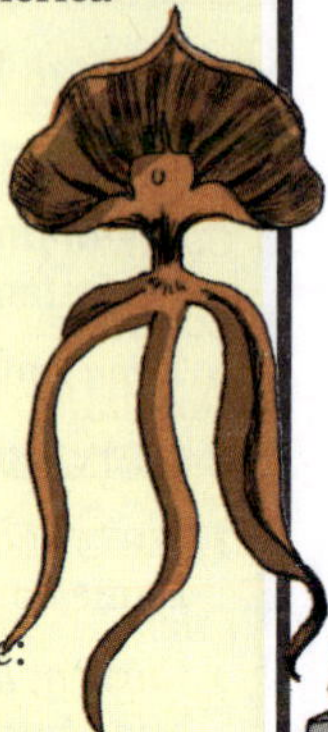

CANADA

- *Location*: Northern America
- *Capital*: Ottawa
- *Languages*: English, French
- *Dominant religion*: Catholicism
- *Time zone*: -3:30 to -8
- *Currency*: Canadian Dollar
- *Current head of state*: King Charles III and Dame Mary Simon
- *Current head of government*: Justin Pierre James Trudeau
- *Type of government*: Federal Parliamentary Democracy under a Constitutional Monarchy

COSTA RICA

- *Location*: Central America
- *Capital*: San Jośe
- *Language*: Spanish
- *Dominant religion*: Roman Catholicism
- *Time zone*: -6
- *Currency*: Costa Rican Colón
- *Current head of state and government*: Rodrigo Chaves Robles
- *Type of government*: Presidential Democratic Republic

CUBA

- *Location*: Caribbean
- *Capital*: Havana
- *Language*: Spanish
- *Dominant religion*: Bermudez Christianity
- *Time zone*: -5
- *Currency*: Cuban Preso
- *Current head of state*: Miguel Diaz-Canel
- *Current head of government*: Manuel Marrero Cruz
- *Type of government*: Communist State

DOMINICA

- *Location*: Caribbean
- *Capital*: Roseau
- *Languages*: English, French patois
- *Dominant religion*: Roman Catholicism
- *Time zone*: -4
- *Currency*: East Caribbean Dollar
- *Current head of state*: Sylvanie Burton
- *Current head of government*: Roosevelt Skerrit
- *Type of government*: Parliamentary Republic

DOMINICAN REPUBLIC

- *Location*: Caribbean
- *Capital*: Santo Domingo
- *Language*: Spanish
- *Dominant religion*: Roman Catholicism
- *Time zone*: -4
- *Currency*: Dominican Peso
- *Current head of state and government*: Luis Abinader
- *Type of government*: Presidential Democratic Republic

EL SALVADOR

- *Location*: Central America
- *Capital*: San Salvador
- *Language*: Spanish
- *Dominant religion*: Roman Catholicism
- *Time zone*: -6
- *Currency*: US Dollar
- *Current head of state and government*: Nayib Armando Bukele Ortez
- *Type of government*: Presidential Republic

GRENADA

- *Location*: Caribbean
- *Capital*: St George's
- *Language*: English
- *Dominant religion*: Protestantism
- *Time zone*: -4
- *Currency*: East Caribbean Dollar
- *Current head of state*: King Charles III and Dame Cécile La Grenade
- *Current head of government*: Dickon Mitchell
- *Type of government*: Parliamentary Democracy under a Constitutional Monarchy

HAITI

- *Location*: Caribbean
- *Capital*: Port-au-Prince
- *Languages*: French, Creole
- *Dominant religion*: Roman Catholicism
- *Time zone*: -5
- *Currency*: Gourde
- *Current head of state*: Vacant (Transitional Presidential Council)
- *Current head of government*: Garry Conille
- *Type of government*: Semi-Presidential Republic

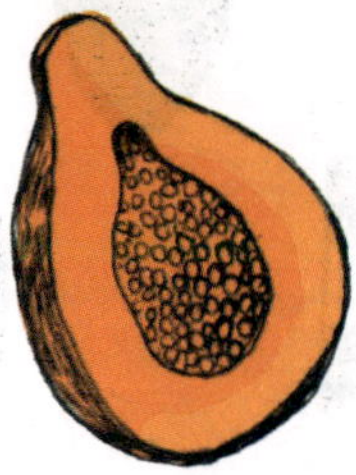

GUATEMALA

- *Location*: Central America
- *Capital*: Guatemala City
- *Languages*: Spanish, indigenous languages
- *Dominant religions*: Christianity, indigenous faiths
- *Time zone*: -6
- *Currency*: Quetzal
- *Current head of state and government*: Bernardo Arévalo
- *Type of government*: Presidential Republic

HONDURAS

- *Location*: Central America
- *Capital*: Tegucigalpa
- *Language*: Spanish
- *Dominant religion*: Roman Catholicism
- *Time zone*: -6
- *Currency*: Lempira
- *Current head of state and government*: Xiomara Castro
- *Type of government*: Presidential Republic

MEXICO

- *Location*: Northern America
- *Capital*: Mexico City
- *Language*: Spanish
- *Dominant religion*: Roman Catholicism
- *Time zone*: -6
- *Currency*: Mexican Peso
- *Current head of state and government*: Andrés Manuel López Obrador
- *Type of government*: Federal Presidential Republic

JAMAICA

- *Location*: Caribbean
- *Capital*: Kingston
- *Languages*: English, Jamaican Patois
- *Dominant religion*: Protestantism
- *Time zone*: -5
- *Currency*: Jamaican Dollar
- *Current head of state*: King Charles III and Sir Patrick Allen
- *Current head of government*: Andrew Holness
- *Type of government*: Parliamentary Democracy under a Constitutional Monarchy

NICARAGUA

- *Location*: Central America
- *Capital*: Managua
- *Language*: Spanish
- *Dominant religion*: Roman Catholicism
- *Time zone*: -6
- *Currency*: Nicaraguan Córdoba
- *Current head of state and government*: José Daniel Ortega Saavedra
- *Type of government*: Presidential Republic

PANAMA

- *Location*: Central America
- *Capital*: Panama City
- *Language*: Spanish
- *Dominant religion*: Roman Catholicism
- *Time zone*: -5
- *Currency*: Balboa
- *Current head of state and government*: Laurentino Cortizo
- *Type of government*: Presidential Republic

ST KITTS AND NEVIS

- *Location*: Caribbean
- *Capital*: Basseterre
- *Language*: English
- *Dominant religion*: Protestantism
- *Time zone*: -4
- *Currency*: East Caribbean Dollar
- *Current head of state*: King Charles III and Sir Marcella Liburd
- *Current head of government*: Terrance Drew
- *Type of government*: Parliamentary Democracy under a Constitutional Monarchy

ST LUCIA

- *Location*: Caribbean
- *Capital*: Castries
- *Language*: English
- *Dominant religion*: Roman Catholicism
- *Time zone*: -4
- *Currency*: East Caribbean Dollar
- *Current head of state*: King Charles III and Cyril Errol Melchiades Charles
- *Current head of government*: Philip J Pierre
- *Type of government*: Parliamentary Democracy under a Constitutional Monarchy

ST VINCENT AND THE GRENADINES

- *Location*: Caribbean
- *Capital*: Kingstown
- *Language*: English
- *Dominant religion*: Protestantism
- *Time zone*: -4
- *Currency*: East Caribbean Dollar
- *Current head of state*: King Charles III and Dame Susan Dougan
- *Current head of government*: Ralph Everard Gonsalves
- *Type of government*: Parliamentary Democracy under a Constitutional Monarchy

TRINIDAD AND TOBAGO

- *Location*: Caribbean
- *Capital*: Port of Spain
- *Languages*: English, Caribbean Hindustani
- *Dominant religions*: Protestantism, Roman Catholicism
- *Time zone*: -4
- *Currency*: Trinidad and Tobago Dollar
- *Current head of state*: Christine Kangaloo
- *Current head of government*: Keith Christopher Rowley
- *Type of government*: Parliamentary Republic

UNITED STATES

- *Location*: North America
- *Capital*: Washington DC
- *Language*: English
- *Dominant religion*: Protestantism
- *Time zone*: -5 to -9
- *Currency*: US Dollar
- *Current head of state and government*: Joseph (Joe) Biden
- *Type of government*: Federal Republic

AUSTRALIA

- *Location*: Oceania
- *Capital*: Canberra
- *Language*: English
- *Dominant religion*: Protestantism
- *Time zone*: +8 to +10:30
- *Currency*: Australian Dollar
- *Current head of state*: King Charles III and David Hurley
- *Current head of government*: Anthony Albanese
- *Type of government*: Federal Parliamentary Democracy under a Constitutional Monarchy

FIJI

- *Location*: Oceania
- *Capital*: Suva
- *Languages*: English, Fijian, Fiji Hindi
- *Dominant religion*: Protestantism
- *Time zone*: +12
- *Currency*: Fijian Dollar
- *Current head of state*: Wiliame Katonivere
- *Current head of government*: Sitiveni Rabuka
- *Type of government*: Parliamentary Republic

KIRIBATI

- *Location*: Oceania
- *Capital*: Tarawa
- *Languages*: English, I Kiribati
- *Dominant religion*: Roman Catholicism
- *Time zone*: +12 to +14
- *Currency*: Australian Dollar
- *Current head of state and government*: Taneti Maamau
- *Type of government*: Presidential Republic

MARSHALL ISLANDS

- *Location*: Oceania
- *Capital*: Majuro
- *Languages*: Marshallese, English
- *Dominant religion*: Protestantism
- *Time zone*: +12
- *Currency*: US Dollar
- *Current head of state and government*: Hilda C. Heine
- *Type of government*: Presidential Republic in Free Association with the US

MICRONESIA (FEDERATED STATES OF)

- *Location*: Oceania
- *Capital*: Palikir
- *Language*: English
- *Dominant religion*: Roman Catholicism
- *Time zone*: +10, +11
- *Currency*: US Dollar
- *Current head of state and government*: Wesley Simina
- *Type of government*: Federal Republic in Free Association with the US

NAURU

- *Location*: Oceania
- *Capital*: Yaren
- *Languages*: Nauruan, English
- *Dominant religion*: Protestantism

- *Time zone*: +12
- *Currency*: Australian Dollar
- *Current head of state and government*: David W.R Adeang
- *Type of government*: Parliamentary Republic

NEW ZEALAND

- *Location*: Oceania
- *Capital*: Wellington
- *Languages*: English, Maori
- *Dominant religion*: Christianity
- *Time zone*: +12
- *Currency*: New Zealand Dollar
- *Current head of state*: Queen King Charles III and Dame Cindy Kiro
- *Current head of government*: Christopher Luxon
- *Type of government*: Parliamentary Democracy under a Constitutional Monarchy

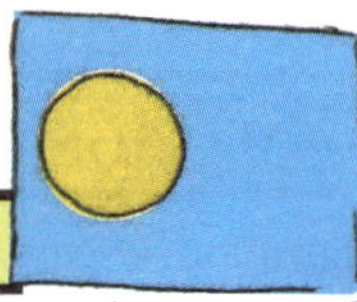

PALAU

- *Location*: Oceania
- *Capital*: Ngerulmud

- *Languages*: Palauan, English
- *Dominant religion*: Roman Catholicism
- *Time zone*: +9
- *Currency*: US Dollar

- *Current head of state and government*: Surangel S Whipps Jr.
- *Type of government*: Presidential Republic in Free Association with the US

PAPUA NEW GUINEA

» *Location*: Oceania

» *Capital*: Port Moresby

» *Languages*: Tok Pisin, English, Hiri Motu

» *Dominant religion*: Roman Catholicism

» *Time zone*: +10

» *Currency*: Kina

» *Current head of state*: King Charles III and Bob Dadae

» *Current head of government*: James Marape

» *Type of government*: Parliamentary Democracy under a Constitutional Monarchy

SAMOA

» *Location*: Oceania

» *Capital*: Apia

» *Languages*: Samoan, English

» *Dominant religion*: Protestantism

» *Time zone*: +13

» *Currency*: Tālā

» *Current head of state*: Afioga Tuimalealiìfano Va‘aleto‘a Eti Sualauvi II

» *Current head of government*: Fiame Naomi Mata'afa

» *Type of government*: Parliamentary Republic

SOLOMON ISLANDS

» *Location*: Oceania

» *Capital*: Honiara

» *Languages*: Melanesian Pidgin, English

» *Dominant religion*: Protestantism

» *Time zone*: +11

Currency: Solomon Island Dollar

Current head of state: King Charles III and Reverend David Vunagi

Current head of government: Jeremiah Manele

» *Type of government*: Parliamentary Democracy under a Constitutional Monarchy

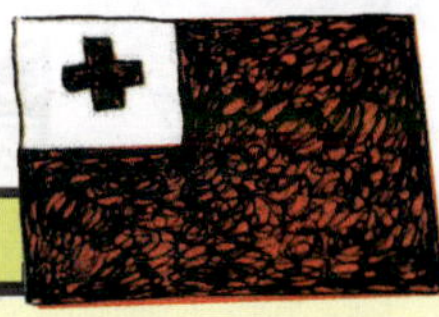

TONGA

» *Location*: Oceania

» *Capital*: Nuku'alofa

» *Languages*: Tongan, English

» *Dominant religion*: Protestantism

» *Time zone*: +13

» *Currency*: Pa'anga

» *Current head of state*: King Tupou VI

» *Current head of government*: Siaosi Sovaleni

» *Type of government*: Constitutional Monarchy

TUVALU

- *Location*: Oceania
- *Capital*: Funafuti
- *Languages*: Tuvaluan, English
- *Dominant religion*: Church of Tuvalu
- *Time zone*: +12
- *Currency*: Tuvaluan Dollar
- *Current head of state*: King Charles III and Tofiga Vaevalu Falani
- *Current head of government*: Feleti Teo
- *Type of government*: Parliamentary Democracy under a Constitutional Monarchy

VANUATU

- *Location*: Oceania
- *Capital*: Port Vila
- *Languages*: Bislama, English
- *Dominant religion*: Protestantism
- *Time zone*: +11
- *Currency*: Vanuatu Vatu
- *Current head of state*: Nikenike Vurobaravu
- *Current head of government*: Charlot Salwai
- *Type of government*: Parliamentary Republic

ARGENTINA

- *Location*: Southern South America
- *Capital*: Buenos Aires
- *Language*: Spanish
- *Dominant religion*: Roman Catholicism
- *Time zone*: -3
- *Currency*: Peso
- *Current head of state and government*: Javier Gerardo Milei
- *Type of government*: Federal Presidential Republic

BOLIVIA

- *Location*: Central South America
- *Capitals*: Sucre and La Paz
- *Languages*: Spanish, Quehcua, Aymara, Guarani
- *Dominant religion*: Roman Catholicism
- *Time zone*: -4
- *Currency*: Boliviano
- *Current head of state and government*: Luis Arce
- *Type of government*: Presidential Republic

BRAZIL

- *Location*: Eastern South America
- *Capital*: Brasília
- *Language*: Portuguese
- *Dominant religion*: Roman Catholicism
- *Time zone*: -2 to -5
- *Currency*: Real
- *Current head of state and government*: Luiz Inácio Lula da Silva
- *Type of government*: Federal Presidential Republic

CHILE

- *Location*: Southern South America
- *Capital*: Santiago
- *Language*: Spanish
- *Dominant religion*: Roman Catholicism
- *Time zone*: -4
- *Currency*: Chilean Peso
- *Current head of state and government*: Gabriel Boric
- *Type of government*: Presidential Republic

COLOMBIA

- *Location*: Northern South America
- *Capital*: Bogotá
- *Language*: Spanish
- *Dominant religion*: Roman Catholicism
- *Time zone*: -5
- *Currency*: Columbian Peso
- *Current head of state and government*: Gustavo Petro
- *Type of government*: Presidential Republic

ECUADOR

- *Location*: Western South America
- *Capital*: Quito
- *Language*: Spanish
- *Dominant religion*: Roman Catholicism
- *Time zone*: -5
- *Currency*: US Dollar
- *Current head of state and government*: Daniel Noboa
- *Type of government*: Presidential Republic

GUYANA

- *Location*: Northern South America
- *Capital*: Georgetown
- *Languages*: English, local dialects
- *Dominant religions*: Christianity, Hinduism
- *Time zone*: -4
- *Currency*: Guyanese Dollar
- *Current head of state and government*: Mohamed Irfaan Ali
- *Current head of government*: Mark Phillips
- *Type of government*: Parliamentary Republic

PARAGUAY

- *Location*: Central South America
- *Capital*: Asunción
- *Languages*: Spanish, Guarani
- *Dominant religion*: Roman Catholicism
- *Time zone*: -4
- *Currency*: Guarani
- *Current head of state and government*: Santiago Peña
- *Type of government*: Presidential Republic

PERU

- *Location*: Western South America
- *Capital*: Lima
- *Languages*: Spanish, Quechua Aymara
- *Dominant religion*: Roman Catholicism
- *Time zone*: -5
- *Currency*: Sol
- *Current head of state and government*: Dina Ercilia Boluarte Zegarra
- *Type of government*: Presidential Republic

SURINAME

- *Location*: Northern South America
- *Capital*: Paramaribo
- *Language*: Dutch
- *Dominant religions*: Hinduism, Protestantism
- *Time zone*: -3
- *Currency*: Surinamese Dollar
- *Current head of state and government*: Chandrikapersad 'Chan' Santokhi
- *Type of government*: Presidential Republic

URUGUAY

- *Location*: Southern South America
- *Capital*: Montevideo
- *Languages*: Spanish
- *Dominant religion*: Roman Catholicism
- *Time zone*: -3
- *Currency*: Uruguayan Peso
- *Current head of state and government*: Luis Lacalle Pou
- *Type of government*: Presidential Republic

VENEZUELA

- *Location*: Northern South America
- *Capital*: Caracas
- *Languages*: Spanish, indigenous languages
- *Dominant religion*: Roman Catholicism
- *Time zone*: -4
- *Currency*: Bolivar
- *Current head of state*: Nicolás Maduro Moros
- *Type of government*: Federal Presidential Republic

AL - Arab League

OACPS - Organization of African, Caribbean and Pacific States

APEC - Asia-Pacific Economic Co-operation

ADB - Asian Development Bank

ASEAN - Association of Southeast Asian Nations

AI - Amnesty International

AU - African Union

CIS - Commonwealth of Independent States

ESCAP - Economic and Social Commission for Asia and the Pacific

EC - European Commission

FIFA - Fédération Internationale de Football Association

G7 - Group of Seven (countries)

G20 - Group of Twenty (developing economies)

GCC - Gulf Cooperation Council

IAEA - International Atomic Energy Agency

IBRD - International Bank for Reconstruction and Development

IDA - International Development Association

INTERPOL - International Criminal Police Organization

IFAD - International Fund for Agricultural Development

IFC - International Finance Corporation

IFRC - International Federation of Red Cross and Red Crescent Societies

IMF - International Monetary Fund

IMO - International Maritime Organization

UNITED NATIONS

UN - United Nations

UN General Assembly

UN Security Council

Economic and Social Council

UN Trusteeship Council

International Court of Justice

United Nations Secretariat

MORE INTERNATIONAL ORGANIZATIONS

INMARSAT - International Maritime Satellite Organization

IOC - International Olympic Committee

ISO - International Organization for Standardisation

ITU - International Telecommunication Union

INTELSAT - International Telecommunications Satellite Organization

MERCOSUR - Trading and Political bloc in Latin America comprising Brazil, Argentina, Uruguay, Venezuela and Paraguay

NAM - Non-Aligned Movement

NATO - North Atlantic Treaty Organization

OAS - Organization of American States

OECD - Organization for Economic Co-operation and Development

OPEC - Organization of the Petroleum Exporting Countries

SAARC - South Asian Association for Regional Cooperation

WIPO - World Intellectual Property Organization

WMO - World Meteorological Organization

WTO - World Trade Organization

WWF - World Wide Fund for Nature

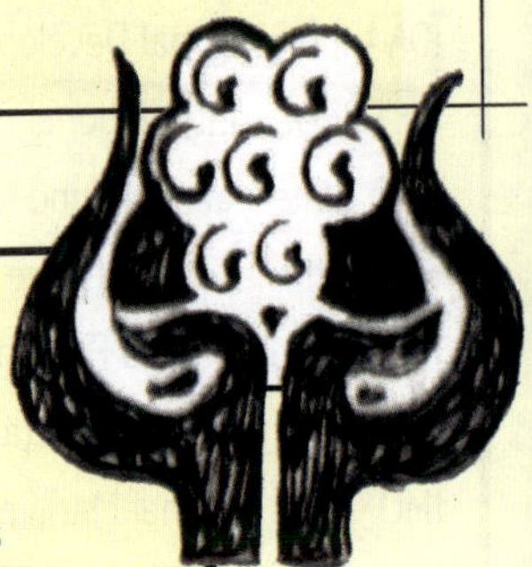

UN SPECIALISED AGENCIES

WHO - World Health Organization

UNESCO - United Nations Educational, Scientific and Cultural Organization

UNICEF - United Nations International Children's Emergency Fund

UNIDO - United Nations Industrial Development Organization

UNDP - United Nations Development Programme

UNHCR - United Nations High Commissioner for Refugees

FAO - Food and Agriculture Organization

UNHRC - United Nations Human Rights Council

IMPORTANT OFFICE HOLDERS

President of the World Bank: Ajay Banga

Secretary-General of the United Nations: António Guterres

Secretary General of Amnesty International: Dr Agnès Callamard

Director-General of UNESCO: Audrey Azoulay

Executive Director of UNICEF: Catherine Russell

Director-General of WHO: Tedros Adhanom Ghebreyesus

ILO Director-General: Gilbert F. Houngbo

President of the International Court of Justice: Judge Yuji Iwasawa

President of the International Olympic Committee: Kirsty Coventry

President of the Fédération Internationale de Football Association: Gianni Infantino

President of the United Nations Human Rights Council (UNHRC): Ambassador Jürg Lauber

Secretary General of the South Asian Association for Regional Cooperation: Ambassador Md. Golam Sarwar

President of the European Commission: Ursula von der Leyen

Director-General of the WTO: Ngozi Okonjo-Iweala

António Guterres

DONALD TRUMP SURVIVES ATTACK AND WINS U.S. PRESIDENTIAL ELECTION

On 13 July 2024, former U.S. President Donald Trump was shot at while campaigning for the presidency in Pennsylvania. A gunman opened fire during one of his rallies, injuring Trump and killing one person who was attending the rally. U.S. Secret Service agents quickly protected Trump and rushed him to safety. Trump was hit in the ear but survived the attack. He later thanked his security team and supporters for their courage and prayers.

Despite the incident, Trump continued his campaign and gained strong support from his followers. On 5 November 2024, he was elected President of the United States for a second non-consecutive term. This makes him the first American leader since Grover Cleveland to hold two separate terms in office. After the election results were announced, Trump promised to work for all Americans and unite the nation. He said his next term would focus on security, job creation, and making America respected worldwide. World leaders congratulated him and expressed hope for stable relations with the U.S. during his presidency.

FAULTY UPDATES LEADS TO GLOBAL COMPUTER OUTAGE

On 19 July 2024, businesses and services around the world faced major problems when a faulty update in Microsoft Windows caused massive IT outages. The unexpected bug brought down computer systems in banks, airports, hospitals, and offices, leaving millions of people unable to work or travel smoothly. Airlines had to delay or cancel flights, while hospitals switched to manual systems to help patients safely.

Microsoft engineers worked through the night to find the cause and released a patch to solve the problem. Experts say this rare event shows how much the world depends on technology and highlights the need for strong backup plans.

BIGGEST PRISONER SWAP HAPPENS BETWEEN AMERICA AND RUSSIA SINCE COLD WAR

On 1 August 2024, the United States and Russia carried out their biggest prisoner exchange since the end of the Cold War. The swap involved dozens of people, including diplomats, journalists, and citizens who had been held for years. Some of the freed prisoners were accused of spying or breaking strict national security laws, while others were arrested during recent tensions between the two countries. Families of those released celebrated the news and thanked both governments for working together.

ISRAEL–HEZBOLLAH TENSIONS RISE AFTER KEY COMMANDER KILLED

On 30 July 2024, Israel carried out an airstrike that killed Fuad Shukr, a senior Hezbollah commander, in southern Lebanon. Shukr was a top military planner for Hezbollah and had been wanted for his role in past attacks against Israel. His death marked a sharp escalation in tensions between Israel and the Lebanese group. In the weeks that followed, cross-border clashes grew more intense along Israel's northern border. Both sides exchanged rocket fire and artillery shells, leading to damage on both sides. Thousands of people living near the border had to move to safer areas for protection.

Around the same time, reports emerged of cyberattacks targeting communication systems used by Hezbollah fighters. Hackers disabled pagers and walkie-talkies, creating confusion among militants during operations. Some of these attacks even caused injuries when equipment failed during clashes. Israel did not officially confirm its involvement in the cyberattacks, but many believe they were part of its broader security strategy.

SHEIKH HASINA STEPS DOWN AS BANGLADESH PM, NOBEL LAUREATE LEADS INTERIM GOVT

On 5 August 2024, Bangladesh's long-time Prime Minister Sheikh Hasina resigned after weeks of large student-led protests in Dhaka. To protect herself, she flew to India in a military plane. On 8 August 2024, Nobel Peace Prize winner Muhammad Yunus, known for helping poor people through micro-loans, was appointed Chief Adviser of the care-taker government in Bangladesh. He pledged to restore peace, improve human rights, and prepare for fair elections.

In October 2024, the International Crimes Tribunal issued an arrest warrant against Hasina over the crackdown on protesters. Meanwhile, Yunus worked on reforms while managing protests about wages and public-sector changes. On 6 June 2025, Yunus announced that the next national election will be held in the first half of April 2026.

SPAIN WITNESSES HISTORIC FLOODING

On 30 October 2024, Spain experienced its worst floods in fifty years. Heavy rains caused rivers to overflow, flooding several areas. More than 200 people lost their lives, and many homes were destroyed. Rescue workers and volunteers helped families reach safety and provided food and shelter. Leaders promised to rebuild damaged areas and improve flood defences to protect people from future disasters.

ICC ISSUES WARRANT FOR ISRAELI PRIME MINISTER

On 21 November 2024, the International Criminal Court (ICC) announced an arrest warrant for Israeli Prime Minister Benjamin Netanyahu. The ICC said the warrant is for alleged war crimes connected to the conflict in Gaza. Many countries reacted differently;

some in support of the court's decision, while others strongly disagreeing and saying Israel has a right to defend itself. The case has drawn global attention and opened big debates about justice and human rights during conflicts.

GAZA CONFLICT CONTINUES

The conflict in Gaza continued with heavy fighting, shortages of food and medicine, and repeated calls for peace. In late 2024, Israel increased its military operations in northern and central Gaza, leading to more evacuations and damage to hospitals and schools. Many people lost their homes, and aid workers struggled to bring food and clean water to affected families. A short ceasefire in January 2025 allowed some hostages and prisoners to be exchanged, but the fighting soon restarted.

In March 2025, airstrikes and ground attacks caused many more casualties, and the UN warned that Gaza faced a serious hunger crisis. By mid-2025, reports showed thousands of children were suffering from lack of food and medical care. In June and July 2025, international leaders, including the United States, Egypt, and Qatar, pushed for a new ceasefire plan. Hamas said it agreed to the proposal, while Israel also joined talks to find a peaceful solution. Many people around the world hope the deal will finally bring an end to the violence and allow families to rebuild their lives safely.

MAJOR UPDATES IN SYRIA'S CIVIL WAR

On 30 November 2024, opposition forces fighting in Syria's long civil war took control of most of Aleppo, one of the country's largest cities. This was the first time since 2016 that so much of Aleppo had changed hands. The takeover led Russia, Syria's main ally, to launch new airstrikes to support the Syrian government. Just a few days later, on 8 December 2024, Syrian President Bashar al-Assad fled the capital, Damascus, and escaped to Moscow after losing power. His departure marked a huge moment in Syria's war, which has lasted for over a decade and displaced millions of people. World leaders called for calm and for talks to help rebuild the country and protect civilians. Many hope this turning point will open the door for lasting peace and a better future for Syrian families.

SOUTH KOREA FACES POLITICAL SHAKE-UP

On 3 December 2024, South Korean President Yoon Suk Yeol surprised citizens by declaring martial law during a late-night TV address. This was the first such move in the country since 1980. The decree briefly restricted protests, media, and lawmakers. However, many people protested, and the National Assembly quickly rejected the order. By early December, the government reversed the decision after just a few hours. The controversy led to Yoon's impeachment by parliament in mid-December 2024, followed by a unanimous Constitutional Court decision on 4 April 2025, officially removing him from office. A

snap presidential election was held on 3 June 2025, and Lee Jae-myung was elected as the new president. He took office in July, promising to fix the economy, strengthen democracy, and improve communication between the government and its people.

FRENCH PRIME MINISTER LOSES CONFIDENCE VOTE

On 4 December 2024, France's Prime Minister Michel Barnier became the first French leader since Georges Pompidou in 1962 to lose a motion of no-confidence in Parliament. Lawmakers voted to remove him after heated debates over new economic reforms and public protests. The no-confidence vote shows how democracy gives people a chance to demand change.

U.S. PAUSES MILITARY AID; UKRAINE SEEKS NEW SUPPORT

On 3 March 2025, President Donald Trump announced a pause on military aid to Ukraine after meeting President Zelenskyy in Washington. Washington said the slowdown was needed to review its stockpiles and focus on global priorities. Ukraine's leaders expressed deep concern, saying the pause could weaken their defence and encourage Russia.

Despite the pause, Ukraine continued to fight back. In July 2025, Russia launched its largest drone and missile attack on Kyiv since the war began, firing over 500 unmanned drones and missiles. Ukraine's defenders successfully intercepted most of them but highlighted the need more air defence tools. Ukraine also struck back, targeting a Russian military airfield in the Voronezh region and stepping up its own missile systems. With alliances shifting and new weapon systems delayed, experts say the conflict may become harder to manage before help arrives.

FORMER PHILIPPINE PRESIDENT DUTERTE ARRESTED

On 11 March 2025, former Philippines President Rodrigo Duterte was arrested at his home in Davao City. The International Criminal Court (ICC) had issued a warrant for his arrest for alleged crimes against humanity linked to his tough anti-drug campaign while in office. The arrest was peaceful, and Duterte was taken to Manila, capital of Philippines, for questioning. Many people in the Philippines and around the world welcomed the move as a step toward justice for victims and their families.

STRONG EARTHQUAKE HITS MYANMAR

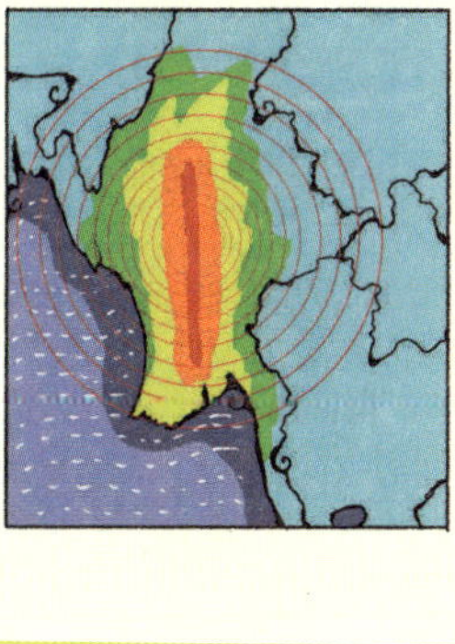

On 28 March 2025, a powerful 7.7-magnitude earthquake struck Myanmar. Sadly, more than 5,400 people lost their lives, and over 11,000 were injured. Many buildings were damaged, and families had to leave their homes to stay safe. Rescue teams and volunteers worked together to help people find shelter, food, and clean water. Countries around the world, including India, sent support to help Myanmar recover. People are now rebuilding their homes and communities with hope for a safer future.

TENSIONS RISE AS ISRAEL AND IRAN CLASH

On 13 June 2025, Israel launched Operation Rising Lion, a large-scale air campaign against Iran's nuclear and military sites, including Natanz, Isfahan, and Tehran. The operation used hundreds of jets and munitions, supported by covert Mossad drone efforts targeting Iranian air-defence systems. Iran retaliated with ballistic missiles and drones, hitting Israeli military bases and launching an attack on the Soroka hospital in Beersheba.

By 17–18 June, Israel had struck dozens of missile launch sites and internal security facilities. Iran responded with waves of missiles and drones aimed at Israeli military hubs and cities such as Tel Aviv and Haifa, prompting evacuations. Civilian damage and casualties were reported on both sides. On 23–24 June, Iran even targeted Al Udeid Air Base in Qatar. By July 2025, tensions continued among the two nations.

GOOD NEWS

SPOTTED HYENA FOUND IN EGYPT AFTER 5000 YEARS OF DISAPPEARANCE

Wildlife experts in Egypt were surprised when they found a spotted Hyena, also known as *Crocuta crocuta*, living in the Elba Protected Area. The discovery was made on 15 November 2025, and is special because the spotted Hyena was, at some point, a common animal in the region but is believed to have disappeared around 5000 years ago.

Scientists had thought that the species had become extinct because of changes in environment and hunting practices. However, with the discovery of the animal, conservationists are optimistic about the healthy conditions in the protected area to support rare wildlife. It has also given a strong push for further protection of Elba Protected Area to ensure that more such rare animals can be rediscovered.

UK BECOMES FIRST G7 COUNTRY TO PHASE OUT COAL POWER

On 30 September 2024, the United Kingdom became the first country in the G7 group to completely phase out coal for producing electricity. This came as a part of country's commitment towards tackling climate change and shifting to greener, more sustainable sources of energy.

Coal has been a backbone of major economies around the world, including the Industrial Revolution in UK. It powered trains, factories, and homes for more than a hundred years. However, coal is also a source of carbon pollution and harmful emissions. This is the reason why the world is looking for greener sources of energy like solar power.

By stopping the use of coal, UK aims to steadily move towards its goal of net-zero emissions by the year 2050. Environmental scientists and organizations have praised the UK for setting an example for other major economies.

LIECHTENSTEIN SAYS YES TO SAME-SEX MARRIAGE

On 1 January 2025, Liechtenstein became the 37th country in the world to legalize same-sex marriage, making it possible for anyone in the country to marry the person they love irrespective of their sex or gender.

The country, known for its beautiful mountains and landscapes, sits between Austria and Switzerland. The new law was approved by Liechtenstein's Parliament in 2024 after many years of debate and discussion. The decision has been celebrated by human rights groups and families across the country. This development has given hope to people around the world that other countries will be inspired to support equal right for everyone too.

KAZAKHSTAN VOTES FOR ITS FIRST NUCLEAR POWER PLANT

More than 60 per cent voters in Kazakhstan supported country's plan to build its first nuclear power plant. On 6 October 2024, the referendum was held, where citizens of Kazakhstan voted in support or against the plan.

With the approval from the citizens, the country will now be able to use its rich uranium deposits to produce energy through a nuclear plant. This will reduce its dependency on coal and natural gas. A successful implementation of the plan will provide a pathway for other countries who can also switch towards cleaner sources of electricity generation. Kazakhstan's nuclear plant is expected to start operating by early 2030s.

By **NAMIT HANS**

4500 BC
Sumerian civilization in Mesopotamia (present-day Iraq) established in this period.

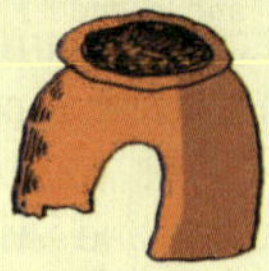

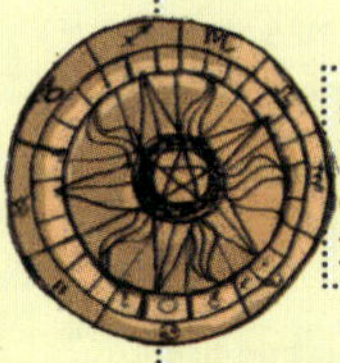

2700 BC
Egyptians create 365-day calendar with the new year beginning in June.

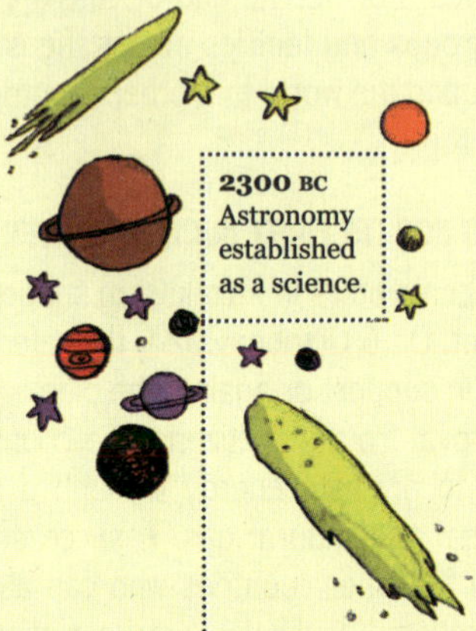

2300 BC
Astronomy established as a science.

2000–1200 BC
Iron Age begins with the discovery of iron. Iron replaces bronze in implements and weapons

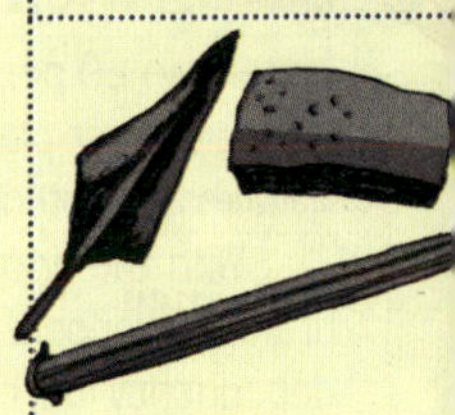

3500 BC
Wheel used for the first time.

5000 BC — 3500 BC — 2500 BC — 2000 BC — 1800 BC

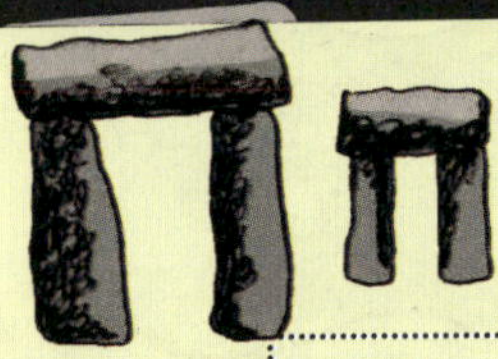

3100 BC
Work begins on Stonehenge.

2500 BC
City of Mohenjo-Daro established in the Indus Valley.

2700-2300 BC
Pyramids built in Egypt.

2000 BC
The Bronze Age reaches Europe.

1500 BC
Rise of the Ganges civilization in northern India. The Rig Veda, the oldest book in Sanskrit or any Indo-European language, compiled around this time.

753 BC
Rome is founded by Romulus. Twelve birds circled overhead during the founding ceremony and legend had it that the city would survive for twelve centuries.

509 BC
Founding of the Roman Republic. The great architecture of Rome can be traced back to this period.

776 BC
First Olympics held in Olympia, Greece.

438 BC
Parthenon in Athens completed after nearly forty years of work.

430 BC
Democritus theorizes that matter is composed of tiny grains called 'atomos' that cannot be subdivided.

1500 BC
The Maya civilization established.

400–200 BC
Hindu epics, the Mahabharata and the Ramayana, composed.

44 BC
Julius Caesar assassinated by Brutus and other conspirators.

6-4 BC
Jesus is born.

1120 BC
Magnetic compass is invented.

1500 BC — 1000 BC — 500 BC — 250 BC — 0 BC

1184 BC Trojan war ends.

347 BC
Death of Greek philosopher Plato.

55 BC
Julius Caesar invades Britain, having already captured Gaul, what is now modern France.

1100 BC
Phoenicians develop alphabetic script.

586 BC
Fall of Jerusalem to the Babylonians.

1000 BC
The Chinese develop gunpowder.

220 BC
Building of the Great Wall of China commences.

850 BC
Iliad and *Odyssey* composed by Homer.

623 BC
Gautama Buddha, founder of Buddhism, born in India.

268 BC
Ashoka is crowned.

1500 BC
Birth of Zoroaster, the founder of Zoroastrianism, in Media, Iran.

650 BC
Earliest coins appear.

336 BC
Accession of Alexander the Great at the age of twenty-two to the throne of Macedon in southeastern Europe.

Not to scale.

1 AD
Since the scholars who designed the new calendar did not have the concept of zero, the new Gregorian calendar is calculated to start at Year 1.

30D
Crucifixion of Jesus Christ.

50 AD
Buddhism reaches China.

64 AD
Great Fire of Rome lasts for six days. Emperor Nero does nothing to stop it.

68–69 AD
Civil War in Rome after Emperor Nero dies.

70 AD
Romans under Titus destroy Jerusalem; 1.5 million Jews die. Gold taken from the temple finances the Colosseum in Rome.

500 AD
Persians use windmills to power irrigation pumps.

570 AD
Birth of Prophet Mohammad, the founder of Islam, in Mecca.

754 AD
Beginning of the state of the Vatican City.

1024 AD
The Chinese start issuing paper money.

1069 AD
Oxford University founded in Oxford, England.

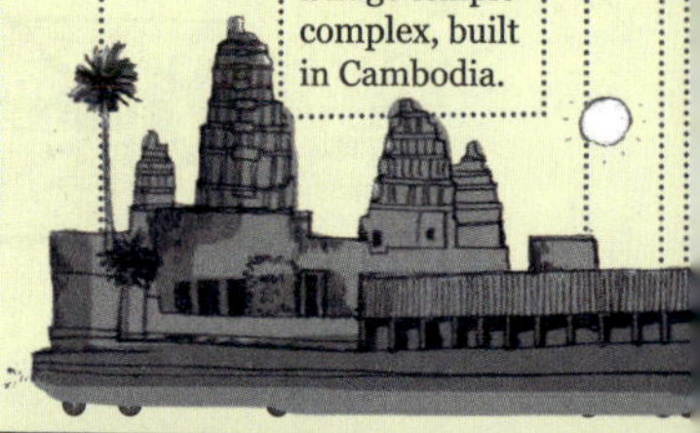

1096–99 AD
First Crusade.

1140 AD
Angkor Wat, a huge temple complex, built in Cambodia.

1187 AD
Ships begin to use the magnetic compass.

1215 AD
King John of England seals the Magna Carta, giving more power to the Barons. Mongols under Genghis Khan conquer Beijing.

1271 AD
Marco Polo starts on his trip to China. He returns to Venice in 1295.

1285 AD
Spectacles for the far-sighted are invented in Italy.

1300 AD
Gunpowder used for warfare in England after being introduced to Europe in 1242.

1315 AD
Great Famine of 1315–17.

0 AD — 500 AD — 1000 AD — 1200 AD

337 AD
Beginning of the 100 Years' War
between England and France,
resolved only in 1453.

1347–50 AD
The Great Plague, popularly called Black Death, ravages Europe.

1431 AD
Joan of Arc, who is credited with leading the French to victory over the English, is burnt at the stake for allegedly practising witchcraft.

1438 AD
The Inca Empire established in Peru.

1498 AD
Vasco da Gama reaches India. He becomes the first European to travel to India by sea.

1558 AD
Commencement of the Elizabethan era in England.

1564 AD
Birth of poet and playwright William Shakespeare in England.

1588 AD
The Spanish Armada is defeated by an English naval force.

1619 AD
Johannes Kepler finally solves the mystery of the motion of the planets.

1350 AD — 1500 AD — 1550 AD — 1700 AD

1455 AD
First Bible printed after the invention of the printing press by German goldsmith Johannes Gutenberg.

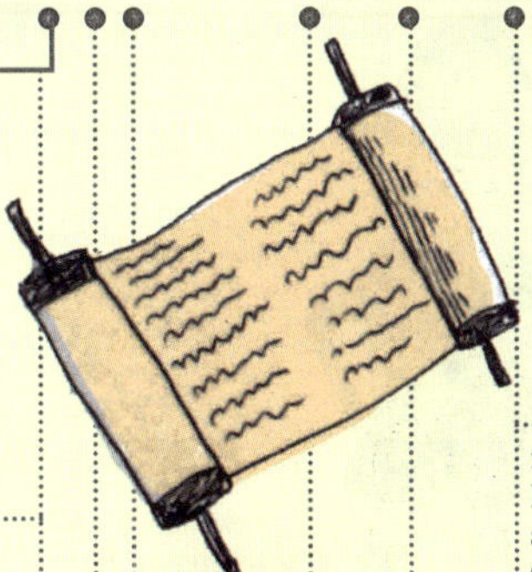

1455–85 AD
The civil wars, or the Wars of the Roses, in England.

1488 AD
Bartholomew Diaz rounds the Cape of Good Hope.

492 AD
hristopher Columbus lands on
ie Americas. He dies in 1506
elieving he had landed in Asia.

1503 AD
Mona Lisa painted by Leonardo da Vinci.

1519 AD
Ferdinand Magellan starts what would be the first circumnavigation of the globe.

1534 AD
King Henry VIII breaks apart from the Roman Catholic Church and appoints himself as the head of the English Church.

1556 AD
Earthquake in China kills 8,30,000.

1666 AD
London engulfed by the Great Fire.

1689 AD
Constitutional Monarchy established in England.

1770 AD
Captain James Cook discovers Australia.

1776 AD
US Declaration of Independence is signed on 4 July. American colonies declare themselves independent of Great Britain.

1783 AD
First manned hot-air balloon flight in Paris by Jean Francoise Pilatre de Rozier and Marquis D'Arlands.

1789 AD
On July 14, the French Revolution begins with the storming of the Bastille to free prisoners and end monarchy. Oddly enough, the Bastille was empty of any real prisoners.

1795 AD
Metric system of measurement introduced in France.

1801 AD
Joseph-Marie Jacquard invents a loom that uses punched cards to create designs in fabric.

1804 AD
Napoleon Bonaparte crowned Emperor of France.

1805 AD
Battle of Trafalgar; British fleet under the command of Horatio Nelson defeats a combined Spanish French fleet.

1812 AD
On September 14, Napoleon takes Moscow, but it is a hollow victory. The city is burned to the ground, yet the Tsar does not surrender. Napoleon and the French army retreat.

1815 AD
Napolean is finally defeated after many attempts in the Battle of Waterloo.

1816 AD
The year without a summer. Mount Tambora erupts and throws up so much dust in the air that it causes 10 inches of snow to fall in June in New England (US). Crops fail and famines are widespread.

1833 AD
England outlaws slavery and frees more than 7,80,000 slaves.

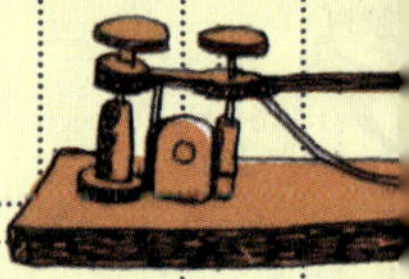

1838 AD
On January 24, Samuel Morse demonstrates the telegraph machine.

1840 AD
The *Nemesis*, built by a Scottish shipbuilder, becomes the first ironclad to round the Cape of Good Hope.

1839–1842 AD
The First Opium War: Hong Kong becomes a British colony.

1845–52 AD
The Great Hunger (aka the Potato Famine) in Ireland. Over 1.5 million die of starvation and disease while Ireland continues to export grain to England to pay rents.

1837–1901 AD
Victoria is Queen of the United Kingdom.

1848 AD
Karl Marx and Friedrich Engels publish the *Communist Manifesto*.

1854 AD
Lord Cardigan leads the British cavalry against the Russians in what would become known as 'The Charge of the Light Brigade'.

1856 AD
Louis Pasteur shows that disease is spread by tiny organisms. Modern germ theory born.

1859 AD
Charles Darwin publishes *On the Origin of Species*.

1861–65 AD
American Civil War; President Lincoln bans slavery; some states attempt to break the Union.

1866 AD
Prussia invades Austria.

1869 AD
Suez Canal opens.

1876 AD
Telephone invented by Alexander Graham Bell.

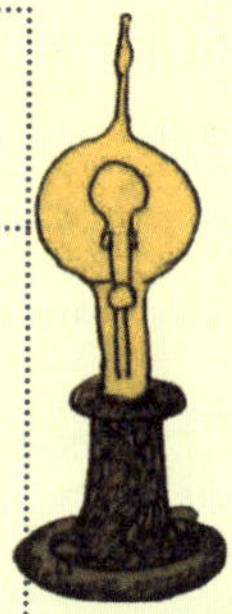

1879 AD
The light bulb is invented by Thomas Edison.

1895 AD
In France, the Lumiere Brothers showcase films for the first time in the history of the world.

1896 AD
The first modern Olympic Games are held in Athens, Greece.

1898 AD
Spanish-American War starts. Reports of atrocities by the Spaniards against Cubans compels the US to intervene.

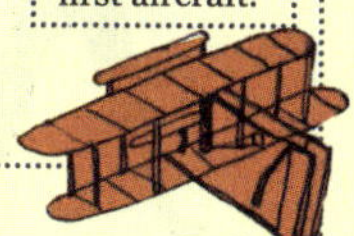

1903 AD
Orville and Wilbur Wright invent, build and fly the first aircraft.

1904 AD
Russo-Japanese war begins: Russians underestimate the modern Japanese fleet, which a year later destroys most of the already depleted Russian navy.

1905 AD
While working as a patent clerk, Albert Einstein publishes his theory of relativity and also states energy equals matter ($e = mc^2$). This is his 'miracle year'.

1860 AD · 1875 AD · 1900 AD

1912–13 AD
The Balkan Wars. Two short wars, fought over the possession of the European territories by the Ottoman Empire.

1914 AD
First World War, commonly known today as World War I, begins. Germany declares war on France and begins the war.

1917 AD
The US enters World War I against Germany. Around ten million military personnel die in the war.

1912 AD
The *Titanic*, which was touted to be the largest luxury liner to sail the open seas sinks with over 1,500 passengers.

1917 AD
The Russian Revolution destroys the Tsarist autocracy and leads to the creation of the Soviet Union.

1944 AD
On 6 June 1944, a date known ever since as D-Day, a mighty armada crosses from England to Normandy, France, and breaks the Nazi grip on western Europe which marks the end of Hitler's Third Reich.

1945 AD
On August 6 an atomic bomb drops on Hiroshima, Japan, killing an estimated 80,000 civilians. On August 9 another bomb is dropped on Nagasaki. On August 14, Japan surrenders and World War II is officially over. The UNO is established.

1916 AD
Easter Rising in Ireland.

1918 AD
At the 11th hour of the 11th day of the 11th month, World War I is officially over.

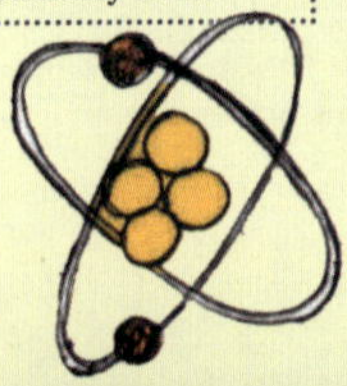

1919 AD
Ernest Rutherford splits an atom for the first time.

1928 AD
British bacteriologist, Sir Alexander Fleming, after many years of research on antibiotics, discovers penicillin.

1930 AD
Planet Pluto is discovered.

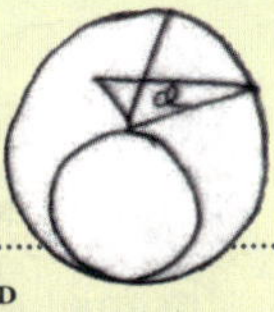

1942 AD
At the University of Chicago, Enrico Fermi conducts the first nuclear reaction and thereby demonstrates the controlled release of nuclear energy.

1939 AD
Hitler invades Poland on September 1. The British Commonwealth and France declare war on Germany, starting World War II.

1938 AD
Adolf Hitler, Chancellor of Germany, launches 'Kristallnacht', a night of terror visited upon the Jews by the Nazis. Hundreds of Jews are killed and the glass from synagogues and businesses is shattered onto the streets.

1950–53 AD
Post-World War II division of Korea leads to the Korean War in which China supports North Korea and the US lends support to South Korea.

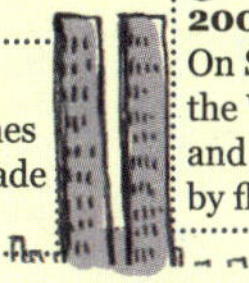

1957 AD
Sputnik I becomes the first man-made satellite.

1960 AD
On January 23, Jacques Piccard and Don Walsh travel to the bottom of the Marina Trench, the lowest point on the earth, in the Bathsyscaphe Trieste. Oddly, no one has ever gone back a second time.

1961 AD
On April 11, Yuri A Gagarin becomes the first human to reach space.

1991 AD
The Soviet Union dissolves, and with it the Cold War.

2001 AD
On September 11, terrorists attack the World Trade Centre in New York and the Pentagon in Washington DC by flying planes into their targets.

2003 AD
US and British forces invade Iraq. Saddam Hussein is caught, and eventually executed in 2006.

2011 AD
Osama bin Laden, the mastermind behind the 11 September 2001, terror attack in the US is killed near Islamabad.

2010 AD
Volcanic eruptions under a glacier in Iceland cause the biggest disruption of international air traffic in recent times.

2009 AD
Barack Hussein Obama becomes the first African-American president in the history of the US. He wins the Nobel Peace Prize.

950 AD ---- 1975 AD ---- 2000 AD ---- 2011 AD

1965–73 AD
Vietnam War.

1969 AD
On July 20, Neil Armstrong lands on the surface of the moon.

1982 AD
Falklands War fought between Argentina and the United Kingdom over the disputed Falkland Islands, South Georgia and South Sandwich Islands.

1989 AD
In November, the Berlin Wall that divided West Berlin from East Berlin is torn down. Berlin united for the first time since World War II.

1990 AD
Apartheid ends in South Africa. Nelson Mandela becomes the president of South Africa in the country's first free elections in 1994.

1990 AD
First Gulf War begins when the US attacks Iraq in response to Iraq's invasion of Kuwait.

1994 AD
Rwanda is engulfed in a huge and bloody civil war.

2004 AD
A huge earthquake near Indonesia on Christmas Day causes a tsunami in the Indian Ocean that kills thousands in Indonesia, Thailand, Sri Lanka, India and other countries.

2007 AD
Benazir Bhutto, the exiled former Pakistani prime minister, assassinated after her return to Pakistan.

2008 AD
Nepal abolishes monarchy. King Gyanendra vacates the Royal Palace and Nepal becomes a democracy.

2013 AD
A near-earth asteroid entered the earth's atmosphere, bursting over Chelyabinsk in Russia, producing many fragmentary meteorites, a powerful shock wave and damaging more than 7,200 buildings.

2013 AD
US scientists successfully created a cloned human embryo, using the same technique used for developing the cloned sheep in 1996.

2015 AD
Scientists have found water on Mars, the first indication that there is possibility of life on the red planet.

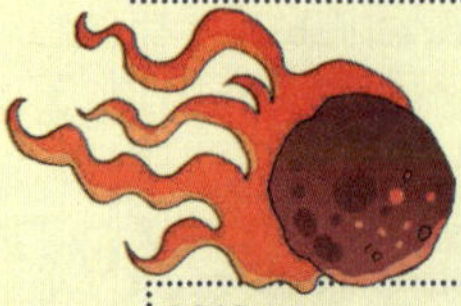

2012 AD
Higgs boson, the particle that is said to give matter mass, is found by scientists at CERN, the European laboratory for particle physics.

2014 AD
Malaysian Airlines flight MH370, carrying 239 people on board, disappeared over the South China Sea and MH17 was shot down over war-torn eastern Ukraine, killing all 298 on board.

2018 AD
NASA launched a spacecraft named the *Parker Solar Probe* on a daring mission to 'touch' the Sun. It will try to answer several questions about our nearest star.

2012 AD
Mars rover *Curiosity* finds landforms that point towards flowing liquid. Has there been life on Mars?

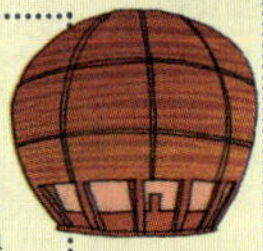

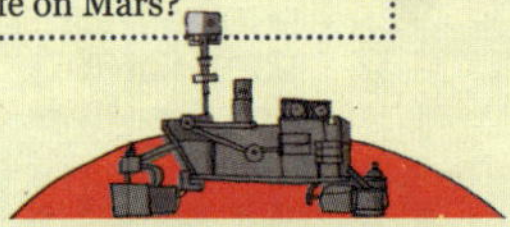

2012 AD — 2013 AD — 2015 AD — 2018 AD

2011–2012 AD
Arab Spring:
Pro-democracy protests overthrow military governments in Egypt and Yemen. In Bahrain and Syria, they challenge the monarchy and the establishment.

2016 AD
In a historic referendum, the United Kingdom voted to leave the European Union.

2017 AD
The Indian Space Research Organization (ISRO) created a space record after it successfully launched 104 satellites in orbit, in a single launch.

2012 AD
Indian American Sunita Williams takes the longest space walk for a woman.

2014 AD
The Ebola Virus, one of the most virulent viral diseases known to mankind, was detected in Guinea. The virus causes haemorrhagic fever and has resulted in over 11,325 deaths so far.

2019 AD
Numerous fires spread throughout the Amazon rainforest causing worldwide concern.

2023 AD
Israel-Hamas war begins, leading to heavy casualties in Palestine.

2020 AD
Covid-19 pandemic gripped the world since early December 2019.

2025 AD
Iran at war with Israel

2020 AD | 2022 AD | 2024 AD

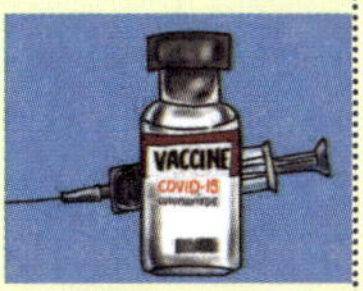

2021 AD
United Kingdom becomes the first country in the world to begin mass vaccination campaign with Pfizer-BioNTech Covid-19 vaccine.

2022 AD
Russia launches full-scale war on Ukraine.

2024 AD
A 7.6 earthquake struck Japan on 1 January 2024, causing major damage and over 200 deaths.

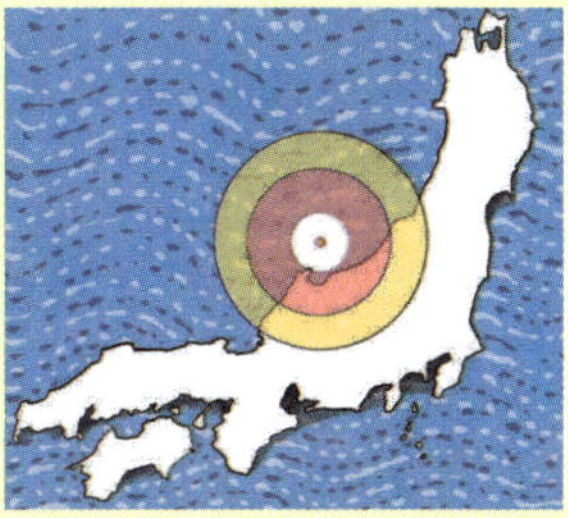

- Wonders of the World
- Top Ten Lists of the Biggest, Longest, Tallest and much more

Seven natural wonders of the world

Grand Canyon, Colorado River, Arizona
Rio de Janeiro Harbour, Brazil
Great Barrier Reef, Australia
Parícutin Volcano, Michoaćan, Mexico
Mount Everest, on the border of Tibet and Nepal
Victoria Falls, borders of Zambia and Zimbabwe
Northern Lights (Aurora Borealis), especially from northern Canada and Alaska

Ten man-made wonders of the world

Pyramids of Giza, Egypt
Great Wall of China, China
Taj Mahal, India
Machu Picchu, Peru
Temples of Bali, Indonesia
Angkor Wat, Cambodia
Forbidden City, China
Bagan Temples and Pagodas, Burma
Karnak Temple, Egypt
Teotihuacan, Mexico

Ten famous monuments in India

Taj Mahal, Uttar Pradesh
Qutub Minar, Delhi
Gateway of India, Maharashtra
Gwalior Fort, Madhya Pradesh
Statue of Unity, Gujarat
Khajuraho, Madhya Pradesh
Sanchi Stupa, Madhya Pradesh
Sun Temple, Odisha
Charminar, Hyderabad
Meenakshi Amman Temple, Tamil Nadu

Longest mountain ranges

Andes, South America - 7,242 km
Southern Great Escarpment, Africa - 5000 km
Rocky Mountains, North America - 4,800 km
Great Dividing Range, Australia - 3,621 km
Trans Antarctic, Antarctica - 3,541 km
Appalachian Mountains, North America - 3,200 km
Brazilian East Coast Range, South America - 2600 km
Himalayas/Karakoram/Hindu Kush, Asia - 2,500 km
Tien Shan, Asia - 2,500 km
Urals, Eurasia - 2,500 km

Longest rivers

Nile, Africa - 6,649 km
Amazon, South America - 6,437 km
Yangtze, Asia - 6,300 km
Huang He, Asia - 5,463 km
Parana, South America - 4,879 km
Zaire, Africa - 4,700 km
Irtysh, Asia - 4,248 km
Mississippi, North America - 3,781 km
Ob, Russia - 3,650 km
Yenisei, Asia - 3,487 km

Highest waterfalls

Angel, Churún River, Venezuela - Drop: 979 m
Tugela, Tugela River, South Africa - Drop: 948 m
Mattenbachfälle, Switzerland - Drop: 930 m
Tres Hermanas, Cutevirini River, Peru - Drop: 914 m
Olo'upena Falls, Hawaii - Drop: 900 m
Yumbilla Falls, Peru - Drop: 896 m
Skorga, Skorga (stream), Norway - 875 m
Vinnufallet, Vinnu River, Norway - Drop: 860 m
Pu'uka'oku Falls, Hawaii - Drop: 840 m
James Bruce Falls, Canada - Drop: 840 m

Largest islands

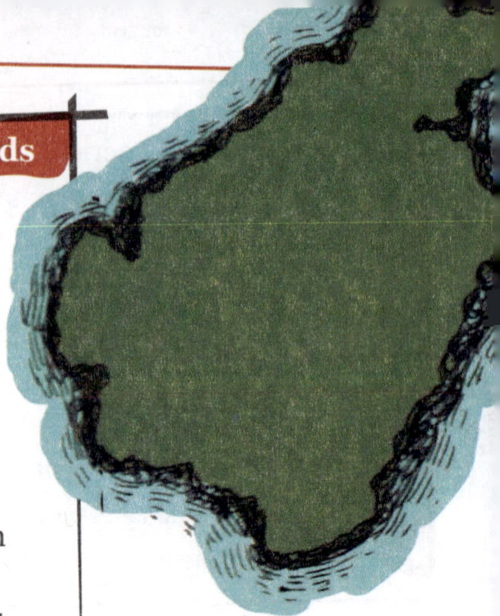

Greenland - 2,166,088 sq km
New Guinea - 8,21,400 sq km
Borneo - 7,48,168 sq km
Madagascar - 5,87,295 sq km
Baffin Island, Canada - 5,07,451 sq km
Sumatra, Indonesia - 4,43,066 sq km
Honshu, Japan - 2,27,898 sq km
Victoria Island, Canada - 2,17,291 sq km
Great Britain - 2,09,331 sq km
Ellesmere Island, Canada - 1,96,236 sq km

Largest freshwater lakes

Superior, Canada/US
Victoria, Kenya/Tanzania/Uganda
Huron, Canada/US
Michigan, US
Tanganyika, Burundi/Tanzania/
Democratic Republic of the Congo/Zambia
Baikal, Russia
Great Bear, Canada
Malawi, Tanzania/Mozambique/Malawi
Great Slave, Canada
Erie, Canada/US

Biggest deserts

Antarctic Desert, Antarctica - 14.2 million sq km
Arctic Desert, Alaska/Canada/Greenland/Iceland/
Norway/Sweden/Finland/Russia - 13.9 million sq km
Sahara Desert, North Africa - 9.1 million sq km
Arabian Desert, Southwest Asia - 2.6 million sq km
Gobi Desert, Central Asia - 1.3 million sq km
Kalahari Desert, Southern Africa - 0.93 million sq km
Patagonia Desert, South America - 0.67 million sq km
Great Victoria Desert, Australia - 0.64 million sq km
Syrian Desert, Middle East - 0.50 million sq km
Great Basin Desert, US - 0.49 million sq km

Largest oceans and seas

Pacific Ocean
Atlantic Ocean
Indian Ocean
Antarctic Ocean
Arctic Ocean
Coral Sea
Arabian Sea
South China Sea
Caribbean Sea
Mediterranean Sea

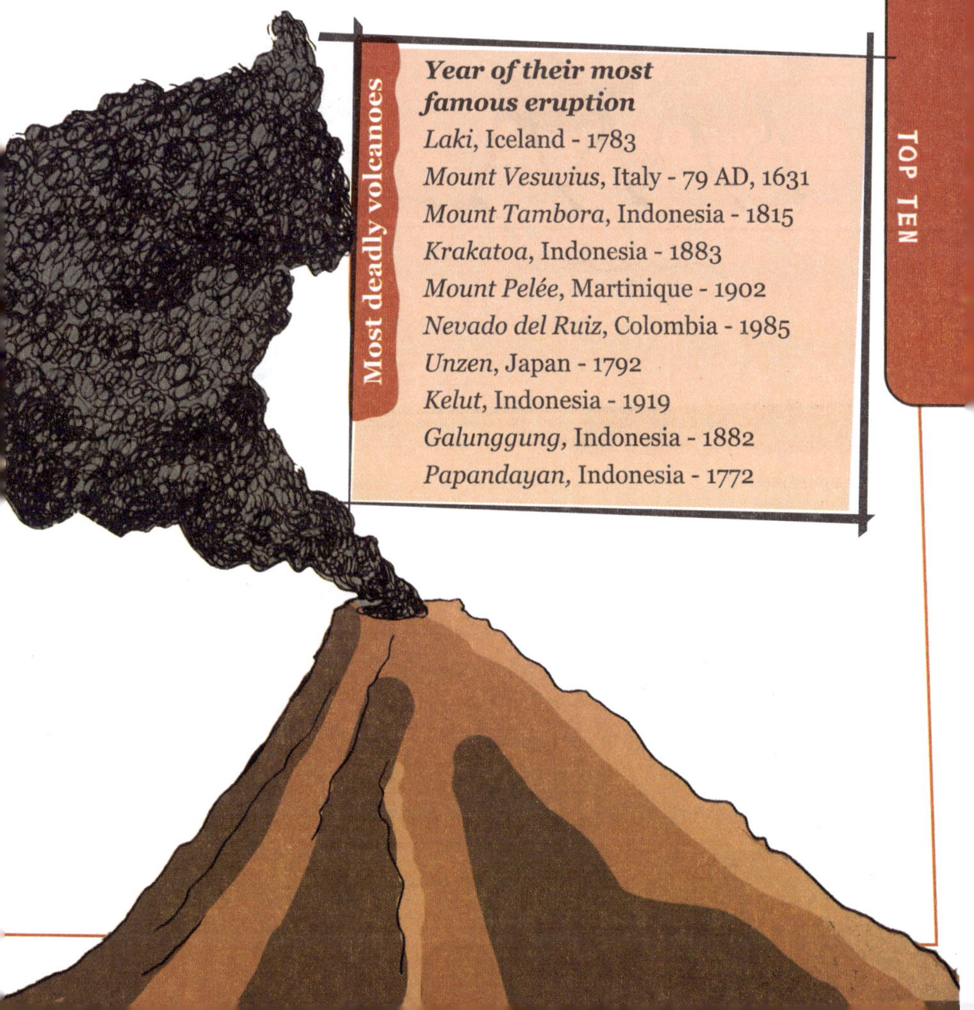

Most deadly volcanoes

Year of their most famous eruption

Laki, Iceland - 1783
Mount Vesuvius, Italy - 79 AD, 1631
Mount Tambora, Indonesia - 1815
Krakatoa, Indonesia - 1883
Mount Pelée, Martinique - 1902
Nevado del Ruiz, Colombia - 1985
Unzen, Japan - 1792
Kelut, Indonesia - 1919
Galunggung, Indonesia - 1882
Papandayan, Indonesia - 1772

Hottest places

Location	*Highest Temperature*
Death Valley, USA	56.7°C
Kebili, Tunisia	55°C
Ahvaz, Iran	54°C
Tirat Tsvi, Israel	54°C
Mitribah, Kuwait	53.9°C
Basra, Iraq	53.9°C
Turbat, Pakistan	53.7°C
Mohenjodaro, Pakistan	53.5°C
Mexicali, Mexico	52°C
Jeddah, Saudi Arabia	52°C

TOP TEN

Coldest places

Location	*Lowest Temperature*
Dome Fuji Ridge, East Antarctic Plateau	–93.2°C
Russia's Vostok Research Station, Antarctica	–89.2°C
Amundsen-Scott South Pole Station, Antarctica	–82.8°C
Dome Argus, Antarctic Plateau	–82.5°C
Denali, Alaska	–73.8°C
Verkhoyansk, Russia	–69.8°C
Klinck Research Station, Greenland	–69.4°C
Oymyakon, Russia	–67.8°C
North Ice, Greenland	–66.1°C
Snag, Canada	–62.7°C

Wettest places

Location	**Total Rainfall**
Mawsynram, Meghalaya, India	11,871 mm
Cherrapunji, Meghalaya, India	11,777 mm
Tutunendo, Colombia, South America	11,770 mm
Cropp River, New Zealand	11,516 mm
San Antonio de Ureca, Bioko Island, Equatorial Guinea	10,450 mm
Debundscha, Cameroon, Africa	10,299 mm
Big Bog, Maui, Hawaii	10,272 mm
Mt Waialeale, Kauai, Hawaii	9,763 mm
Kukui, Maui, Hawaii	9,293 mm
Emei Shan, Sichuan Province, China	8,169 mm

Places with the lowest population densities

People per square km

Greenland - 0.1
Falkland Islands (Malvinas) - 0.3
Mongolia - 2.2
Western Sahara - 2.2
Namibia - 3.2
Australia - 3.5
Iceland - 3.7
French Guiana - 3.9
Suriname - 4
Libya - 4

Places with the highest population densities

People per square km

Macao SAR - 21,608.7
Monaco - 17,360.4
Singapore - 8,430
Hong Kong - 7,139.7
Gibraltar - 3,274.3
Bahrain - 1,897.1
Maldives - 1,726.3
Malta - 1,677.3
Bangladesh - 1,342.1
Sint Maarten - 1,303.8

Richest countries

GDP (current US$ in billions)

United States - 30,510 billion
China - 19,230 billion
Germany - 4,740 billion
India - 4,190 billion
Japan - 4,180 billion
United Kingdom - 3,840 billion
France - 3,210 billion
Italy - 2,420 billion
Canada - 2,230 billion
Brazil - 2,120 billion

Most populous cities

Tokyo - 37,115,035
Delhi - 33,807,403
Shanghai - 29,867,918
Dhaka - 23,935,652
Sao Paulo - 22,806,704
Cairo - 22,623,874
Mexico City - 22,505,315
Beijing - 22,189,082
Mumbai - 21,673,149
Osaka - 18,967,459

Countries with the lowest HDI*

Somalia - 0.380
South Sudan - 0.381
Central African Republic - 0.387
Niger - 0.394 (tie)
Chad - 0.394 (tie)
Mali - 0.410
Burundi - 0.420
Yemen- 0.424
Burkina Faso - 0.438
Sierra Leone - 0.458

***HDI = Human Development Index**

Tallest buildings

Burj Khalifa, Dubai, UAE - 2,717 ft, 163 storeys

Merdeka 118, Kuala Lumpur, Malaysia - 2,227 ft, 118 storeys

Shanghai Tower, Shanghai, China - 2,073 ft, 128 storeys

Makkah Royal Clock, Mecca, Saudi Arabia - 1,972 ft, 120 storeys

Ping An Finance Centre, Shenzhen, China - 1,965 ft, 115 storeys

Lotte World Tower, Seoul, South Korea - 1,819 ft, 123 storeys

One World Trade Center, New York City, US - 1,776 ft, 94 storeys

Tianjin CTF Finance Centre, Tianjin, China - 1,740 ft, 98 storeys

CTF Finance Centre, Guangzhou, China - 1,739 ft, 111 storeys

CITIC Tower, Beijing, China - 1,731 ft, 109 storeys

Longest bridges

Danyang-Kunshan Grand Bridge, China	1,64,800 m
Changhua-Kaohsiung Viaduct, Taiwan	1,57,317 m
Cangde Grand Bridge, China	1,15,900 m
Tianjin Grand Bridge, China	1,13,700 m
Weinan Weihe Grand Bridge, China	79,732 m
Hong Kong-Zhuhai-Macao Bridge, Hong Kong	55,717 m
Bang Na Expressway, Thailand	54,000 m
Beijing Grand Bridge, China	48,153 m
Wuhan Metro Bridge, China	37, 000 m
Lake Pontchartrain Causeway, US	38,398 m

Countries with the highest HDI

Switzerland - 0.967

Norway - 0.966

Iceland - 0.959

Hong Kong - 0.956

Denmark - 0.952 (tie)

Sweden - 0.952 (tie)

Germany - 0.950 (tie)

Ireland - 0.950 (tie)

Singapore - 0.949

Australia - 0.946 (tie)

Languages

English - 1.5 billion speakers

Mandarin - 1.1 billion speakers

Hindi - 609.5 million speakers

Spanish - 559.1 million speakers

French - 309.8 million speakers

Standard Arabic - 274 million speakers

Bengali - 272.8 million

Portuguese - 263.6 million speakers

Russian - 255 million

Urdu - 231.7 million

Space Round-up
Science And Technology
The Internet
Gadgets
SCIENCE

SOLAR ACTIVITY PEAK THRILLS AURORAE WATCHERS GLOBALLY

In 2024-2025, the sun reached its peak of this 11-year cycle, with intense solar activity. In the second half of the year, a dazzling array of phenomena like sunspots, solar flares, prominences, and aurorae were visible. While several geomagnetic storms were recorded, a thrilling display of northern and southern lights coming all the way down to low latitudes was recorded, including at Hanle in Kashmir. This rare visibility at such southern locations amazed scientists and skywatchers alike. The event sparked renewed interest in space weather and its impact on satellites, power grids, and communication systems. Observatories across the world recorded unprecedented solar data during this period.

SUNITA WILLIAMS GETS STRANDED; SETS SPACEWALK RECORD

Sunita Williams flew to the International Space Station last year on a Boeing Starliner, becoming the first person to pilot it. However, upon docking at the ISS, the vehicle was found to have system malfunctions because of which Suni (as she is known to those around her) and crewmate Butch Wilmore couldn't not fly back after eight days as intended. Instead, they stayed in the ISS for over nine months until they returned to Earth in March.

SPACEWALK RECORDS

While she was aboard the ISS, Sunita Williams also completed her ninth spacewalk in January. She has now accumulated over 62 hours of spacewalk, setting the time record for a female astronaut and fourth overall for time spent spacewalking.

In December, two Chinese astronauts, Cai Xuzhe and Song Lingdong, completed the longest spacewalk ever done by humans—nine hours and six minutes. They worked in space outside China's space station Tiangong, performing activities like installation of space debris protection devices and inspection of the facilities and equipment.

The first ever commercial spacewalk was also conducted in September with the Polaris Dawn mission.

FIRST SUCCESSFUL PRIVATE LANDER ON THE MOON

The American company Firefly Aerospace successfully landed its robot on the moon in March this year, becoming the first commercial company to successfully do so. It was a part of NASA's Commercial Lunar Payload Services program, which aims to send private robotic rovers to the moon to scout the surface.

The mission functioned for one lunar day or 15 Earth days, after which it was officially declared ended.

TWO MISSIONS LAUNCH TO BEYOND MARS

In October, both the European Space Agency (ESA) and the American NASA launched spacecraft to fly beyond Mars. ESA's Hera spacecraft will arrive at the asteroid Didymos in 2026 to inspect the effects of the DART mission which collided into the asteroid's moon to change its orbit last year. NASA's Europa Clipper is presently en route to Jupiter's orbit, from where it will conduct fly-bys and study the icy moon Europa.

CLOSEST FLY-BY OF A PLANET AT MERCURY

The BepiColombo mission, a joint mission between ESA and Japan's JAXA, performed the closest fly-by of a planet in September. The spacecraft flew by Mercury, coming a mere 165 km from its surface. The distance is comparable to the record for the lowest orbiting satellite around earth, Japan's Tsubame or Super Low Altitude Test Satellite, which orbited at 167 km in 2017-2019. For comparison, the distance between the earth to the moon is over 380,000 km. During the fly-by, BepiColombo captured high-resolution images of Mercury's surface and collected crucial data on its magnetic field. This close approach also helped refine the spacecraft's trajectory as it prepares to enter Mercury's orbit in 2025. Scientists hope the mission will reveal more about the planet's mysterious iron-rich core and extreme temperature variations.

NEPTUNE'S COLOUR IS UPDATED

The highest resolution pictures available today of Neptune were taken in 1989 when the Voyager 2 mission flew by it, giving the first and only close-up images of the planet we have. After the image was processed to show features visible on the surface, NASA scientists released it, depicting the planet to be a deep, bright blue color. This was a false color image, but is widely used to show Neptune in media all around us. At the same time, Uranus's image was depicted with a pale blue color.

Now, scientists have reanalyzed the Neptune raw data from Voyager 2 and have updated the planet's color to resemble Uranus's pale, hazy blue.

SATURN DOUBLES ITS MOON COUNT

Early this year, astronomers using the Canada-France-Hawaii Telescope announced the discovery of a whopping 128 new moons orbiting around Saturn. All the moons are irregularly shaped, and are possibly fragments of multiple larger rocks that broke up in the past. They are all merely 2-4 km wide. But with now a total of 274, Saturn has more natural satellites than the rest of the seven planets combined. Many of these moons follow distant, tilted, and eccentric orbits, suggesting they were likely captured objects rather than ones formed with the planet. This discovery provides vital clues about Saturn's dynamic past and the chaotic history of its outer moon system. It also opens new avenues to study how moons form and evolve in gas giant systems.

ISRO SUCCESSFULLY PERFORMS TWIN DOCKING WITH SPADEX

The Indian Space Research Organisation (ISRO) launched its test technology to demonstrate the ability to rendezvous, dock, and perform formation flying by satellites in December of last year. The Space Docking Experiment or SpaDeX mission consisted of two satellites that were launched together and released into two different orbits.

Subsequently, the two spacecrafts carried out manouvers to come close together and dock with each other, and then undock successfully. This makes India the fourth country after USA, Russia (USSR) and China to have achieved docking in space.

AXIOM'S MISSION WITH INDIAN GAGANYATRI SHUBHANSHU SHUKLA

The first of India's new astronaut corps, Shubhanshu Shukla, flew to space on a private crewed commercial mission aboard the Axiom-4 in June, becoming the first Indian astronaut to visit the ISS. He flew as a pilot, and was accompanied by astronauts from USA, Poland, and Hungary. For India, Poland, and Hungary, this mission hosted the second astronaut to fly from the country with the first having all been in a USSR mission. The mission carries seven microgravity experiments from India and are managed by ISRO, including studying muscle regeneration, food crop yield, reproduction of microscopic animals and more.

By **SANDHYA RAMESH**

WORLD'S FIRST LUNG CANCER VACCINE

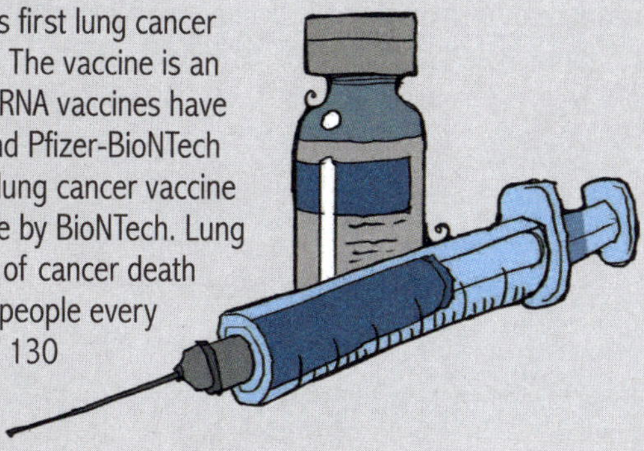

In August, the trials for the world's first lung cancer vaccine began in seven countries. The vaccine is an mRNA one, and so far, only two mRNA vaccines have been approved—the Moderna and Pfizer-BioNTech Covid vaccines. The cutting-edge lung cancer vaccine is called BNT116 and is also made by BioNTech. Lung cancer today is the leading cause of cancer death worldwide, killing over 1.5 million people every year. After initial trials with around 130 lung cancer patients in UK, USA, Hungary, Poland, Germany, Spain, and Turkey, the vaccine will progress to the next round of trials with more volunteers.

FIVE PEOPLE SEE IMPOSSIBLE NEW COLOR

In an experiment that involved shooting precise and controlled lasers into the eye, participants reported seeing a brand-new color outside of the visible spectrum to human eyes. Cells called cones in the eye detect color and are of three types—S, L, and M. When light activates M cones, it also activates one of S or L cones, thus preventing M cones from activating alone. The new technique allows to deliver light only to M cones and the brand-new shade of color visible to the study participants was described as an extremely highly saturated aquamarine.

E-TASTE TECHNOLOGY IS BORN

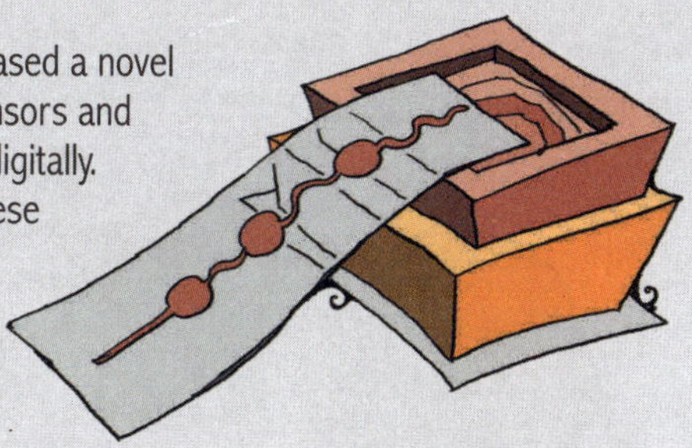

Engineers at Ohio State University released a novel technology called e-Taste that uses sensors and chemical dispensers to simulate taste digitally. The interface uses a combination of these sensors and wireless dispensors to directly fit in the mouth. It recognizes molecules that represent the basic tastes of sweet, salty, sour, bitter, and umami. The prototype device was able to vary the intensities of various flavours safely using an interface directly into the mouth fitted with a small electromagnetic pump. This could pave the way for immersive applications in virtual reality, digital dining, and even healthcare. It also opens up possibilities for taste experiences without actual food consumption, which could benefit dietary control or therapeutic interventions.

ICELAND VOLCANOES ERUPT AGAIN AND AGAIN, AND AGAIN!

Eruptions in the Grindavik region of Iceland began in December of 2023 as lava began to flow in the evacuated area. However, it did not stop, and eruptions occurred in the Sundhnukur volcano in the months of January, February, March, May, August, and November of last year, making a total of seven volcanic eruptions from the same volcano in one year. Eruptions continue in 2025, with another one having occurred in April of this year. The volcano began spewing molten rock after a series of earthquakes in November 2023, leading to significant damage to both towns as well as existing geological landscape. The eruptions changed magma pathways underground, and some volcanologists believe these eruptions could continue for months or even years.

ALCHEMY COMES TO LIFE INSIDE CERN

Scientists working on the ALICE (A Large Ion Collider Experiment) at CERN's Large Hadron Collider (LHC) have announced the detection of transmutation of lead into gold inside the collider. Extremely high energy movement of lead nuclei resulting in near-miss collisions generated intense electromagnetic fields that could knock out protons from the lead atom and transform it into a gold nucleus. However, these continue travelling at high speeds and hit the walls of the reactor, immediately breaking up into protons and neutrons.

ELEPHANTS CALL THEIR RELATIVES BY NAME

Scientists studying elephants in Africa have analysed their sound patterns when communicating with each other, and concluded that elephants might be using specific sound patterns to call an individual elephant, similar to names humans have for each other. The team captured more than 450 unique calls made by the various elephants in the experiment, and noticed a call-and-response system where various animals used the same pattern of sound to call the same elephant. Parrots and dolphins are known to address specific individuals by imitating the sounds they make, but elephants are now the only other species apart from humans that have names or a unique identifying sound for each individual.

SMALLEST QUANTUM COMPUTER MADE UP OF ONE PHOTON

Taiwanese engineers and physicists built the world's smallest quantum computer which is the size of a desktop PC and is powered by a single photon. The technology demonstration machine uses photons as alternative to supercomputing qubits or basic units, and also operates at room temperature. The machine can perform complete but basic mathematical operations such as prime number factorization. This marks a major step towards making quantum computing more accessible and practical for everyday use. Its compact size and low power requirement could revolutionize how we integrate quantum processors into future technologies.

CHINA REFUELS THORIUM REACTOR WHILE IT IS ON

China has been able to refuel a thorium reactor in the Gobi desert without shutting it down during the process—a world first. The development indicates great strides in use of safe and efficient nuclear power. Thorium reactors use thorium as fuel instead of the traditional uranium used by reactors world over, offering advantages such as availability, less nuclear waste, less chances of being used in bombs, more efficiency, and safer mining. While India has the largest supply of thorium in the world, there is still only one reactor in the country that produces moderate power—the Kalpakkam Mini reactor or KAMINI.

SEE-IN-THE-DARK INFRARED CONTACT LENSES

A team in China has created infrared contact lenses which allow wearers to see in the dark for the first time. Additionally, since infrared passes through skin, the lenses make people see even with their eyes closed. The lens contains tiny particles that absorb infared light and convert it to visible wavelengths, and operate in various wavelengths in the near-infrared region of the spectrum. This breakthrough could lead to revolutionary applications in security, rescue operations, and medical diagnostics. Soldiers, firefighters, or emergency responders could use them in low-light or smoke-filled environments. The ability to perceive through obstacles like skin may also open new doors for non-invasive health monitoring. Unlike traditional night vision gear, these lenses are compact and hands-free. Researchers are now working to ensure safety, comfort, and long-term wearability for real-world use.

2024 BECOMES FIRST YEAR TO BREACH 1.5°C PARIS AGREEMENT LIMIT

The last few years have consistently broken temperature records, with 2024 being the hottest ever year on record. Global average temperatures also crossed the 1.5°C above pre-industrial age thresholds for the first time, breaching the lower limit set in the Paris Agreement goals of 2015 to limit global heating. The rate of acceleration of temperature increase spells bad news for the world, and new research warns that the 2°C limit above pre-industrial temperatures will be crossed as early as 2050.

By **SANDHYA RAMESH**

WORLD'S FIRST DOUBLE FOLDING PHONE

Huawei released the Mate XT, the world's first phone that folds on the screen not only once, but twice. The triple-fold phone is sleek and slim with four cameras and three batteries. It launched last year in China and is now available globally. The phone runs on Huawei's Harmony OS, and comes with reverse charging, which allows users to charge other devices from the phone. It also comes with a kickstand case and foldable keyboard. When fully unfolded, the screen expands into a small tablet-sized display, ideal for productivity and media consumption. Despite its complex folding mechanism, the Mate XT is remarkably durable, with reinforced hinges tested for thousands of folds. Its multitasking features lets users run multiple apps simultaneously across different panels. Huawei aims to redefine mobile versatility with this device, blurring the lines between phones, tablets, and laptops.

LENOVO ROLLABLE LAPTOP

Lenovo introduced the ThinkBook Plus Gen 6, the world's first laptop that has a flexible OLED screen that rolls out from the edge. The screen then opens up straight from the bottom, extending upwards into a long rectangular screen from the keyboard. This rollable display transforms the device from a compact laptop into a taller, scroll-like format, ideal for reading, coding, or multitasking with vertical apps. The innovative mechanism is motorized and can expand the screen at the touch of a button. Despite its flexibility, the screen maintains high resolution and brightness, offering a seamless viewing experience. Lenovo designed the hinge and rolling mechanism to withstand thousands of cycles without damage. The concept also points toward a future where foldable and rollable displays become mainstream in portable devices. Battery life and performance remain comparable to traditional laptops, making it a practical innovation rather than just a futuristic prototype.

HI-TECH TINY DRONE

The veteran brand DJI has introduced a mini drone that can fit in the palm of one's hand for beginner drone photography. The compact drone, called DJI Neo, looks like a small robotic bird with four wings and has a built-in 4K camera that can store 40 minutes of footage. It can take off from your hand and fly for about 18 minutes between charges. Despite its size, it includes intelligent flight modes like auto-tracking, one-tap cinematic shots, and obstacle avoidance. The drone connects easily to a smartphone app for live viewing and quick editing. Its lightweight design makes it perfect for travel, outdoor adventures, or even indoor practice. DJI has aimed this model at hobbyists, content creators, and students looking to explore aerial photography without the bulk or complexity of larger drones.

A VISUAL EAR-CLEANER

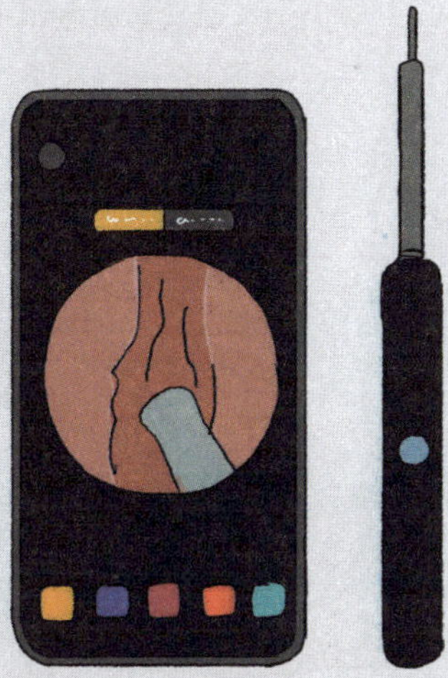

It might look like a pair of sophisticated wireless headphones, but Bebird's EarSight Flow is a medical device. Upon wearing, the 'headphones' actually begin cleaning your ear and removes buildup of ear wax. In fact, it projects the live video of the entire cleaning process on to your phone or a screen while doing so.

The cleaning is done through water, which is filled up into the device. The EarSight Flow warms up the water and gently shoots it into the ear canal to clean it.

ANKER SOLAR UMBRELLA

Surprisingly, only for the first time, umbrellas now might carry solar cells that can power other gadgets. Anker launched its Solix Solar Umbrella that looks like a regular outdoor umbrella. However, the cells on top and its USB-C connectivity helps power gadgets for those sitting underneath it. It's designed for patios, cafes, and outdoor workspaces, offering sustainable energy while providing shade. The umbrella can charge phones, tablets, and even small laptops during sunny hours. This innovation blends comfort and clean energy in an everyday setting.

COLOUR KINDLE

While digital readers have been pervasive in the market for a few years now, the standout has continued to be Amazon's Kindle. Until 2024, the Kindle e-book reader was available only in black and white. However, this year, the tech giant has released one with the first 'colour e-ink' display, allowing for comics and graphic novels to also be read on the reader in their original, vivid format. The new display retains Kindle's signature glare-free readability while adding a whole new visual dimension to the experience. It also supports subtle color variations without compromizing battery life. This marks a major leap for digital reading, especially for visual content like textbooks, cookbooks, and children's books.

By **SANDHYA RAMESH**

ALL MY SAVINGS ARE GONE!

India has the dubious distinction of being the source of one of the highest numbers of online scams in the world. In addition to it being a massive blow to the country's reputation across the globe, some of the highest number of victims of online scams are Indians themselves, especially senior citizens and those who are not so tech savvy.

In addition to many awareness campaigns and messages, the government has taken a number of steps to prevent such online attacks, despite which such cases keep growing by the day. As some methods of scamming get outed and become outdated, new methods are invented to rid people of their money.

In addition to financial loss, victims have reported severe mental strain that can manifest for years. As all financial interfaces get integrated into the smartphone, the risk of getting scammed is very high despite several checks and measures being in place.

GLOBAL SHUTDOWN? NEITHER SIMPSONS NOR TRUMP

Sometimes, the Internet itself is in the news for weird reasons. In January 2025, there was a rumour doing the rounds claiming that the entirety of the global Internet would shut down on 16 January, according to a prediction made in the American TV show *The Simpsons*. The rumour itself was false. No such prediction was made in any episode and the video was fake and edited. Also, according to the rumour, the global shutdown was to coincide with the inauguration of Donald Trump as president of USA, which actually took place on 20 January. So much for believing whatever is said on the Internet, even if it concerns the Internet itself!

...AND HEADING FOR THE STARS

Internet users in India have more to celebrate as satellite Internet services are also expected to grow in a big way. In addition to the Bharti Airtel–Eutelsat OneWeb and Reliance Jio–SES ventures, Elon Musk's Starlink has also received permission to operate in India. There's more! An Indian private company, Ananth Tech, is expected to launch satellite broadband services by 2028, while Vodafone Idea (Vi) is partnering with AST SpaceMobile to provide satellite broadband in remote areas. The age of satellite Internet has truly arrived in India!

GROWING BY LEAPS AND BOUNDS...

A report from the Internet and Mobile Association of India (IAMAI) and KANTAR predicted India's Internet user base to cross 900 million by 2025. This growth is driven by two factors: The rise of Indian language content, such as Tamil, Telugu, Malayalam, Hindi and Bengali, and greater penetration in rural areas. According to the report, the rural population accounted for 55 per cent of the country's Internet user base in 2024. India already has the second highest number of Internet users in the world after China, although the number of average users is still not very high when compared to developed western or far eastern nations. With Internet service providers offering attractive plans, greater availability of cheaper handsets, and newer generations more technologically aware, this number is only expected to rise.

GROUNDED

But all is not so bright and shiny. India also has the dubious distinction of being the number one country to block access to the Internet in the first half of 2025, in a report by virtual private network (VPN) provider Surfshark tracking 10 countries that restricted Internet access in that period. In addition to affecting information access and communication, such blockages cause great losses in both the private and public sectors, especially at a time when the country is moving towards a greater reduction of the digital divide.

BUT WAIT!

A massive global Internet outage actually did take place, not on 16 January, but on 12 June. Sure, it was not predicted by any TV series, but a number of services, including Google, Spotify, Discord, Cloudflare and many others stopped working for a few hours due to a bug in Google's cloud services.

WAR IS NO JOKE!

With major conflicts going on in the world, especially in Russia-Ukraine and also in West Asia, it is to be expected that the Internet and social media would be harnessed and weaponized for propaganda and disinformation purposes. Even during the brief Operation Sindoor in the aftermath of the deadly terrorist attacks in Pahalgam, there was a profusion of fake news, some of which downright ludicrous and comical, from trolls on all sides. As a result, for a long time during the fog of war, few people actually knew the truth behind what actually was taking place.

REAL OR FAKE? YOU DECIDE!

It was around two years ago that artificial intelligence (AI) started becoming a buzzword. Many applications today are powered by AI without us even knowing. AI has made life easier in many professions, and social media apps can also not do without it. Even game development has started incorporating AI into it, with levels or character dialogues being generated by it with no human intervention.

One area where the use of AI has been contentious is art. The ethics and legality of training a model on copyrighted artwork has often been debated. The art and illustration community has been vocal in its protests against AI, and have been shaming those who use it. On the other side of the debate are those who argue that AI is just like any other tool, and artists and illustrators will only benefit from it in the long run.

One aspect of AI images that is beyond any debate, however, is its use in creating fake 'photos' or 'videos' of real persons or events, which are then used to spread fake news or to blackmail. Social media today is filled with such photos and videos, and users will have to be discerning enough to differentiate the real from the fake.

HENCE, META PLANS

Facebook parent company Meta has announced plans of creating a new division called Meta Superintelligence Labs (MSL). Meta CEO Mark Zuckerberg has said that as AI progresses at a great pace, and the time has come to develop a powerful superintelligence that is integrated into personal uses such as Meta's social and messaging platforms. Apple is also planning to utilize third-party advanced AI models from Anthropic and OpenAI to develop its customized large language models (LLM) for its cloud infrastructure and Siri.

By SOURAV DUTTA

Environment

ENVIRONMENT NEWS

GLOBAL WILDLIFE POPULATION DECLINED BY NEARLY THREE-QUARTERS

In the last 50 years, the global wildlife population declined by 73 per cent according to a World Wildlife Fund (WWF) report. Between 1970 and 2020, freshwater populations were hit the hardest, shrinking by 85 per cent. Terrestrial populations fell by 69 per cent, and marine populations dropped by 56 per cent during the same period. Across the world, Latin America and the Caribbean saw the most significant decline (95 per cent), followed by 76 per cent in Africa and 60 per cent in Asia-Pacific. Meanwhile, the decline in Europe, Central Asia and North America was less than 40 per cent. The biggest threat to wildlife is habitat degradation and loss caused by human food production. Other major threats include overexploitation, invasive species, and diseases. Climate change was another critical threat linked to population decline in Latin America and the Caribbean, while pollution has had the greatest impact in North America, Asia, and the Pacific.

Declines in wildlife populations can signal increasing extinction risk and loss of healthy ecosystems. When the number of a certain species becomes too low, they may fail to carry out their usual role within the ecosystem—whether that is seed dispersal, pollination, grazing, nutrient cycling, or the many other processes that keep ecosystems functioning. Improved conservation efforts, along with an accelerated transformation to sustainable food production and clean energy, can help slow down these declines. Additionally, we should change our financial systems to support businesses and activities that help meet global goals for nature, climate, and sustainable development.

GLACIERS ARE MELTING FASTER THAN EVER

The world's glaciers have lost over 6,500 billion tonnes of ice–nearly 5 per cent of their ice–since 2000, accelerating global sea-level rise. The pace of melting increased by 36 per cent between 2012 and 2023 compared to the first decade of the study period. This is the most comprehensive scientific analysis on the matter so far, combining over 230 regional estimates from thirty-five research teams across the world. Climate change causes glacier melting, as global temperatures continue to rise due to human activities, mainly burning fossil fuels for energy.

Glaciers lost an average mass of approximately 273 billion tonnes each year between 2000 and 2023. To put this into perspective, this corresponds to the water consumption of the entire global population in thirty years, assuming each person consumes 3 litres per person. Glacier ice is the largest reservoir of the world's freshwater. If they melted entirely, the global sea level would rise by 32 centimetres.

Since 2000, the loss of glacial ice has added 18 millimetres (mm) to global sea levels. Rising sea levels can submerge important cities, damage critical infrastructure, displace millions of people and threaten food security.

OVER 50 PER CENT OF INDIAN DISTRICTS AT HIGH HEAT RISK, HOTTER YEARS AHEAD WORLDWIDE

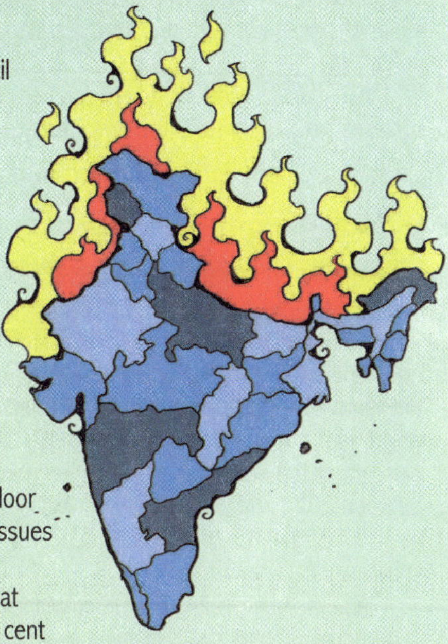

India faces serious risks from rising temperatures. A recent study by the Council on Energy, Environment and Water (CEEW) shows that 57 per cent of Indian districts, which are home to over 75 per cent of the population, are at high to very high heat risk. This heat isn't just a daytime issue anymore. Nearly 70 per cent of districts have experienced more than five unusually warm nights a year from 2012 to 2022. Warmer nights make it hard for people to cool down and recover from daytime heat, which can lead to serious health problems. Those most at risk include the elderly, outdoor workers, children, and people with health issues like hypertension and diabetes.

India urgently needs to improve its heat action preparedness as there is an 80 per cent probability that at least one of the next five years (2025-2029) will be hotter than 2024, the hottest year on record, according to the World Meteorological Organisation (WMO). There is also an 86 per cent chance that at least one year will exceed 1.5°C above the pre-industrial level. This is significant as the current level of warming is already causing extreme heatwaves, heavy rainfall, severe droughts, melting ice sheets, and rising sea levels.

The South Asian region will continue to receive heavier rainfall from 2025 to 2029. According to another CEEW study, the majority of India is already seeing a surge in southwest monsoon rainfall, with 55 per cent of sub-districts seeing a significant increase of over 10 per cent in the last decade. The increased rainfall frequently comes in short bursts of heavy rainfall, which often leads to flash floods.

THE CLIMATE COST OF WARS IN UKRAINE AND GAZA

The war with Russia has become Ukraine's largest source of carbon emissions. Of the estimated 230 metric tons of carbon dioxide equivalent (MtCO2e), 36 per cent is directly from warfare and 27 per cent from rebuilding what was destroyed. Wildfires were the third largest contributor, releasing nearly 46 million tonnes of greenhouse gases (GHG) from war-driven landscape fires alone. That's 20 to 25 times more than Ukraine's pre-war average. The summer of 2024 was drier than usual in Ukraine and helped fuel these fires. Most fires occurred near the front lines and border areas, where battles raged on. Explosions, shelling, and missile strikes can ignite vegetation instantly.

The long-term climate cost of the war in Gaza could add up to over 31 million tonnes of carbon dioxide equivalent (tCO2e). This is more than the combined 2023 annual GHG emissions by Costa Rica and Estonia. Most of the emissions, nearly 29 million tonnes, are expected to be from the reconstruction of Gaza post-war. Direct emissions from war activities have resulted in around 1.9 million tonnes of emissions so far.

War involves widespread environmental destruction, not just emissions. It releases toxic chemicals, destroys infrastructure, pollutes soil, air, and water resources, and accelerates climate and environmental disasters.

GOOD NEWS

RENEWABLES BOOM HELPS WORLD SURPASS 40 PER CENT CLEAN POWER

The world generated over 40 per cent of its electricity without burning fossil fuels last year, according to a new study. This is significant as heatwaves, AI, and data centres are leading to a surge in power demand. Solar power generation, which doubled in the last two years, is driving the clean electricity transition. The total solar generation worldwide is now enough to power India. China led the way, adding more than 50 per cent of the global increase in solar power. India also doubled its solar capacity between 2023 and 2024. The EU increased its solar generation twofold in the three years leading up to 2024, and produced 71 per cent of its electricity from clean sources, including nuclear.

In September 2024, The UK ended its 142-year-long coal-fired electricity generation when its last remaining coal power plant at Ratcliffe-on-Soar in Nottinghamshire ended operations. This country was home to the world's first coal-fired power station, the Holborn Viaduct, which began generating electricity in 1882. Coal power made up 40 per cent of the UK's electricity as recently as 2012. The rise of cheap renewables and high carbon taxes led the UK to become the first major economy to exit coal power.

Investments in low-carbon energy rose by 11 per cent in 2024, reaching a record US$ 2.1 trillion in 2024. China was the largest market for investments. However, estimates suggest that the world needs to invest about US$ 5.6 trillion annually from 2025 to 2030 to meet the net-zero emissions target by 2050.

WORLD'S LARGEST CORAL DISCOVERED IN THE PACIFIC OCEAN

In 2024, scientists discovered the world's largest coral reef near the Solomon Islands in the Pacific Ocean. It is three times larger than any previously discovered coral. The mega coral, 32 metres long and 34 metres wide, is about the size of two basketball courts and could be about 300 years old. It is so large that it can be seen from space. Unlike a reef, which is made up of many coral colonies, this is a single gigantic coral made of tiny creatures called coral polyps. A group of scientists working from the Pristine Seas research vessel found the coral. They initially thought it was part of a shipwreck because of its size until they took a closer look.

Coral reefs cover only 1 per cent of the world's oceans, but provide habitat for at least 25 per cent of marine life. Many reef species are still unknown. Coral reefs play a critical role in protecting coastlines from erosion, and support the livelihoods of millions through tourism and fishing. However, climate change has been warming oceans and harming corals. Scientists fear the reefs have reached a critical point, with the world in the midst of the largest coral bleaching event on record—the fourth mass coral bleaching event in history.

INDIA DRAFTS EMISSIONS TARGETS FOR INDUSTRY

The Ministry of Environment, Forests and Climate Change (MoEFCC) has released a draft notification that sets greenhouse gas (GHG) emissions intensity targets for high-emitting industries. This includes 282 industrial units across four sectors: aluminium, cement, chlor-alkali, and pulp and paper. The cement sector, responsible for 5.8 per cent of India's carbon emissions, has the most industries (186) with targets. Other industries such as fertilizers, iron, steel, petrochemicals, petroleum refineries and the power sector, the largest emitter, have not been included yet.

The targets are a step towards finalizing India's first compliance-based carbon market, expected to launch in 2026. The notification requires the listed industrial units to meet the targets. If a unit reduces emissions beyond the given target, it can generate credits and sell them in the carbon market. Units that struggle to cut emissions can meet their goals by purchasing these credits. Failure to meet targets would mean payment of a fine in the form of environmental compensation to the Central Pollution Control Board (CPCB).

The targets are designed to push industries towards a low-carbon growth trajectory using sustainable technologies and practices. For instance, a cement plant can cut emissions by adopting cleaner and greener processes at different stages of production. It can switch from coal to biomass and use cleaner, more energy-efficient kilns. These targets are part of India's broader strategy to reduce its GHG emission intensity by 45 per cent by 2030, compared to 2005 levels, and align with the country's commitments to reduce emissions under the Paris Agreement.

INDIA DOUBLES TIGER POPULATION IN A DECADE

India's tiger population has grown to over 3600, which means the country is home to nearly 75 per cent of the world's tigers. The population doubled between 2006 and 2018 as a result of a scientific strategy combined with political support and community buy-in. Tiger populations are usually threatened by habitat destruction, infrastructure projects like roads, railways, power transmission lines, and human settlements, poaching, armed conflict and human-wildlife conflict.

In response to the Global Tiger Recovery Programme, launched in 2010, India aimed to double its tiger population by 2022. Communities were relocated from national parks and sanctuaries to create human-free zones that now support 85 per cent of India's breeding tigers. The country also created habitat corridors and adopted land-use practices that reduce conflict between humans and tigers, enabling them to coexist with over 66 million people.

However, the level of co-existence varies. Tigers share land with people at high densities in wealthier states like Madhya Pradesh, Maharashtra, Uttarakhand, and Karnataka, where people benefit from tiger-related tourism and receive government compensation for conflict-related losses. In other regions like Odisha, Jharkhand, Chhattisgarh, and parts of northeastern India, where poaching and bushmeat eating are prevalent, tigers are either absent or extinct.

By **MILAN GEORGE JACOB**

Entertainment

- ☑ Cinema
- ☑ Art
- ☑ Theatre
- ☑ Indian Dance and Music
- ☑ Music
- ☑ Television
- ☑ Books

PAYAL KAPADIA'S GLOBAL DOMINATION

Filmmaker Payal Kapadia's big win at the Cannes 2024 for her film *All We Imagine As Light* was just the beginning of all the global recognition that has come her way in the past year. Since then, Payal and her film has earned laurels at various film festivals and awards. Payal even secured a Best Director nomination at the 2025 Golden Globes for the film, even though the film was not India's official entry at the awards. She lost the award to Brady Corbet for *The Brutalist*. The film also earned a BAFTA Award for Best Film Not in the English Language.

Payal's rise in world cinema has been meteoric ever since her Cannes win. She also served as a jury member at the Cannes Film Festival 2025.

OSCAR RACE: 'LAAPATAA LADIES' VS 'ALL WE IMAGINE AS LIGHT'

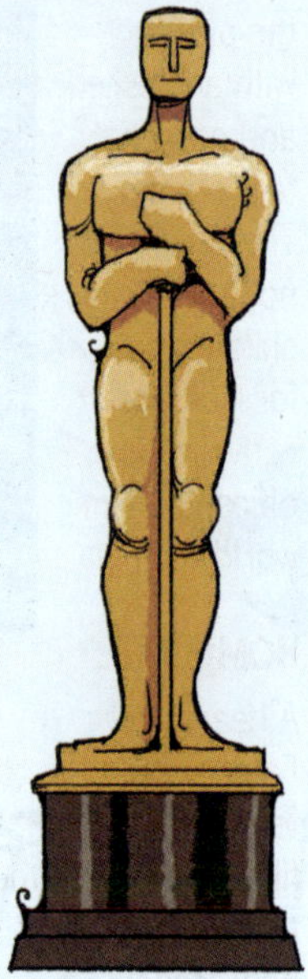

Kian Rao's *Laapataa Ladies* and *All We Imagine As Light* were the finest that Indian cinema produced in 2024. Both films earned critical praise. But only one could be chosen to represent India at the international stage. While cinema fans felt Payal's film had better chances of winning at various International film awards, it was *Laapataa Ladies* that was selected as India's official entry to the Oscars 2025 in the Best International Film category. Rao's film was a heartwarming story about two lost brides, who end up finding themselves and rediscovering their identity even as their families try desperately to look for them. While the film represented India and also delivered a positive message on women empowerment, many felt Kapadia stood a bigger chance at getting an Oscar nomination as the film had already earned a Grand Prix at Cannes 2024. Amid uproar and heated discussions on which film stood a better chance, *Laapataa Ladies* launched an extensive campaign in the US ahead of the Oscar awards. But despite the film's content and producer Aamir Khan and filmmaker Alfonso Curon backing it, *Laapataa Ladies* could not impress the Oscar jury and did not make it to the final nomination list.

ALEC BALDWIN ACQUITTED

Nearly two and a half years after he first faced charges of involuntary manslaughter on the sets of the movie *Rust*, which led to the death of the film's cinematographer Halyna Hutchins, actor Alec Baldwin could breathe a sigh of relief after a US judge dismissed the case against him. The judge found the state had withheld evidence on how live rounds ended up on a film set in the first place. The case was dismissed due to the misconduct of the police and prosecutors in withholding evidence from the defence in the 2021 incident. The judge also stated that the case could not be refiled. The judgment marked the end of criminal culpability for Baldwin after a nearly three-year-long ordeal. On the fateful day Baldwin was pointing a gun at Hutchins and rehearsing lines when the revolver went off, killing the cinematographer and wounding director Joel Souza. *Rust* was released in theatres in May 2025 but got a lacklustre response from the audience.

INSIDE OUT 2 BECOMES HIGHEST GROSSING ANIMATED FILM OF ALL TIME

Inside Out 2 came to the cinemas, and not only did it heal the audience with its beautiful take on mental health, but also created magic at the box office as well. A sequel of the 2015 film, *Inside Out 2* introduced new emotions, like Embarassment, Anxiety, Envy, and Boredom, as the protagonists with whom Riley enters her teens. With adolescence comes new complex emotions and new challenges, and the film beautifully tackled mental health without being too preachy. The result was for everyone to see. The film not only struck a chord with young adults and children but also with adults. Even though meant for kids, the animated film was able to open up conversation about mental health. At the box office, the film earned a whopping USD 1.69 billion worldwide, making the highest-grossing animated film ever.

HOMEBOUND AT CANNES

A heart wrenching story of friendship and loss stirred the audience at Cannes Film Festival 2025. Karan Johar backed *Homebound*, directed by Neeraj Ghaywan and featured Ishaan Khatter and Vishal Jethwa became one of the most talked about films of 2025 at the prestigious film festival. The story was based on a news article that appeared in *New York Times* and was set in 2020, when India witnessed an unprecedented migrant crisis during the first phase of lockdown due to COVID-19. Homebound, a sensitive story of friendship, of survival and claiming what's theirs, spoke an universal language of humanity, thus making it a hit at the French Riviera.

STREE 2 SUCCESS: PR WAR

Whose film is it anyway? As *Stree 2* struck gold at the box office and became the biggest hit of 2024, a cold war ensued off-screen between the publicity teams of Shraddha Kapoor and Rajkumamr Rao, the lead actors of the film. Reason: Who should be given credit for the success of the film? While the tussle played out in media, with each team pumping their own star as the sole reason for the success of the film, director Amar Kaushik and fellow actors Aparshakti Khurana and Abhishek

Banerjee were left clarifying and giving politically correct statements that a film's success is always attributed to the full team.

YEAR OF BLOCKBUSTER SEQUELS

From *Stree 2* to *Singham Again* to *Bhool Bhulaiyaa 3*, 2024 box office was dominated by sequels of hit franchises. The year's biggest hit came from Maddock Films' *Stree 2*, a sequel of *Stree* (2018), the film brilliantly infused folklore, mythology and more to create a horror comedy for all ages. The film earned over ₹800 crore globally, creating history at the box office. With a plot that borrowed heavily from Ramayana, and a host of A-list Bollywood stars playing cameo roles, *Singham Again* had blockbuster written from the word go. The film may have received mixed reviews from critics, but fans showered love, and the film earned over ₹300 crores. Kaartik Aaryan, a formidable crowd puller, weaved his magic the second time around in *Bhool Bhulaiyyaa 3*. Another horror-comedy franchise, the film's biggest draw was a dance-off between Vidya Balan and Madhuri Dixit. While the story was absurd on many occasions, it struck a chord with the audience for its message on inclusivity. The film earned over ₹400 crores at the box office.

Not just in Hindi cinema, but in Hollywood, too, sequels ruled the box office. *Inside Out 2* was a gigantic hit, and *Despicable Me 4*, the sixth film in the franchise, earned over US$ 972 million worldwide.

SITAARES ARE BORN

After delivering two duds at the box office, Aamir Khan—the actor and producer—went back to the basics. For years, Aamir Khan has been associated with feel good-message-driven cinema. In 2025, Aamir Khan, the producer, launched 10 neurodivergent actors in his film *Sitaare Zameen Par*, a spiritual sequel of his critically acclaimed film *Taare Zameen Par*. In *Sitaare Zameen Par*, Khan played a basketball coach who is given charge to train a bunch of neurodivergent players for a national championship. Initially reluctant to train them, Aamir's character eventually warms up to them and learns important life lessons along the way. Khan, with years of experience in front of the camera and having delivered memorable performances in blockbusters, was easily overshadowed by the debutant actors who breathed life into an otherwise predictable plot.

DEEPIKA PADUKONE VS SANDEEP REDDY VANGA

Deepika Padukone's big comeback on screen post welcoming daughter Dua Padukone Singh, along with husband Ranveer Singh is highly anticipated. The actress who has been part of blockbuster hits in 2024 like *Singham Again*, *Kalki 2898 AD* and *Fighter*, came in news in early 2025 not for signing a new project but for walking out of one. Sandeep Reddy Vanga's *Spirit*, co-starring Prabhas, was set as the big-budget comeback movie for Deepika. However, the actress and the director had a fallout over work hours and profit share. Initially, no party spoke about the fallout openly, but later Vanga went on a rant on X, conforming all the rumours. While he did not name Deepika, he did accuse the actress of 'ousting his story' and 'putting down a younger actress'. Deepika maintained a stoic silence on the matter; however, the incident did lead to conversations on whether the 8-hour shift demand on the film sets is justifiable or not. Meanwhile, Vanga promptly replaced Deepika with Triptii Dimri in the project. Deepika is yet to open up about the incident and announce her next project.

OTT: THE NEW HOPE OF INDIAN CINEMA?

While theatres failed to attract audiences and big budget films bombed at the box office left right and centre, OTT delivered gems like *The Mehta Boys*, *Stolen* and *Mrs. Mrs* was a copy of *The Great Indian Kitchen*, and led to conversation around sexism and misogyny in Indian household like never before, *The Mehta Boys* was a poignant story of a father and son, rediscovering each other and forming a new bond after the loss of the wife/mother. Stolen, meanwhile, was a thriller that not only tested the bond between two brothers while on the run as they tried to search for a missing baby. Filmmakers have been more experimental on OTT in the last few years, and these films were a testament to the fact that the audience was hungry to watch solid stories on screen, irrespective of the star cast.

TOURIST FAMILY SUCCESS

Directed by Abhishan Jeevanth, Tamil film *Tourist Family* was the surprise hit of 2025. The film, which narrates the story of a Sri Lankan Tamil family fleeing to Tamil Nadu, India after political turmoil in Sri Lanka forces them to relocate, struck a chord with not just the audience but also with critics. Starring M Sasikumar and Simran, the film successfully blended humor with emotional beats, making even the most poignant scenes enjoyable. The film made at a modest budget, created magic at the box office and did well even on its OTT release.

BOYS CREATE BOX OFFICE HISTORY

Based on a real-life incident that took place in 2006 at the Guna Caves, *Manjummel Boys* was a survival thriller that starred a bunch of known faces from Malayalam cinema, including Soubin Shahir. The film, where a bunch of friends fight odds and help to save one of their friend stuck in a deep pit at the Guna Caves, made for a deeply engrossing and engaging watch. *Manjummel Boys* went on to earn over ₹200 crore and became the highest-grossing Malayalam film of all time- making the film and the boys create a permanent space in the history of Malayalam films.

By **SHOMINI SEN**

INSIDE THE 2025 AGENT WISHLIST

Every publishing season brings with it a quiet buzz behind the scenes—agents scanning slush piles, reading pitches, and making mental notes about what readers are responding to and what might strike next. In 2025, that buzz turned into a clear signal: readers wanted stories that were gripping, inclusive, emotionally layered, and unafraid to challenge the status quo. Literary agents were refreshingly open about what caught their attention, and these patterns of preference helped shape the most talked-about trends in both fiction and non-fiction.

A. In fiction, five genres stood out. Young Adult remained a powerhouse, attracting teens and adults alike with its crossover appeal. Dominant sub-genres included fantasy, romance, and thrillers. The growing enthusiasm for YA likely stems from its vivid characters and clear storytelling, making it especially well-suited for screen adaptations—a trend that continues to gain momentum. LGBTQ+ fiction also gained well-earned momentum, with agents actively seeking stories that centred queer protagonists and were written by queer authors. Horror made a strong comeback, especially when infused with speculative twists, gothic tones, and layered social commentary. Commercial fiction, with its focus on accessible storytelling and wide appeal, remained a firm favourite among agents scouting for books that could speak to large, diverse audiences. And finally, women's fiction held its ground, offering nuanced, character-driven explorations of identity, family dynamics, and personal transformation—genres often resonating with the majority-female fiction readership.

B. In non-fiction, agents were equally clear about what worked. Pop culture analysis thrived, with books offering sharp, research-backed takes on internet culture, fandoms, and entertainment trends. History books that unearthed lesser-known narratives or challenged conventional perspectives drew particular interest. Investigative journalism continued to attract attention, especially works that engaged with political developments, social justice, and global crises. LGBTQ+ non-fiction—from personal memoirs to essay collections and historical overviews—was recognized as both timely and necessary. Lastly, memoir remained a consistently sought-after genre, with agents drawn to authentic voices telling emotionally honest, layered stories from personal experience.

THE BOOKS THAT BROKE THROUGH

A. If agents set the tone, it's the readers—and their collective enthusiasm—that truly crown the year's book champions. In 2025, clear trends emerged across genres. Readers gravitated toward fiction that combined emotional intensity with high-concept premises. In speculative fiction, there was a marked rise in high-stakes narratives exploring power, survival, and imagined futures—epic fantasy sagas like *Onyx Storm* and *Fearless*, dystopian returns like *Sunrise on the Reaping*, and science-led dramas like *Atmosphere* reflected this appetite. Simultaneously, emotionally intelligent romance remained a stronghold, with stories by Emily Henry (*Great Big Beautiful Life*) and Ali Hazelwood (*Deep End*) offering love alongside grief, ambition, and vulnerability. Psychological thrillers and domestic suspense surged, too, fuelled by chilling mysteries and emotionally complex protagonists, as seen in *The Crash* by Freida McFadden and *Broken Country* by Clare Leslie Hall. Across all these categories, a few through-lines stood out: a preference for female-led narratives, emotionally layered conflicts, and heightened or unusual backdrops—from icy blizzards to space shuttles to reimagined totalitarian arenas.

B. Adding to this trend, speculative and literary fiction tackling themes of labour, gender, and systemic injustice saw renewed energy—books that blurred realism with allegory to examine who gets to survive, dream, and narrate in the face of precarity. From Chimamanda Ngozi Adichie's *Dream Count*—a rich, multi-threaded story of three Nigerian women reckoning with memory, power, and failed dreams—to Han Kang's haunting *We Do Not Part*, which blends dream and history in a story of two women uncovering buried trauma, 2025's best fiction was as formally inventive as it was emotionally resonant. Torrey Peters' *Stag Dance* pushed genre boundaries with trans-centered tales ranging from historical fantasia to romantic thrillers, while Abdulrazak Gurnah's *Theft* offered a quiet, powerful meditation on postcolonial adolescence. Natasha Brown's biting *Universality* satirized identity politics and media spectacle, and Ocean Vuong's *The Emperor of Gladness* gave readers a tender, ensemble-driven view of survival and solidarity in America's forgotten corners. These works didn't just reflect the moment—they reshaped how fiction engages with history, intimacy, and power.

C. And on the non-fiction shelf, titles like *Is a River Alive?* by Robert Macfarlane and Imani Perry's *Black in Blues* pointed to a growing hunger for ecological reflection and cultural excavation. If 2025 taught us anything, it's that the most enduring books are those that unsettle, illuminate, and reshape the way we imagine our lives and futures.

THE INDIAN CHAPTER

Indian publishing in 2025 saw a clear shift towards bold storytelling, regional language translations, and the rising prominence of short fiction. The year's most defining moment came when *Heart Lamp*, a Kannada short story collection by Banu Mushtaq, won the International Booker Prize, marking a historic win for regional Indian literature on the world stage. This recognition signalled a growing global appetite for stories that emerge from India's linguistic and cultural diversity, especially when carried by powerful translation.

Back home, the year was shaped by books that embraced introspection, experimentation, and a fearless engagement with the times. Memoirs and autobiographical reflections carved a strong presence—Arundhati Roy's *Mother Mary Comes to Me* and Pico Iyer's *Learning from Silence* offered poignant explorations of inner worlds, while Sudha Murty's *The Circle of Life* struck a warm, nostalgic chord. Fiction, too, pushed boundaries: from Kiran Desai's diasporic love story *The Loneliness of Sonia & Sunny* to Jeet Thayil's surreal *The Elsewhereans*, authors weren't afraid to experiment with form or subject. Queer narratives found a bolder voice in *On the Brink of Belief*, while regional storytelling shone brightly in *Loal Kashmir*. History and politics continued to provoke and inform, with Pankaj Mishra's *The World After Gaza* and Shashi Tharoor's *The Constitution of India: A Short History* capturing pressing global and national debates. 2025, in short, was a year where the written word in India reached both inward and outward—anchored in memory, yet alive to the urgencies of the moment.

NOTABLE LITERARY PRIZE WINNERS

Edna O'Brien (27 July 2024), Irish novelist

Barry N. Malzberg (19 December 2024), American science fiction author

M.T. Vasudevan Nair (25 December 2024), Indian novelist and screenwriter

Andrew Pyper (3 January 2025), Canadian literary thriller writer

James Carlos Blake (11 January 2025), American novelist

Humra Quraishi (16 January 2025), Indian journalist and author

Geoff Nicholson (18 January 2025), British novelist and non-fiction writer

Raosaheb Rangnath Borade (11 February 2025), Indian author

Clive Wilmer (13 March 2025), British poet and critic

Panchakshari Hiremath (14 March 2025), Indian poet, critic and translator

Rose Kerketta (17 April 2025), Indian tribal activist and writer

Caroline Knox (24 April 2025), American poet

Paul Durcan (17 May 2025), Irish poet

Ngũgĩwa Thiong'o (28 May 2025), Kenyan novelist and activist

H.S. Venkateshamurthy (30 May 2025), Indian poet and playwright

Frederick Forsyth (9 June 2025), British thriller novelist

SELECT AWARD WINNING CHILDREN'S BOOKS FROM 2023-24

Erin Entrada Kelly, *The First State of Being* - Winner of the 2025 John Newbery Medal for the most outstanding contribution to children's literature

C.G. Esperanza, illustrator of *My Daddy is a Cowboy* - Winner of the 2025 Coretta Scott King Award for Illustration, recognising African American illustrators of outstanding books for children and young adults

Jason Reynolds, *Twenty-four Seconds from Now...* - Winner of the 2025 Coretta Scott King Author Award, recognising African American authors of outstanding books for children and young adults

Ame Dyckman (author) and Mark Teague (illustrator), *Vacation* - Winners of the 2025 Theodor Seuss Geisel Award for books for beginning readers.

Marcelo Verdad, illustrator of *The Dream Catcher*; Karla Arenas Valenti, author of *Lola*; and Carolina Ixta, author of *Shut Up, This Is Serious* - Winners of the 2025 Pura Belpré Awards, celebrating Latino/a authors and illustrators of outstanding books for children and young adults

Nitin Kushalappa MP, *Dakshin: South Indian Myths and Fables Retold* - Winner of the 2025 Sahitya Akademi Bal Sahitya Puraskar in English

By ANURIMA CHANDA

What is art? Like beauty, it must also lie in the eyes of the beholder because a fresh banana duct-taped to a wall sold for US$6.2 million at a Sotheby's auction on 20 November 2024. A piece of conceptual art by Italian visual artist Maurizio Cattelan, the artwork titled 'Comedian' set the internet on fire with debates on what qualifies and succeeds as art. The art that comes with a duct tape, instructions on how to install and a certificate of it being an authentic work, was bought by Chinese crypto entrepreneur Justin Sun.

MOST EXPENSIVE INDIAN ARTWORK!

MF Husain is the perhaps the most recognizable name in Indian art. Always in the news for his unique style and artworks, one of the legendary artist's paintings '(untitled) Gram Yatra' sold for a whopping US$13.8 million (₹118.7 crore) at a Christie's auction in New York recently, making it the most expensive Indian art sold at an auction ever. Interestingly, the 1954 painting, spanning 14 ft, had been off public viewing for almost seven decades. According to reports, the huge canvas, that beautifully captures Indian pastoral life, was placed at a Norway based hospital and had been donated by a family of a surgeon.

Prior to this, Husain's 'Battle of Ganga and Jamuna: Mahabharata 12', a large painting from the Hindu epic, had fetched a record breaking US$1.6 million in 2008.

ART

AWARDS AND RECOGNITION

The multidisciplinary Indian artist Sohrab Hura won the Eye Art and Film Prize in May 2025. He received ₹30000 and a solo presentation at Amsterdam's Eye Film museum. The jury loved his hybrid forms of work, noting he was not bound by discipline and that he traversed smoothly between photography, film and painting, and he explored a wide range of themes – violence, inequality, religion, mental health and the distortion of reality through the digital flow of images. Hura, who started his career as a photographer, has moved to several mediums since, with his paintings having been exhibited at New York's MoMA PS1 for four months in 2024. His latest series *Things Felt But Not Quite Expressed* comprises of illustrations about everyday life in playful pastels.

Jyoti Bhatt, an iconic Indian artist received the Balkrishna Doshi: Guru Ratna Award in August 2024. Instituted by the Vastu Shilpa Foundation, the award was given to the great painter, printmaker and photographer for his 'transformative impact on the art world through his innovative practice and philosophical approach to art education'. The nonagenarian artist won the Padma Shri in 2019.

CENTENARY CELEBRATIONS

One of India's greatest artists, Krishen Khanna, turned a glorious 100 on 5 July 2025. To celebrate the occasion, the exhibition *The 100th Year of A Legacy* was held at Mumbai's Tao Art Gallery between August and September 2024. The last surviving member of the Progressive Artists Group that comprised of greats like SH Raza, FN Souza, KH Ara, MF Husain and Tyeb Mehta among others, Khanna has had an illustrious career of almost five decades in which he has chronicled the human condition almost to a perfection. His work is prolific and distinctive, with paintings, sculptures, tapestries et al finding a place in his rich repertoire. Some of his famous works like 'Bandwallahs', 'News of Gandhiji's Death' and 'The Migrants' are not just iconic, they speak tons about the society we live in. Khanna won the Padma Bhushan in 1999.

As a tribute to the great artist and architect Satish Gujral on his centenary year, the Gujral Foundation presented the exhibition *Ear to the Ground*. It was curated by Vishal K Dar and showcased many of Gujral's architectural drawings, sculptures, photographs of his murals and mixed-media. The exhibition, that was held in February 2025, also had on display a previously unexhibited work titled 'The Condemned' (1957) from the Cyrus and Ruth Prawer Jhabvala family collection. According to Dar, the idea was to present a complete image of the extraordinary modernist who refused to be stereotyped or categorized.

DALI COMES TO INDIA!

Spanish surrealist Salvador Dali has held the imagination of art lovers of the world for decades. In fact, his influence on surrealism has been singular. In February 2025, New Delhi became the first place in India to showcase more than 200 of Dali's original sketches, etchings and watercolour paintings. Curated by Christine Argillet, daughter of Pierre Argillet, a French collector and friend of Dalí's, the collection comprised of his famous works like 'Pegasus', 'Corridors of Kathmandu', 'Flower Woman at the Piano', and 'Secret Poems by Apollinaire' among many others.

ART FAIRS GET BIGGER, MORE INCLUSIVE

The 16th India Art Fair had over 120 galleries participating, making it the largest edition yet. It was held in February 2025 and saw reputed galleries like David Zwirner and Lisson Gallery return post-pandemic and first-time entrants like Lagos' ko. Along with artworks of legends like SH Raza and MF Husain were modern pieces by artists like Gurjeet Singh, Jayeeta Chatterjee and designers like Thamshangpa (Merci) Maku and Anikesa

Dhing. Interestingly, one work that caught everyone's attention was Deborah Fischer's piece 'The Whisperers' that was placed at the entrance. The installation, that evolved though collaborations with the Public Arts Trust of India and the Villa Swagatam initiative by the Institut Français in Delhi (2024) was created by Fischer and *master charpai* or cot weaver Dinesh Solanki from Rajasthan. The piece that debuted in Jodhpur Arts Week in October 2024, is an 'exploration of the symbolism of walls, through the presence of the *charpais*, where beds become walls and walls become beds, blurring the boundaries between home and the city, between intimacy and shared space', in the words of Fischer.

The 60th Venice Biennale held in 2024 had the highest number of Indian artists till date. The prestigious event curated by Adriano Pedrosa, had artworks by Indian artists like Francis Newton Souza, Jamini Roy, Ram Kumar and B Prabha among several others. For instance, the master artist Amrita Sher-Gil's 'The Head of a Girl', a young girl with big, almond-shaped eyes with a striking resemblance to the artist herself, was on display. In a section that focused on works by queer artists, was Indian painter Bhupen Khakhar's 'Fishermen in Goa'. 'Diaspore', a 100 ft long mural work by the trans-members of Aravani Art Project, a Bengaluru based art collective that creates collaborative space for the transgender community via public art, was also present.

ONCE STOLEN, NOW RETURNED

While all art is open to appreciation and interpretation, stolen art is not exactly a compliment. Fortunately, a lot of amends were made in the past year with many extraordinary artworks being returned to their rightful places.

'The Return of the Holy Family from the Flight into Egypt' by Jacob Jordaens was looted from the resistance fighter Joseph Scheppers de Bergstein when he was held and sent to the Buchenwald concentration camp by the Nazis in the 1940s. In 2022, the painting was found in Ardèche, France. Finally, in 2025, the valuable piece was returned to Joseph's grandsons.

Lebanon also received three stolen artifacts from the Swiss Embassy in 2025. As reported by L'Orient, a blue-tinted glass bottle with embossed motifs, a small statue of the goddess Aphrodite dating back to the 2nd or 3rd century BC and a small bronze statuette from the 2nd century BC were received by the Lebanon Cultural Ministry in February 2025.

By Runa Mukherjee Parikh

GOING BEYOND THE STAGE

Theatre in 2025 proved that performances no longer need to be confined to proscenium arches and neatly arranged seats. Immersive experiences and hybrid formats, blending in-person and digital elements, moved beyond their post-pandemic origins to become deliberate and imaginative artistic choices. Audiences didn't just watch; they took part. From navigating multi-sensory environments to solving on-site mysteries or influencing the plot in real time, theatre-goers were drawn into the action. Long-running favourites like *You Me Bum Bum Train* (still evolving since its 2004 debut) stood alongside new titles such as *Rhythm and Ruse* and *Elvis Evolution*, which embraced this interactive ethos.

Digital streaming of plays and musicals also continued to grow, especially for audiences unable to attend in person. Theatres large and small shared online-exclusive versions of their productions, enriched with behind-the-scenes footage, cast interviews, and even virtual watch parties. Initiatives like *National Theatre Live* remained central to this digital shift, bringing high-quality recordings to cinemas and homes around the world. The Royal Court Theatre and the Young Vic were among those leading the charge, offering paid streams and partnering with broadcasters for limited-time events that added a sense of occasion. These offerings didn't attempt to replace live performance, but instead opened new doors, helping theatres reach global audiences while preserving the intimacy of the stage.

Meanwhile, technological innovation played an increasingly dynamic role in reshaping storytelling in powerful new ways. Virtual and augmented reality became more than gimmicks; they brought fresh emotional layers and visual depth to the theatrical experience. A standout example was *Briar & Rose*, a magical collaboration between Norway's Nordland Teater, Teater Vestland, Teatret Vårt, and Glitch Studios. As Europe's first one-of-its-kind live stage production to incorporate AR, it invited audiences—each wearing a headset—into a fairytale land where animated dragons and mythical creatures shared the stage with live actors. With 'Far Throw AR' technology enabling full-stage immersion, and a dragon character animated by one of Europe's top talents, the production proved that cutting-edge tech could feel enchanting rather than cold. Having toured 50 venues and earned major awards, *Briar & Rose* showed how digital innovation can elevate storytelling, especially for younger audiences.

GREEN LIGHTS

One of the quieter but significant revolutions in theatre has been the growing seriousness with which the stage world has begun to think about the planet. This year, while Broadway continued to rely on big, glitzy productions, a growing number of theatres—particularly indie and educational ones—embraced bold eco-conscious choices. Paperless tickets, LED lighting, recycled sets, and upcycled costumes became increasingly common. Directors challenged themselves to stage low-waste productions, sometimes involving audiences in the process, inviting them to build sets or contribute old clothes for costume swaps.

Sustainability also began to influence storytelling itself, with more plays addressing climate change, endangered species, and ecological justice. Crucially, these weren't just grim warnings; many plays offered humour, hope, and a sense of agency. Major theatres signalled change too: the Royal Shakespeare Company implemented energy and waste reduction strategies, the Wooster Group experimented with repurposed materials in their sets, and Edinburgh's Traverse Theatre invested in greener lighting and heating systems. On larger stages, Broadway's *Hadestown* drew attention for its LED lighting and sustainable set design, while the National Theatre's *The Curious Incident of the Dog in the Night-Time* used a set made entirely of recycled materials. For many young theatre-makers, 'sustainable theatre' in 2025 was less a limitation than a creative provocation; a way to reimagine what theatre could be in an age of climate crisis.

LIGHTS, LEGENDS, AND NEWCOMERS

Theatre in 2025 dazzled with a thrilling mix of star power and fresh talent. Big names like Rosamund Pike (*Inter Alia*), Cate Blanchett (*The Seagull*), Rami Malek (*Oedipus*), and Brie Larson (*Elektra*) shared stages alongside bold new musicals and absurdist revivals, showcasing a diverse slate spanning Greek tragedy, Shakespeare, satire, and original works. From the provocative family drama *Unicorn* to a musical adaptation of *Clueless*, themes ranged from political intrigue in *The Estate* to complex relationships in *My Master Builder*.

Across the Atlantic on Broadway, star debuts by George Clooney and Sarah Snook captivated audiences, while veterans like Audra McDonald continued to shine. Rich narratives explored family tensions, mortality, and American history, ranging from a dream-cabaret imagining of Mary Todd Lincoln's afterlife to gripping McCarthy-era newsroom dramas. Revivals thrived with *The Seagull*, *Elektra*, and Gary Oldman's haunting *Krapp's Last Tape*. Meanwhile, theatres across the UK brought bold reinterpretations to classics: *Romeo and Juliet* was remixed with hip-hop and soul, while *Come Fall in Love*, inspired by Aditya Chopra's *Dilwale Dulhania Le Jayenge*, brought Bollywood vibrancy to Broadway's diaspora storytelling.

Globally, the year was marked by a genuine embrace of plurality as artistic and cultural expansion—not tokenism. African, South Asian, and Scottish voices rang out powerfully: Wole Soyinka's *Death and the King's Horseman* (directed by Mojisola Kareem) offered a stirring meditation on ritual and colonial rupture, while Martin O'Connor's *Through the Shortbread Tin* interrogated Highland identity with dark humour and poetry. Surreal and psychologically intense works like *Rhinoceros* (translated and directed by Omar Elerian) and *4.48 Psychosis* (directed by James Macdonald) challenged audiences with bold, unsettling aesthetics.

Comedy took a sharp, confessional turn, with Amy Gledhill's *Make Me Look Fit* and Jordan Brookes' *Fontanelle* delivering self-aware humour, while Julio Torres's *Color Theories* transformed stand-up into a dreamlike experience. True crime drama also gained prominence through Robert Icke's *Manhunt*, which probed the ethics of spectacle.

THE INDIAN ACT

In 2025, Indian theatre reaffirmed its position as a dynamic, evolving space—honouring tradition while embracing global thought. The stage became not just a place for storytelling, but a forum for dialogue, experimentation, and cultural resilience. This was seen most vividly at the third edition of the International Festival of Theatre Schools (IFTS), held in Kerala, which brought together over 300 participants from around the world. Hosted by the School of Drama and Fine Arts, the festival promoted progressive approaches to theatre pedagogy and curriculum development, with a focus on student-led learning. Workshops led by international educators explored diverse subjects such as intercultural performance, sustainable scenography, Noh theatre, Indian folk music, and physical theatre. Panel discussions and academic talks highlighted key themes such as decolonising theatre practices and the ethical responsibilities of performance-making.

The 15th edition of the International Theatre Festival of Kerala (ITFoK) in Thrissur affirmed its place as one of India's most inclusive and socially engaged theatre events. Centred on the theme 'Cultures of Resistance', it featured bold works tackling themes such as same-sex desire (*Be-Loved*, Mumbai), female sexuality (*Project Darling*, Bengaluru), and indigenous rights (*Aboriginal Cry*, Manipur), alongside powerful international entries like *Amal* (Iraq) and *Dear Children, Sincerely...* (Sri Lanka). Its lasting impact lay in its egalitarian spirit and its role as a genuinely democratic cultural space. In Delhi, the Triveni Theatre Fest, launched in 2024, continued to spotlight emerging talent; this year's standout was *Nazeer Katha Kirtan* by Khel Tamasha Theatre Group, a musical celebrating 18th-century poet Nazeer Akbarabadi, which won Best Play. In Jaipur, the *Irrfan Theatre Festival* paid tribute to the iconic actor while also offering space for new voices, with productions like *The Verdict*, *Qisse Kinaron Ke*, and *Maharathi* blending legacy with innovation. Sanhita Manch 2025, a theatre festival that aims to spark dialogue not just about theatre-making but about the very soul of storytelling in India today, was held in Mumbai from 1st to 3rd August. It brought together bold new plays, rich conversations, and a celebration of Indian playwriting. Known for championing the written word in performance, the festival continued to nurture original voices and meaningful storytelling in contemporary Indian theatre. This year, Meera Sitaraman won in the English category for *All That Matters*, while *Romeo and Shakuntala* by Avinash Matta received a special mention.

Adding to the year's expansive theatrical landscape was the silver jubilee edition of *Bharat Rang Mahotsav* (BRM), which went international for the first time. Organized by the National School of Drama, BRM 2025 featured over 200 productions across 13 cities in India, Sri Lanka, and Nepal under the theme *One Expression, Supreme Creation*. In Colombo, the festival was hosted in partnership with the Swami Vivekananda Cultural Centre and the Visual and Performing Arts University, with standout performances like *Tajmahal Ka Tender* and *Babuji* in Hindi, and *Romeo and Juliet* and *Sindu Kirilli-2* in Sinhala. This expansion reflected not only NSD's growing international ambition but also the enduring cultural relevance of Indian theatre on the global stage.

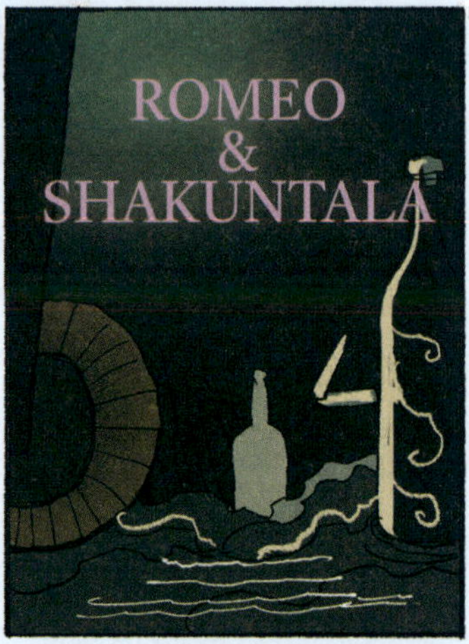

The 20th edition of the Mahindra Excellence in Theatre Awards (META) continued to champion India's theatrical diversity. Out of 367 plays from 20 states and 32 languages, only 10 made the cut—showing just how diverse and powerful theatre is right now. Big winners included *Nihsango Ishwar* (Best Production and Script) and *Swang: Jas Ki Tas* (Best Director for Akshay Singh Thakur). The plays didn't shy away from tough stuff like caste, gender, mythology, and rebellion, mixing bold storytelling with fresh formats—like arena-style staging in *Mattiah 22:39* or the sharp take on caste in *Bob Marley*. New voices shone too, like first-time director Anirudh Sarkar's *Chandaa Bedni*, featuring performers who flew for the first time just to be there. META also honoured the legendary Shanta Gokhale with the Lifetime Achievement Award, recognising her six decades of writing, translating, and inspiring the theatre world.

WORLD THEATRE DAY 2025

World Theatre Day 2025 stood out as a powerful reminder of the role of the stage in a world on edge. Since its inception in 1961, the day has united global theatre communities every 27 March to celebrate storytelling as a force for connection and peace. This year, the International Theatre Institute invited Greek director Theodoros Terzopoulos to deliver the annual message—one that resonated deeply. In it, he questioned whether theatre could still respond to the world's cries: digital isolation, ecological breakdown, and rising intolerance. He urged theatre-makers to confront, not just reflect and to use myth as a radical language of resistance and healing. His invocation of Dionysus wasn't nostalgic; it was a challenge to reimagine theatre's power in our fractured age.

By **Anurima Chanda**

C.V. CHANDRASHEKHAR: BHARATNATYAM DANCER AND SCHOLAR PASSES AWAY AT 89

On 19 June 2024, India lost one of its legends in classical dance form Bharatnatyam. C.V. Chandrashekhar was a renowned choreographer, dancer, and scholar of the art form. He passed away at the ripe age of 89. Chandrashekhar had dedicated his entire life to the dance form, and, as a researcher, he explored ancient dance traditions in India while also writing about the history and meaning of classing Indian dance forms.

KHAJURAHO DANCE FESTIVAL SETS GUINNESS WORLD RECORD

An impressive Guiness World Record was set during the Khajuraho Dance Festival in February 2025. A total of 139 artists from across the country performed continuously for more than 24 hours and showcased classical Indian dance forms like Kuchipudi, Kathak, Bharatnatyam, Odissi, and Mohiniyattam. The festival took place in the backdrop of majestic Khajuraho temples in Madhya Pradesh. This record-breaking performance was not only a celebration of India's rich classical dance traditions but also a tribute to the dedication and hard work of the artists and their gurus.

SANGEET NATAK AKADEMI HOSTS INTERNATIONAL DANCE FESTIVAL IN MYSURU

From 29 April to 3 May 2025, the Sangeet Natak Akademi hosted a grand six-day International Festival on Indian Dance in Mysuru, Karnataka. Indian and international dancers gathered to perform both classical and folk-dance forms, including Manipuri, Odissi, Kathak, and Bharatnatyam. The festival celebrated rich cultural diversity of India and provided young dancers an opportunity to learn from experienced teachers. Visitors enjoyed colourful costumes, beautiful music, and stories told through graceful dance movements.

LEGENDARY KATHAK CHOREOGRAPHER KUMUDINI LAKHIA PASSES AWAY AT 94

On 12 April 2025, India's dance community mourned the loss of Kumudini Lakhia, a legendary Kathak choreographer, who passed away at the age of 94. She was known for her efforts to modernize Kathak dance form while also respecting its deep traditions. Lakhia had trained many dancers through her academy and

INDIAN DANCE AND MUSIC

had choreographed several memorable group performances. Her graceful style, creative ideas, and love for storytelling on stage inspired generations of performers in India and internationally.

PADMA SHRI HONOUR FOR ODISSI GURU DURGA CHARAN RANBIR

In January 2025, renowned Odissi dance guru Durga Charan Ranbir was awarded the Padma Shri, one of India's highest civilian honours, for his outstanding contributions to Odissi dance. He is celebrated for his graceful performances, dedication to teaching, and tireless work to preserve the rich tradition of Odissi. Charan trained many students who now perform on major stages around the world. His award is a tribute to his lifelong efforts to keep this classical dance form alive and inspire new generations to learn and cherish it.

GOKUL CHANDRA DAS: FIRST DHAKI HONOURED WITH PADMA SHRI

In January 2025, Gokul Chandra Das made history by becoming the first-ever Dhaki (traditional Bengali drum player) to receive the prestigious Padma Shri award. The dhak is a large drum played during Durga Puja and other festivals in Bengal. Gokul Chandra Das had kept the tradition alive by training many young performers, including women, breaking old traditions. By teaching women and encouraging them to perform on prominent stages, Das played a crucial role in empowering them and opening new doors for female artists in rural Bengal. His Padma Shri award celebrates not only his own talent but also his efforts to protect folk culture and give opportunities to people who dream of performing and carrying this tradition forward.

PADMA SHRI FOR MANIPURI DANCE TO THIYAM SURYAMUKHI DEVI

In January 2025, Thiyam Suryamukhi Devi, a celebrated Manipuri classical dancer, was awarded the Padma Shri for her remarkable contributions to the dance form. She is known for her dedication to keep this beautiful dance form from Northeast India alive and training many young dancers. Her students have gone on to perform at prestigious stages in India and abroad. Through her contributions, Devi helped Manipuri to be recognized internationally. Her award is a proud moment for the Manipuri dance community and inspires young artists to keep the tradition alive.

REPUBLIC DAY PARADE SETS GUINNESS RECORD WITH FOLK DANCE

On 26 January 2025, India's Republic Day Parade in New Delhi made history with a new Guinness World Record for 'The Largest Indian Folk Variety Dance.' More than 5,000 folk artists from across the country performed together, showcasing over

50 different folk and tribal dance forms on Rajpath. This colourful performance celebrated India's rich cultural diversity and brought together dancers from every region. The record highlighted how traditional dances keep communities connected and preserve age-old stories for new generations to enjoy.

INDIAN MUSICIANS SHINE AT THE GRAMMYS AND BEYOND

Indian artists made the country proud on the global music stage. Renowned flautist Rakesh Chaurasia added two Grammy Awards to India's tally in 2024 for his soulful performances blending Indian classical music with international sounds. At the same 67th Grammy Awards, sitar player Anoushka Shankar and singer Varijashree Venugopal, along with other artists of Indian origin, earned nominations in categories like Best New Age and Global Music Performance. In 2025, Ricky Kej, known for his powerful environmental music, received another Grammy nomination for his inspiring work focused on nature and climate awareness. He was also honoured with the Padma Shri, India's fourth-highest civilian award, for his outstanding contribution to music and environmental activism. These achievements show how Indian musicians continue to make their mark worldwide while staying rooted in rich musical traditions.

LEGENDARY TABLA MAESTRO ZAKIR HUSSAIN PASSES AWAY AT 73

In late 2024, the legendary Tabla virtuoso, Zakir Hussain, passed away at the age of 73 in San Francisco. Zakir Hussain was admired worldwide for his masterful performances and his ability to blend Indian classical music with global traditions. He played with the best musicians around the world and was one of the founding members of the famous fusion band Shakti, which brought Indian musical rhythms to jazz and Western music lovers. Hussain received many awards in his lifetime, including the Padma Bhushan, for his dedication to the art form. Fans and fellow artists remember him not only for his incredible speed and complex rhythms but also for his warm smile and love for teaching. His legacy will continue through his recordings and students.

By **Namit Hans**

VIDEO KILLED THE STREAMING STARS

Whenever we think of music streaming services, the first names that come to mind are Spotify and iTunes or Apple Music. Their biggest competitor today, however, is YouTube. The company has revealed that YouTube Music and Premium services have crosses 125 million subscribers globally. Spotify is still the biggest music industry partner with over 236 million subscribers. The biggest advantage YouTube has over other music streaming services is that they are able to offer music videos. This is a throwback to the time when the visual media of music television channels like MTV became more popular than radio stations back in the 1980s.

OASIS IS BACK! WHAT'S THE STORY?

Those old enough to remember Britpop giants Oasis will know that they split back in 2009. The two main members, brothers Liam and Noel Gallagher, have not been on the best of terms since then. In 2025 they reunited for a July to November world tour across five continents in what the British newspaper *The Guardian* has called 'the most anticipated tour of the century'.

FROM ARMY TO ARMY

Oasis is not the only band whose reunion is hitting the headlines. South Korean K-pop stars BTS are said to be planning a comeback following their hiatus in 2022, now that the members' 18 months of mandatory military service is over. This is great news for their fans, who are known as the BTS Army.

BREAKING RECORDS IN INDIA AND THE WORLD

Seeing global music acts live in India is a bit of a rarity. Back in January 2025, however, fans in Mumbai and Ahmedabad were treated to Coldplay concerts as part of their *Music of the Spheres* world tour, which included a record-breaking 134,000 thousand attendance in Ahmedabad's Narendra Modi Stadium. This was not Coldplay's first time in India though. They had previously visited in 2016.

Not to be left behind, singer Ed Sheeran also performed in India—Hyderabad, Chennai and Delhi among others—as part of his global *Mathematics* tour.

Meanwhile, Taylor Swift's 2023-24 *Eras* tour, which did not include India, has been declared the highest grossing concert tour of all time and the first and only to cross US$ 2 billion.

BIGGEST HITS

Some of the biggest hits of 2025 included 'Baile Involvidable' by Bad Bunny, Alex Warren's 'Ordinary', Lana Del Rey's 'Bluebird', 'Hampstead' by Ariana Grande, and 'Abracadabra' by Lady Gaga. 'APT' by ROSÉ and Bruno Mars, a big hit in 2024, continued its run in 2025. Some of the best albums of the year were Bad Bunny's *Debí Tirar Más Fotos*, Blondshell's *If You Asked for a Picture*, and Ariana Grande's *Eternal Sunshine Deluxe: Brighter Days Ahead*, a re-issue of her 2024 album *Eternal Sunshine*.

67TH ANNUAL GRAMMY AWARDS

The Grammy Awards, hosted by comedian and TV host Trevor Noah, were dominated by Kendrick Lamar, who won in five categories, including Record of the Year and Song of the Year for 'Not Like Us'. Beyoncé won in the Album of the Year category with 'Cowboy Carter'. She also became the first African American woman to win a Grammy in the Country category and the first female artist to receive 11 nominations in one year, breaking her own record she previously shared with Lauryn Hill. Chapell Roan was awarded the Best New Artist award. Interestingly, The Beatles won a Grammy after many years for the Best Rock Performance, after also being nominated in the Record of the Year category. Their song 'Now and Then' is also remarkable for being AI enhanced.

THE TIME OF AI MUSIC IS HERE!

The Beatles hit is surely not the only record produced with the help of AI. Generative AI—the use of AI to create or modify music—is quickly getting popular, like all other things AI. This technology relies on datasets of music that it analyses and looks for patterns and structures, which are then used to create original compositions. This gives musicians and composers the ability to quickly create music, including vocals that sound as if being sung by a famous singer. AI is also used to restore voices on existing tracks and add them to new ones. Music streaming services are also integrating AI in their search functions.

A FAKE BAND

With AI making it so easy to create original music, it was only a matter of time before AI generated music would become the real thing. That's exactly what happened with The Velvet Sundown, an AI band with AI music with more than one million monthly listeners on Spotify. Listeners had already suspected that something was off about the band, its promo material, its music and lyrics, and photos, until the 'band' itself revealed that they were indeed AI, 'Not quite human. Not quite machine. The Velvet Sundown lives somewhere in between.'

WHAT'S NEW IN CLASSICAL AND JAZZ?

Western classical music has been getting more and more experimental ever since the early 20th century to the extent that contemporary classical music has become a niche genre. Some of the better known albums of 2025 have been *Rathlin From a Distance* by French composer Yann Tiersen, who is well known for his soundtrack to the film *Amelie*. Other classical and crossover albums have been Abel Selaocoe's *Hymns of Bantu*, a mix of traditional Bantu music and pieces by Bach and others, *Night* by Nils Frahm, *All Living Things* by Korean composer Park Jiha, *Song of the Earth* by Dave Longstreth, and *Aguas de Amazonia* by Philip Glass.

Some of the hits in jazz this year are the albums *Apple Cores* by James Brandon Lewis, *A Joyful Holiday* by Samara Joy, *Remembrance* by Chick Corea and Bela Fleck, and *About Ghosts* by Mary Halvorson.

In video games soundtracks, the highlight of the year was the soundtrack to *Claire Obscur: Expedition 33* by Lorien Testard.

Those who have passed

- Francoise Hardy (17 January 1944 – 11 June 2024). French singer.
- John Mayall (29 November 1933 – 22 July 2024). British rock and blues singer and guitarist.
- Kris Kristofferson (22 June 1936 – 28 September 2024). American country singer.
- Marianne Faithfull (29 December 1946 – 30 January 2025). British singer.
- Roberta Flack (10 February 1937 – 24 February 2025). American soul and pop singer.
- Sly Stone (15 March 1943 – 9 June 2025). American soul and funk singer, member of band Sly and the Family Stone.
- Ozzy Osbourne (3 December 1948 – 22 July 2025). British singer, vocalist of the band Black Sabbath.

By **SOURAV DUTTA**

ALWAYS YES TO ROMANCE!

Love has always been in the air, especially young love. No wonder then, shows like *The Royals* and *Heartstopper* on Netflix find a wide audience. And even though *The Royals* plays on the well-worn premise of a prince going bankrupt while searching for meaning and love, it trended on Netflix India for weeks, proving some formulas never grow stale. *Heartstopper*, a British series about Nick Nelson and Charlie Spring, two young adults who find love, friendship and purpose, also lapped up the adulation it got in its third season and decided to gift its fans with an upcoming movie for its finale!

This year, there were quite a few shows with broad LGBTQ themes like *Heartstopper*. Amazon Prime's *Overcompensating* was funny, entertaining and highlighted an issue many young queer people face – of being closeted and hiding their true selves in order to fit in. In contrast however, was JioHotstar's sitcom *Mid-Century Modern*. The breezy show put the spotlight on three gay best friends in their forties and fifties, who decide to live together while taking on life's many adventures.

Interestingly, *Four Seasons* on Netflix gave us a rare take on mature romances. Co-created by Tina Fey, Lang Fisher, and Tracey Wigfield, it showcased the dynamics of four middle-aged couples with their unique dysfunctionalities. As the couples met from one vacation to another, love, heartbreak, parenting and mundanity, all found space in this bittersweet story of how life and age happen to one and all.

WHO DOESN'T ENJOY A GOOD THRILLER?

Thrillers remained a mass favourite with Amazon Prime's *Pataal Lok* keeping the audience at the edge of their seats. The story and tension moved to India's serene North East in this season and the character arcs were close to perfect, making the long wait for its second season worth it. Sony LIV's *The Hunt - The Rajiv Gandhi Assassination Case* was yet another feather in the streaming giant's cap, with taut performances and a well-researched tale that toed the line between fact and fiction smartly.

This time around, the stakes got even higher, with everyone rooting for their hero, participant 456 (aka Lee Jung-jae) to take down the dastardly men and their ghastly games! While the show ended on a meaningful note, it is set to come back in its American avatar soon!

Cloning, AI, enshittification and various other tech-centric concepts and their possible (terrible) consequences found a voice in Netflix's popular anthology series *Black Mirror* that dropped its seventh season this year.

And finally, fans of the Apple TV+ show *Severance* breathed a sigh of relief as its second season was released after a gap of three years! The Ben Stiller and

Dan Erickson run series had a plethora of surprises in its kitty this time with the lines between outies and innies blurring. Ideas of philosophy merged with morality and gave way to dilemmas with no clear right or wrong in sight. Television at its best.

In 2022, a wave of shock ran through the world when Netflix dropped its sensational Korean thriller *Squid Games*. The audience were stunned by its unique story line—a bleak survival game which treats poor people as pawns for the entertainment of the rich. The first season ended too quickly and we waited with bated breath for the next one…for three whole years! Finally, the show makers gave us a double treat by releasing season 2 in December 2024 and season 3 in June 2025!

SOMETHING TO THINK ABOUT

The English miniseries *Adolescence* trended on Netflix worldwide for weeks in March 2025 with good reason. A compelling and gut-punching story about a teenager accused of murder, the show got rave reviews from critics, artists and parents alike. The British series was lauded for throwing light on the manosphere and its harmful impact on the young. It also made headlines for shooting entire episodes on single takes!

The Danish miniseries *Secrets We Keep* was also similar in its messaging. It showed the misuse of technology by young boys and the class divide that most affluent seem to overlook or worse, dismiss. These shows raked in large viewership while pointing to a bigger problem that might be plaguing teenagers today.

SHOCK VALUE APLENTY

The year's shock value was provided by the second season of the HBO series *The Last of Us.* In its second episode, the series killed off a major character, sending ripples in the audience world and dividing loyal fans. The success of this show, along with Amazon Prime's hit post-apocalyptic Los Angeles fare *Fallout*, proved that video game adaptations make for spectacular television.

MYTHOLOGY WITH TWISTS

Mythology came with a wicked twist in Netflix's *Kaos*, a dark version of the Greek gods we know and revere. The plot was typical enough; three ordinary people hold the key to saving the world, much to the annoyance of the high and mighty residing in Mount Olympus. What made the series great was the reimagining of the story and some great acting from Jeff Goldblum who was none other than Zeus!

In a sweet contrast was the Sony Liv series *Veer Hanuman: Bolo Bajrang Bali ki Jai.* The endearing tales of Lord Hanuman when he was just a child who was slowly becoming aware of his growing powers and great destiny found a loyal audience.

LIVE EVENTS ON NETFLIX!

The boxing world saw the comeback of legend Mike Tyson in a match against YouTuber turned boxer Jake Paul and it was streamed live by Netflix. The fight, an 8-round bout at AT&T Stadium in Arlington, Texas attracted an estimated global audience of 60 million in 15 November 2024.

Moving ahead with full steam, Netflix went on to add a classic line up of WWF/WWE content in 2025. In fact, live events like *WWE SummerSlam* along with fresh episodes of *RAW* and *SmackDown* have become instant hits on the platform.

WELCOME TO THE RESORT LIFE

It is well documented on the internet how the Mike White led cult series *The White Lotus* has its fans in a chokehold. In its third instalment, the show made its way to Thailand, Asia, and explored concepts of life and death in Buddhism—yet again making for an interesting view, especially on the rich. And this year's cast had a surprise for BLACKPINK fans; singer Lisa was a part of the show!

While this season made the talented British actress Aimee Lou Wood an instant internet darling, some took jabs at her appearance. Her gap teeth made more headlines than her acting, with the actress herself slamming the SNL comedy team for making poor jokes at her expense. *You* star Madeline Brewer was also booed by netizens for not looking 'pretty enough' in their favourite Netflix murder series. Body shaming in 2025? Not cool.

UNIQUE VOICE OF INDIAN DOCUMENTARIES

In Amazon Prime's *Angry Young Men*, cinephiles discovered the untold journey of the dynamic Indian writer duo Salim-Javed, who wrote 24 films in a decade. The pieces of the puzzle; of how the careers and stars of Salim Khan and Javed Akhtar came together, of how their families and personas were impacted by their relationship and what brought about the duo's climax, all fit in this neatly shot three-part documentary.

It was a double rush of nostalgia for Indians when Netflix released *The Roshans* in January 2025. The four-part docuseries focussed on the iconic Roshan family—the talented composer Roshan Lal Nagrath, his sons, filmmaker Rakesh and composer Rajesh, and finally, his grandson, the heartthrob actor Hrithik Roshan.

Rapper Yo Yo Honey Singh's controversial rise and success was also put together with a certain sensitivity and soul baring finesse in the Netflix documentary *Yo Yo Honey Singh: Famous.*

In sports, Netflix came up with a fascinating albeit a little one-sided docuseries, *The Greatest Rivalry: India v Pakistan.* It focussed on the thrumming pulse of the one rivalry that never seems to die off, that of India and Pakistan. Interviews of cricketing greats like Sourav Ganguly and Shoaib Akhtar made the three-part docu worthwhile.

Saudi Pro League: Kickoff, an interesting documentary on the rise of football in Saudi Arabia was also released on Netflix in November 2024. Full of tête-à-têtes with celebrity players like Ronaldo and Neymar Jr., it gave football fans a good look into the rising dominance of football clubs with their roots in Saudi Arabia.

FAMILY FUN GUARANTEED

Wizards Beyond Waverly Place, which is a sequel to the much-loved *Wizards of Waverly Place,* premiered on JioHotstar in October 2024 and got glorious reviews and a high viewership. In fact, the final episode of the show saw the return of Selene Gomez aka Alex Russo, the wizard sister from the original! Gomez is now set to star in the second season that will drop soon! Netflix's *Tales of the Teenage Mutant Ninja Turtles* also made for some great kid-friendly watch.

MEANINGFUL ENDS

How many of us remember the shock we felt when *The Handmaid's Tale* aired on our screens for the first time? The horror of repression and exploitation played out quietly even as our insides wanted to scream. In 2025, after five seasons, June Osborne and her army of handmaids took one last swing at the villainous patriarchy of Gilead and won! Freedom never looked better than when the dystopian story flung its oppressive red out forever. The show, that was adapted, and in the later seasons, inspired by Margaret Atwood's bestselling novel, gave us a story for the ages, award-winning performances and an iconic female character, never to be forgotten.

And finally, Pat Sajak, the host of the super popular *Wheel of Fortune*, won the test of time and adulation by becoming the longest tenured game show host in U.S. history. Sajak started hosting the popular game show in 1981 and retired in 2024, having worked in the same show for 43 years!

By **RUNA MUKHERJEE PARIKH**

SPORTS

CRICKET

ICC CHAMPIONS TROPHY 2025

India secured their third ICC Champions Trophy title on 9 March 2025, in Dubai, defeating New Zealand by four wickets in the final. Skipper Rohit Sharma led from the front with a crucial 76 in the final. New Zealand's Rachin Ravindra was named Player of the Series for accumulating 263 runs in the tournament, while fellow Kiwi Matt Henry took 10 wickets, the most in the competition. India remained unbeaten and set global viewership records.

VIRAT KOHLI, ROHIT SHARMA AND R ASHWIN RETIRE FROM TEST CRICKET

Indian cricket legends Virat Kohli, Rohit Sharma, and Ravichandran Ashwin have announced their retirement from Test cricket, marking the end of a golden era. The trio, instrumental in India's dominance over the past decade, leave behind a legacy of stellar performances and leadership. Their contributions have shaped modern Indian Test cricket and inspired countless young cricketers.

TIM SOUTHEE AND JAMES ANDERSON RETIRE FROM INTERNATIONAL CRICKET

Veteran pacers Tim Southee of New Zealand and James Anderson of England have announced their retirement from international cricket. Both players leave behind illustrious careers, having led their respective bowling attacks for over a decade. Anderson retires as the most successful fast bowler in Test history, while Southee is celebrated for his consistency and leadership in New Zealand cricket.

BORDER GAVASKAR TROPHY 2024-25

Australia clinched the Border-Gavaskar Trophy 2024–25 with a 3–1 series victory over India, marking their first triumph in the rivalry since 2014. Jasprit Bumrah earned Player of the Series honour with a record-breaking 32 wickets at an average of 13.06 in an overseas Test series. Australia's Travis Head topped the scoring charts with a total of 448 runs.

INDIA-BANGLADESH SERIES 2024

India showcased their dominance during the 2024 series against Bangladesh, held from September to October, with a commanding 2–0 win in the Test series and a 3–0 sweep in the T20Is. Yashasvi Jaiswal led the batting in Tests with 189 runs, while Jasprit Bumrah and R Ashwin took 11 wickets each. Sanju Samson sealed the T20I series with a century.

INDIA-NEW ZEALAND TEST SERIES 2024

New Zealand scripted history with a 3–0 whitewash against India in the October–November 2024 Test series—their first-ever Test series win on Indian soil. Spinners dominated, with Mitchell Santner taking 13 wickets and Ajaz Patel bagging 11. Will Young led the scoring charts with 244 runs. This marked India's first home Test series defeat since 2012, significantly impacting the World Test Championship standings.

WORLD TEST CHAMPIONSHIP FINAL 2025

South Africa scripted a landmark victory in the 2025 World Test Championship Final (June 11–14) at Lord's, defeating Australia by five wickets. Led by skipper Temba Bavuma and Aiden Markram's brilliant 136, the Proteas ended their 27-year wait for an ICC title. Kagiso Rabada's nine-wicket haul was instrumental in securing South Africa's first-ever WTC crown.

WOMEN'S T20I WORLD CUP 2025

New Zealand clinched their maiden Women's T20 World Cup title with a 32-run victory over South Africa in Dubai on 20 October 2024. All-rounder Amelia Kerr delivered a match-winning performance, scoring 43 runs and taking three wickets, earning both Player of the Match and Series honours. New Zealand posted 158/5, and restricted South Africa to 126/9, ending a 10-match losing streak.

WOMEN'S PREMIER LEAGUE 2025

Mumbai Indians secured their second Women's Premier League title on 15 March 2025, with an eight-run win over Delhi Capitals in a thrilling final at Mumbai's iconic Brabourne Stadium. Skipper Harmanpreet Kaur scored 66, while English all-rounder Nat Sciver-Brunt shone with a match-winning all-round display, earning Player of the Match. Sciver-Brunt won the Orange Cap (523 runs), and Amelia Kerr took the Purple Cap (18 wickets).

INDIAN PREMIER LEAGUE 2025

Royal Challengers Bengaluru captured their first-ever IPL title in 2025, edging out a valiant Punjab Kings by six runs in a nail-biting final at Ahmedabad's Narendra Modi Stadium on 3 June 2025. Gujarat Titan's Sai Sudharsan claimed the Orange Cap with 759 runs, while his teammate Prasidh Krishna secured the Purple Cap with 25 wickets. Led by captain Rajat Patidar, RCB won all their away league games, creating another unique record.

ATHLETICS

PARIS OLYMPICS 2024

The 2024 Paris Olympics, held from 26 July to 11 August, featured 10,714 athletes from 206 countries competing in 329 events, including debut sports like breaking, kiteboarding, and kayak cross. Set against iconic backdrops like the Seine River and Eiffel Tower, the Games focused on sustainability. Highlights included Simone Biles's beam routine, a record pole vault, and Neeraj Chopra's stellar Silver Medal winning javelin performance.

MANU BHAKER

Manu Bhaker etched her name in history at the Paris 2024 Olympics by securing India's first-ever Olympic medal in women's shooting, winning bronze in the 10m air pistol final with an impressive score of 221.7. She continued her stellar performance by clinching another bronze alongside Sarabjot Singh in the mixed 10m air pistol event. With these achievements, Bhaker became the first Indian woman—and the first athlete from independent India—to win two medals at a single edition of the Olympic Games.

NEERAJ CHOPRA

Neeraj Chopra delivered a stellar performance in the men's javelin final at the Paris 2024 Olympics, clinching the silver medal with a season's best throw of 89.45m. He narrowly missed gold to Pakistan's Arshad Nadeem, who set a new Olympic record with 92.97m. Despite struggling with a recurring groin injury, Chopra showcased his resilience and consistency, becoming only the fourth Indian athlete in history to win medals at two consecutive Olympic Games—a remarkable achievement in Indian sporting history.

VINESH PHOGAT

At the Paris 2024 Olympics, Vinesh Phogat made history by becoming the first Indian woman wrestler to reach an Olympic final, advancing to the gold-medal match in the women's 50kg freestyle. She secured remarkable wins over reigning champion Yui Susaki and Pan American Games gold medallist Yusneylys Guzman. However, in a heartbreaking turn, she was disqualified for exceeding the 50-kg weight limit by just 100gms. Despite the setback, her exceptional run marked a significant milestone in Indian wrestling history.

PARALYMPICS

India achieved its best-ever result at the Paris 2024 Paralympics (28 August-8 September), winning a record 29 medals—7 gold, 9 silver, and 13 bronze—surpassing its Tokyo 2020 tally. With 84 athletes competing across 12 disciplines, India made debut entries in para-cycling, para-rowing, and blind judo. Highlights included Avani Lekhara's second Paralympic gold, Sumit Antil's record-breaking title defence in javelin (F64), Preethi Pal's double in track events, and Harvinder Singh's historic gold in para-archery, marking a landmark Paralympic campaign.

DIPA KARMAKAR RETIRES

Indian gymnastics icon Dipa Karmakar announced her retirement at the age of 31 in October 2024, concluding a pioneering two-decade career. The Tripura-born athlete made history as the first Indian woman gymnast to compete at the Olympics, finishing fourth in the vault final at Rio 2016. Renowned for performing the daring Produnova vault, Karmakar battled numerous injuries—including ACL tears and a shoulder injury. Her resilience culminated in a stunning comeback, winning gold at the 2024 Asian Championships in Tashkent, cementing her legendary status.

CHESS

GUKESH D BECOMES YOUNGEST WORLD CHAMPION

Eighteen-year-old Indian chess sensation D Gukesh Dommaraju created history by defeating China's Ding Liren 7½–6½ in the 14-game 2024 World Chess Championship final in Singapore, becoming the youngest undisputed World Chess Champion ever, eclipsing the record held by Garry Kasparov. His win marked India's second world title and the first since Viswanathan Anand, bringing the crown back to Indian soil and igniting national pride and celebrations across the country for the teenage grandmaster's extraordinary triumph.

DIVYA DESHMUKH BEATS HUMPY KONERU TO BECOME WORLD CHAMPION AT 19

Nineteen-year-old Indian chess prodigy Divya Deshmukh made history by defeating Grandmaster Humpy Koneru to clinch the FIDE World Championship title on 28 July 2025. Her remarkable victory marks a pivotal moment in Indian chess, highlighting the emergence of a new wave of talent. Battling one of the nation's most celebrated players, Divya demonstrated remarkable poise and tactical excellence. This triumph not only establishes her among the game's elite but also serves as a powerful inspiration for aspiring young chess players across the country.

NORWAY CHESS CHAMPIONSHIP

The 13th edition of Norway Chess 2025 took place in Stavanger from 26 May to 6 June this year, featuring an elite line-up, including home favourite Magnus Carlsen, reigning World Champion and Indian sensation D Gukesh, Hikaru Nakamura, Fabiano Caruana, India's Arjun Erigaisi, and China's Wei Yi. Carlsen retained his crown with 16 points, narrowly ahead of Caruana (15.5) and Gukesh (14.5). In the women's tournament, Anna Muzychuk emerged victorious with 16.5 points. The event followed a double round-robin format with thrilling Armageddon tiebreaks.

CHESS OLYMPIAD 2024

India scripted history at the 2024 Chess Olympiad by winning gold in both the men's and women's team events for the first time. The men's team, led by D Gukesh, Arjun

Erigaisi, and Vidit Gujrathi, edged out top seeds USA and China. The women's team, captained by Koneru Humpy and supported by Vaishali Rameshbabu and Harika Dronavalli, delivered a flawless campaign. Their dual victories marked a landmark moment for Indian chess and cemented the country's dominance on the global stage.

THE COMEBACK OF KONERU HAMPI

In 2025, veteran Indian woman chess sensation Koneru Humpy made a stunning comeback, reestablishing herself as a leading figure in the circuit. Following a subdued 2024, the 37-year-old Grandmaster bounced back by clinching the Women's Candidates Tournament in April, securing a World Championship title shot. Her consistent, high-level play throughout the year, marked by wins over top-ranked opponents, highlighted her skill and determination. Humpy's return to peak form has reignited national hopes of seeing India once again at the summit of women's world chess.

TATA STEEL CHESS MASTERS 2025

India's R Praggnanandhaa claimed a landmark victory at the Tata Steel Masters 2025 in Wijk aan Zee in the Netherlands, edging out reigning World Champion and fellow countryman Gukesh Dommaraju in a thrilling blitz tiebreak after both finished with 8½ points in the classical segment. The prestigious tournament featured top players, including Wei Yi and Arjun Erigaisi. In the Challengers category, Czech grandmaster Thai Dai Van Nguyen emerged victorious. The event followed a round-robin format, with rapid Armageddon playoffs deciding the winner in the case of a tie.

FOOTBALL

SUNIL CHHETRI CALLS OFF HIS RETIREMENT

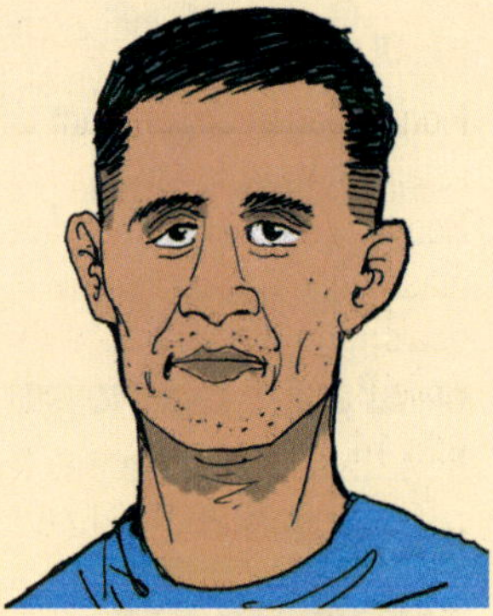

At 40, Indian football icon Sunil Chhetri made a stunning return from international retirement, rejoining the national squad for the March 2025 FIFA window. Selected by coach Manolo Márquez for friendlies against Maldives and Bangladesh ahead of the AFC Asian Cup 2027 qualifiers, Chhetri made an immediate impact as he netted his 95th international goal in India's 3–0 win over Maldives. His performance reignited national hopes and injected fresh energy into India's qualification campaign.

UEFA NATIONS LEAGUE 2025

On 8 June 2025, Portugal secured their second UEFA Nations League title with a thrilling victory over Spain at Munich's Allianz Arena. The match ended 2–2 in regular time, with talismanic player Cristiano Ronaldo scoring a vital equalizer before getting substituted. Portugal triumphed 5–3 in the penalty shootout, with Nuno Mendes winning Player of the Match. This historic win

made Portugal the first team to claim the Nations League trophy twice, capping off an unforgettable Iberian showdown.

UEFA CHAMPIONS LEAGUE 2025

Paris Saint-Germain secured their maiden UEFA Champions League crown with a dominant 5–0 win over Inter Milan at Munich's Allianz Arena on 31 May 2025. Goals from Achraf Hakimi, Khvicha Kvaratskhelia, Senny Mayulu, and a brace by teenage star Désiré Doué sealed the biggest final victory in the tournament's history. Under Luis Enrique, PSG completed a historic treble, having already won the French Ligue 1 and the Coupe de France. Doué was named Player of the Match for his standout performance.

PREMIER LEAGUE 2024-25

In a stellar debut season, Arne Slot guided Liverpool to their 20th league title and second Premier League crown, finishing with 84 points—ten ahead of runners-up Arsenal. Mohamed Salah was in sensational form, topping the charts with 29 goals and 18 assists, totaling a record 47 goal involvements. Tottenham's late slump saw Newcastle grab the final Champions League spot, while Aston Villa missed out. Southampton, Ipswich, and Leicester faced relegation, as Nottingham Forest impressed under Nuno's leadership.

INDIAN SUPER LEAGUE 2024-25

Mohun Bagan Super Giant achieved a remarkable double in the 2024–25 ISL season, retaining the League Shield with 56 points and clinching the Cup final 2–1 against Bengaluru FC, courtesy of Jamie Maclaren's extra-time strike. NorthEast United's Alaaeddine Ajaraie emerged as the star performer, winning both the Golden Boot (23 goals) and Golden Ball. Vishal Kaith secured the Golden Glove with 15 clean sheets, while Brison Fernandes was named Emerging Player. At 40, Sunil Chhetri impressed with 14 goals.

HOCKEY

JUNIOR HOCKEY WOMEN'S ASIA CUP

India secured their second successive Junior Women's Hockey Asia Cup title with a hard-fought win over China in the final, showcasing grit and skill on both ends of the field. With disciplined defence and sharp attacking play, the young Indian side held firm to retain their continental crown. Following a nail-biting 1-1 score line after the regulation time, India came out on top in the penalty shoot-out with a 3-2 margin. This consecutive triumph not only reflected the growing depth and consistency in India's junior women's hockey program, but also signaled a bright and promising future for the national team on the global stage.

ASIAN CHAMPIONS TROPHY 2024 (MEN'S)

India retained their Men's Asian Champions Trophy title with a hard-fought 1–0 win over hosts China in the final at Hulunbuir, capturing a record fifth crown. The decisive goal came in the 51st minute when Jugraj Singh netted a field goal after a precise assist from captain Harmanpreet Singh. Despite China's determined challenge, India's defence stood firm to seal victory. Meanwhile, Pakistan secured the bronze medal by defeating South Korea 5–2, concluding an exciting edition of the continental hockey tournament.

ASIAN CHAMPIONS TROPHY 2024 (WOMEN'S)

India retained their Women's Asian Champions Trophy crown with a gritty 1–0 win over Olympic silver medalists China in the final held in Rajgir, Bihar. Striker Deepika netted the decisive goal in the 31st minute via a penalty corner and emerged as the tournament's top scorer with 11 goals. Japan beat Malaysia to claim bronze. With this triumph, India matched South Korea's record of three titles, underscoring their growing dominance in Asian women's hockey and delivering another proud moment for home fans.

TENNIS

RAFAEL NADAL RETIRES

Rafael Nadal, hailed as the 'King of Clay', retired at the age of 38 after an illustrious 23-year career, ending with his final match for Spain in the 2024 Davis Cup finals in Málaga on 19 November 2024. A 22-time Grand Slam winner—most notably 14 French Open titles—he also claimed two Olympic gold medals. Honoured with a farewell at the 2025 Roland-Garros (French Open), Nadal thanked his supporters and rivals. With 92 ATP titles and 209 weeks as World No. 1, he exited as one of tennis's all-time greats.

AUSTRALIAN OPEN 2025

The 2025 Australian Open delivered a memorable showcase of tennis excellence as Jannik Sinner made history by becoming the first Italian to win consecutive Australian Open men's singles titles, defeating Alexander Zverev of Germany in straight sets. Madison Keys of the US earned her first Grand Slam title with a hard-fought win over Belarusian Aryna Sabalenka. Harri Heliövaara and Henry Patten won the men's doubles, while Kateřina Siniaková and Taylor Townsend triumphed in women's doubles. Australians Olivia Gadecki and John Peers captured the mixed doubles title on home soil.

US OPEN 2024

The 2024 US Open witnessed historic moments and record-breaking excitement as Jannik Sinner became the first Italian man to win the Grand Slam, defeating Taylor Fritz to claim his second Major title. Aryna Sabalenka earned her maiden US Open crown with a dominant win over Jessica Pegula. In doubles, Max Purcell/Jordan Thompson and Lyudmyla Kichenok/Jeļena Ostapenko emerged victorious, while Sara Errani and Andrea Vavassori took mixed doubles honours. The event made history by attracting over one million spectators for the first time.

ROLAND-GARROS 2025

The 2025 Roland-Garros delivered unforgettable tennis drama and milestones. Spanish sensation Carlos Alcaraz successfully defended his French Open title by outlasting Jannik Sinner in a thrilling five-set final, saving three match points in what became the tournament's longest championship match. Coco Gauff of the US made history by clinching her first French Open and becoming the first American woman to win the tournament since the legendary Serena Williams. In doubles, Marcel Granollers and Horacio Zeballos took the men's crown, while Italians Sara Errani and Andrea Vavassori triumphed in the mixed doubles event.

WIMBLEDON 2025

The 2025 Wimbledon witnessed remarkable milestones and dominant performances as Jannik Sinner once again created history by winning his first Wimbledon title, beating Carlos Alcaraz in four sets and becoming the first Italian man to triumph at the All England Club. Iga Świątek of Poland produced a flawless performance in the women's final, defeating Amanda Anisimova of the US 6–0, 6–0 to claim her maiden Wimbledon crown. British pair Julian Cash and Lloyd Glasspool ended an 89-year wait for an all-British men's doubles title, delighting the home crowd.

By **MURUKESH KRISHNAN**

ABOUT THE CONTRIBUTORS

Thirumoy Banerjee is a journalist with over thirteen years of experience. He has worked with leading media houses in the country, including The Times of India, Business Standard, Press Trust of India, The Indian Express, and The Telegraph. He has translated a book (*Yamraaj 5003*) from Odia to English, and has been a visiting faculty at premier institutes, including the Indian Institute of Mass Communication, several DU colleges, and Bharatiya Vidya Bhavan (Kolkata), among others. He has been contributing to the Scholastic Yearbook since 2019 and can be reached on X (formerly Twitter) and Instagram at @thiru_the_moy.

Dr Anurima Chanda is currently an Assistant Professor in the Department of English of Birsa Munda College, University of North Bengal. She completed her PhD in Indian English Children's Literature from Jawaharlal Nehru University. She was a pre-doctoral DAAD fellow at the University of Würzburg, Germany, and a SUSI 2023 Fellow at the University of Montana. She is also a literary translator and a children's author.

Karan Audichya is a practicing advocate at Rajasthan High Court. He is also a columnist for 'Youth Ki Awaaz'.

Namit Hans is an academic researcher and writer. He has worked as a journalist with organizations like Indian Express and has taught Mass Communication at University of Delhi. He continues to write for various organizations.

Murukesh Krishnan is a journalist with over twelve years of experience in reporting and editing on politics, current affairs, foreign affairs, business, and sports, across various vibrant newsrooms such as Hindustan Times, Times Now, and India Today. A polyglot, he spends his spare time learning new Indian languages as he believes there lies the fabric of our nation. You can reach him at: *krishnanmurukesh@gmail.com.*

Runa Mukherjee Parikh is an independent journalist with over fifteen years of experience in writing on education, art and pop culture for both national and foreign publications. She has reported for media mammoths like Times of India and India Today. Runa has also authored a collection of six short stories on new age relationships titled *Your Truth, My Truth* in 2017 and made a documentary about the economic after-effects of the pandemic on the idol makers of Kolkata titled *Mother will Arrive* in 2021.

Milan George Jacob is a multimedia storyteller. With an interdisciplinary background, he has collaborated with researchers, filmmakers, artists, and development practitioners to raise awareness and inspire action on climate change, sustainable development, and public health-related issues. He currently works as a Communications Specialist at the Council on Energy, Environment and Water (CEEW), a New Delhi-based policy research institution.

Sandhya Ramesh is a senior editor of science at *ThePrint.* Her work focuses on all kinds of science, especially in the Indian subcontinent. She loves to write and create videos about space and astronomy. She can be reached on X (formerly Twitter) at @ sandygrains.

Shomini Sen has over fourteen years of experience in the media industry. A film critic and journalist at WION currently, she has worked with CNN News18, Zee News, and Times Group in the past.

Sourav Dutta has worked with numerous Indian and international publishing and media houses, including Oxford University Press, Tehelka, Down to Earth, and many others. He is also a writer for graphic novels and comic books.